Democracy Is Power

Rebuilding Unions from the Bottom Up

by Mike Parker
and Martha Gruelle

A Labor Notes Book
Detroit

We dedicate this book to the memory of Mary Milgram Parker (1914-1997) and Ben Parker (1911-1998), life-long socialists, labor activists, and Workmen's Circle leaders who supported this project, other Labor Notes work, and much more in their commitment to make the world a better place for all.

About the publisher:

The Labor Education and Research Project publishes *Labor Notes,* a monthly magazine of labor news and analysis intended to help activists "put the movement back in the labor movement." The Labor Education and Research Project also holds a biennial conference for all labor activists, acts as a resource center, and puts on schools and workshops on a variety of topics. See the ad at the end of the book for more information on Labor Notes publications.

Cover design: Ricardo Levins Morales.
Cover photo: Jim West. Background photos: Earl Dotter, Jim West.

Library of Congress Catalog Card Number: 99-071521
ISBN: 0-914093-11-8

 133

Contents

Why membership control is essential for strong unions; the forces against union democracy; and a look at the most common views on how unions should work.

More than a good set of bylaws, democracy means a special relationship between leaders and members. What does a democratic union culture look like? What kind of leadership works for the members?

Chapter 3. Inclusion and Equality:
Keys to Democracy 67

Democracy means women and people of color know the union works for their particular interests as well as the concerns they share with others. How can we get beyond erasing internal discrimination—a necessary start—to making union activity worthwhile for everybody?

Chapter 4. Promoting Involvement
in the Union 85

Bargaining is the basic place where members' activity is needed—and thus where democracy counts big. A look at motivations shows how member control inspires involvement. Meetings can help, or hurt, democratic functioning.

Chapter 5. Elections 113

What procedures help make officers elections a healthy part of member control? How can campaigning increase members' choices (including the choice to keep the incumbents)?

Chapter 6. Taking Power in the Local:
The Campaign Continues 127

Winning local union office is a huge challenge for reformers; there's a lot of pressure to operate the union more or less like your predecessor. The key to real change is the same organizing strategies that probably got you elected (and will help get you reelected).

Chapter 7. Structures and Bylaws 161

How unions are organized—for instance, who gets to vote on which positions, decision-making power of officers, which members should be grouped together in which locals—affects democracy and power. When we look at external solutions for abuses, we see it's still up to the rank and file to keep their union on track.

Chapter 8. International Conventions and Elections 199

Democracy at the national or international level means organizing to affect convention decisions and choice of top officers.

Acknowledgments

Two people played such a large role in this project that they can rightly claim co-authorship. Jane Slaughter, former Labor Notes director and now a free-lance labor writer, served as editor. But she did far more, drawing on her own labor and political experience to help us determine priorities, shape the arguments, and find examples. Ken Paff, TDU National Organizer, was part of the conceptualization of this project, the early discussions, and outlines. He read and commented on drafts of many of the chapters and in a number of cases pointed us in a different direction. Our work could easily have lost its course without either of these two.

As the reader will quickly discover, this book draws heavily on the experiences of Teamsters working for democracy in their union. Countless rank and filers have made the Teamster reform movement an inspiration to us; many of them directly contributed to our understanding of the issues. Chapter 6 is based heavily on workshop material by Dan Campbell, a co-chair of Teamsters for a Democratic Union. We also learned much from workshops by Joe Fahey, another TDU co-chair; some of his exercises and examples appear here. Rob Hickey helped us understand the relationship of budgeting to democracy. Many others in and around TDU assisted us in gathering material, information, and insights.

We also relied heavily on unionists throughout North America for information and ideas as well as debate and hard criticism. Particularly we're indebted to activists in reform groups like REAP (in the UFCW), New Directions (in the TWU), New Directions (in the UAW), and the Caucus for a Democratic Union in the California State Employees Association/SEIU Local 1000.

Carl Biers, executive director of the Association for Union Democracy, wrote one of the cases used in this book and provided us with suggestions and relevant material. We cite, and use, AUD resources in several places in this book and hold in high regard their many contributions to union democracy over the years.

Attorney Ellis Boal was a great help on several points including information on the law and on the UAW Public Review Board.

Our thanks for input and information along the way go to those who prefer to remain anonymous and to those whose names we may have missed, as well as to Lewie Anderson, Dean Braid, Bill Breihan, Amy Bromsen, Danny Campbell, Cathy Carroll, Ajamu Dillahunt, Jed Dodd, Steve Downs, Steve Early, Dave Eckstein, Kay Eisenhower, Theresa El Amin, Mike Goldfield, Cathy Hackett, Jim Hard, Wayne Horman, Dan La Botz, Ron Landingham, Michael Laslett, Elly Leary, Paul Levy, Nelson Lichtenstein, Tony Mazzocchi, Paul McLennan, Ann Newman, Bill Parker, David Pratt, Ron Ruth, Sarah Ryan, Simone Sagovac, Tim Schermerhorn, George Smilnak, Dave Staiger, Chris Townsend, Steve Trossman, Jerry Tucker, Rand Wilson, Bob Wages, and Dave Yettaw.

We also got considerable cooperation from a number of unions. We particularly thank the UE for providing copies of the materials they use for leadership training, and the OCAW for information on the union's history. The California Nurses Association made a generous financial contribution in support of this work.

A project like this puts a heavy burden on the Labor Notes staff. Kim Moody, Labor Notes director, did much of the writing on Chapter 3. Jim West, our long-time editor, did the design and layout and provided several photographs. All of the staff, including Linnelle Mogado, Teofilo Reyes, Leah Samuel, Brenda Smith, Jenny Van Proeyen, and Rachel White, provided important guidance as well as sharing much of Martha's assignments to free her for writing. Elissa Karg, a long-time Labor Notes supporter and writer, volunteered to provide the index.

This project turned out to be much larger than we planned; both of us worked on it alongside other responsibilities. Mike thanks Margaret Jordan and Johanna Jordan Parker for their strong support, advice, assistance, and patience.

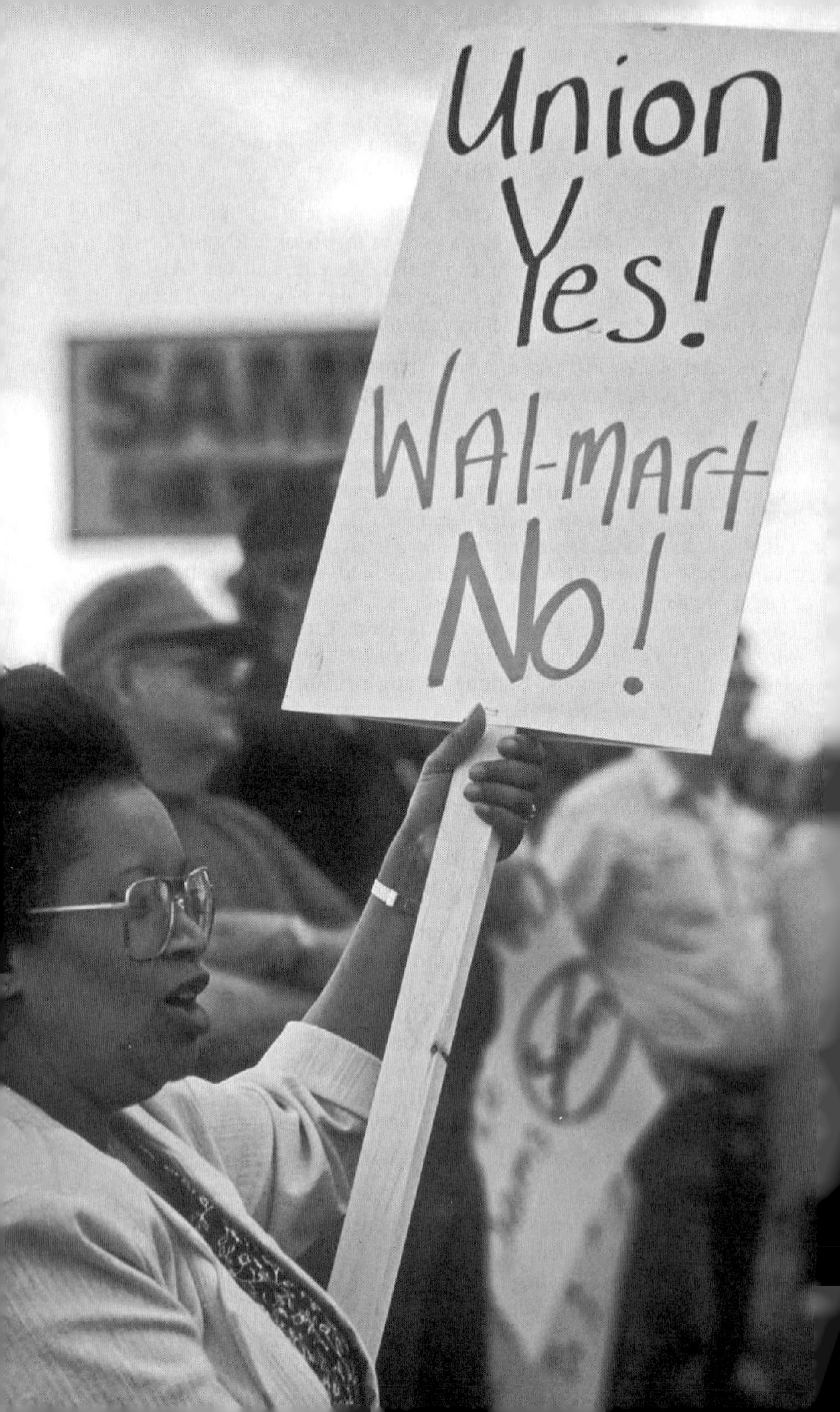
Union
Yes!
WAl-mart
No!

Foreword

by Ken Riley and Leonard Riley

In our time as activists in the International Longshoremen's Association (ILA), we've come to believe that, as the book says, "democracy is power." In other words, democracy is the best avenue we see for strengthening our union.

Many times we've felt victimized by a lack of inclusion in the decision-making process, and we know our members have shared this frustration. This lack of member involvement leads to unchecked power for union leadership and creates a bureaucracy that's almost impossible to penetrate. People say "the cream rises to the top"—but in our union, if the cream does rise, it's by happenstance, not by design.

At the same time, there are many natural leaders in the rank and file—the real cream of the crop—who are not recognized officially because they never run for office. They are recognized by the members, though, because they step up when something is wrong, they inform the members about their rights, and they ask questions. These leaders are proof that even in an undemocratic union, there are ways to get members involved. For activists who want to create a movement for democracy in their union, *Democracy Is Power* is the instruction manual.

BUILDING CAMPAIGNS

When our master contract was negotiated in 2004, we opposed the proposal from the International union, which included three-tiered wages. The reform movement in the ILA, the Longshore Workers Coalition, decided to fight it.

Members helped organize rallies up and down the East Coast. Caravans went from city to city, passing out literature and talking to dockworkers face to face. Convincing people that they could make a difference wasn't easy. When the caravans went to Norfolk, Virginia, for example, members there said, "It's a done deal; there's nothing we can do about it." But Coalition members talked with people about the vote-no campaign and gave them opportunities to get involved and have their voices heard.

When the votes were counted, members in Norfolk voted approximately 1,200 "no" to less than 200 "yes." Overall, it was the largest "no" vote in recent ILA history, nearly 47 percent opposed.

DEVELOPING LEADERS

More than that, we helped build new leaders. Many of the people on the caravans are now more confident and have established roles among the rank and file. They have more credibility with the members than they did before.

Although we did not block the contract, our campaign was a victory. We were able to agitate and mobilize people around issues that count—we shook out that feeling of apathy and helplessness. Bringing so many members together in opposition to the contract let them know that we can be powerful if we force the democratic process to work.

LONG-TERM VISION

That's one of the things *Democracy Is Power* teaches us—that building strong unions is a long fight. Sometimes you'll lose in the short term, but if you're keeping the long-term vision in mind—thinking about how to get members involved and create a democratic culture for members—you can build on those losses, and they can make you stronger. Since you already have *Democracy Is Power* in your hands, you have a great tool for maintaining that long-term vision. Read this book, share it with your union sisters and brothers, and keep fighting.

Ken Riley is president of ILA Local 1422 in Charleston, South Carolina, an international vice-president of the ILA, and a former co-chair of the Longshore Workers Coalition. Leonard Riley is a member of Local 1422 and a current co-chair of the Longshore Workers Coalition.

Introduction to the Second Printing

by Mike Parker and Martha Gruelle

Looking over *Democracy Is Power*, we come to the unhappy conclusion that what we had to say seven years ago is even more relevant today. Why unhappy? Because the labor movement is weaker today than it was only a decade ago.

The book's central point, as the title indicates, is that democracy is not just a desirable option—it's not the icing on the cake. Union democracy—defined as rank-and-file power—is the essential ingredient for restoring the power of the labor movement. Those who say we have to choose between democracy and effectiveness are wrong. Without member power, our successes will be numbers on paper.

Let's be clear: the goal of our movement is not just bigger unions. It's for working people to function as human beings—not bootlickers, not cogs—starting with our jobs, where we spend most of our waking hours. When we leave our jobs at the end of the day, we should be as healthy as when we started. We should be able to look at the next day, and our retirement years, with a feeling of security, not dread. Our larger goal is for workers to exert power collectively in the workplace and society—and for that you need much more than bigger unions. You need powerful workers.

The Great Debate

The 2005 debate in the AFL-CIO opened up crucial questions. Some leaders were clear that drastic change—more than rearranging the deck chairs—was necessary. But power for members wasn't part of anyone's script, and although the open debates on the Internet were a good step forward, there was almost no membership discussion—let alone vote—on splitting or on taking action to prevent a split. A promising debate got muddied by issues of personal power and grabbing dues rebates.

One of the contested issues was how to organize new members when labor laws favor the employers. Should we focus the bulk of our resources on organizing, to grow our numbers and thereby boost our political relevance? Or should we focus on lobbying and electoral campaigns, so that we can get laws passed that will make organizing easier?

History Lesson

To answer this question, we can learn from the last two times that American workers' mass movements rocked the status quo: the union drives of the 1930s and the civil rights/black power movement of the 1960s. We learned then that organizing and political power proceed together, but organizing leads the way; it can't wait for new laws.

The civil rights movement found that the only way to win legal rights for black Americans was through actions that challenged the unjust laws and demanded change. It began with small numbers who were willing to take risks in the name of a moral vision. In the early 1960s the Kennedy administration had decided not to raise any further civil rights legislation. But mass action in Birmingham in May 1963 made the government suddenly decide to push a voting rights bill. And mass action continued to force more civil rights legislation.

In the 1930s, organizing also forced political openings that allowed still more organizing. The epic battles of 1934 that were decisive in reviving the labor movement were fought and won despite anti-worker laws: the Toledo Auto-Lite strike, the Minneapolis Teamsters strike, and the San Francisco general strike. All the power of local governments, including police violence and mass arrests, was brought to bear against these mass mobilizations, and yet workers prevailed. Even defeats like that of the massive 1934 Southern textile strike added to the general sense that the union movement would not be denied.

Today's alarm about the difficulty of organizing under current laws is valid, but it's put in perspective when we look at the 1930s. Workers then faced not only laws that made union activities illegal but also employer-funded blacklists, goons and Pinkertons, police, troops, and courts, and yet the union movement succeeded. It succeeded because there was a social movement that would not wait for the law. Likewise, in the 1937 sit-down strikes that organized GM or the transit workers' sit-ins in New York, the unions had leaders and members who did what had to be done, including ignoring unjust laws, at considerable risk to their safety, their jobs, and their savings.

Structures for Power

A second lesson from history also has relevance for the debates of 2005. The movements for unions and for civil rights were not built by first restructuring the movement organizations into an ideal form. The movements grew because they attracted organizers and members with their vision, their winning strategies, and the deep feeling of sisterhood and brotherhood they engendered among the activists. As the movements grew, new structures—like the CIO—arose to meet new needs, even as old structures, like the AFL unions, adapted and began a new wave of organizing.

Today's labor movement, however it's structured, can't grow in power or numbers by acting as a business with smart hired guns. We have potential power in our numbers, our skills, and our strategic positions in the economy. But this power becomes real only when our members are willing to act on their own behalf. In both organizing and politics, we need to put the movement back in the labor movement, as the Labor Notes slogan says.

Today's union culture is not one that gives rise to legions of volunteer activists committed to social justice. In many unions, members do union work only if they're paid as staff or get "lost time." To build a movement capable of taking on global corporations, we need to rebuild the democratic culture of member power.

Do We Really Need Democracy?

Many leaders of the labor movement know the history. They know that they need members in motion if they're to win anything. But too many envision a mobilized labor movement as troops ready to respond to the commands of their officers. Top-down control seems so efficient, and times are desperate. Do we really need democracy to have a movement? After all, aren't people interested in results—not procedures?

There's a grain of truth to this argument. In Chapter 1, we write about members' desire for a "powerful provider" to fight management for them. But even if top-down leadership could get results in the short term, in the long term a union without active members is a union without power—and the bosses know it.

One reason is the very conditions of global capitalism. Global competition means first and foremost that the labor movement must constantly spread. There is no security in organizing one workplace, one industry, or one company. If the organizing does not keep spreading to "take labor out of competition," union conditions will die.

This process of continuous organization requires not thousands but millions of organizers—millions of workers who tell their sisters, cousins, friends, and lovers they'd be crazy not to join a union. Not millions of members who, when asked, answer, "Yeah, I was in a union once, they didn't do anything for me."

If we want members to go out and recruit, then the union has to deliver in the workplaces of the already organized. Members who see their union as a partner with management or as another boss will not carry a strong union vision to their non-union sisters and brothers.

After all, workers who want a union where they work are the ones that management calls troublemakers. It takes only a few moments with these troublemakers to understand that those who refuse to accept injustice from management will not accept it from union leaders either. If we are to recruit, organizers have to be able to look these potential members in the eye when they say, "Your union will belong to you."

Preparing the Ground

And that leads us to a third lesson from history. Unions have grown the most in surges, when hundreds of thousands of workers were inspired to act, rather than by slow accretion, one drive at a time. No one knows what will touch off the next upsurge in American history. We do know that we can't make it happen just by having the right ideas and working hard. Movements grow in part when people respond to big changes in the economy and society.

The civil rights movement, for example, grew thanks to those who laid the groundwork in the South but also because of events elsewhere in the world. Anti-colonial movements in Africa were inspirational to black people in America, and the federal government was vulnerable to pressure because of its Cold War competition with the communist states. The militant strikes of 1934 and 1937 depended on committed leaders but also on the up-ticks in the economy that promised some relief from the Depression.

Does this mean we should just sit back and wait? Far from it. We need to do everything we can to grow now, but in a way that prepares our organizations. We need democratic unions today, to train thousands of leaders and members who'll be able to step up when the time demands. *Democracy Is Power* is about how to use union structures and processes to build a democratic union culture and democratic leaders.

Structure and Democracy

The structures and procedures that unions use are not principles. Different forms of organization have advantages and disadvantages, and they can be implemented in good and bad ways.

For example, it's a good thing for members in the same industry to bargain together. That's an advantage of large, region-wide, industry-based locals. On the other hand, especially if the bylaws or the culture give all power to the staff, such mega-locals may be almost impossible for members to own. That makes the union weaker. Could one solution be smaller locals with a joint bargaining council? The particulars of each situation have to be weighed, with the goal of maximizing member power—and willingness—to act against the boss.

It's possible to get mired in the procedures and miss the point. Building rank-and-file confidence and power has to be the priority. We hope that this book shows how to figure out which are the most useful procedures, by keeping our eyes always on that prize.

Introduction: About Power

This book is about democracy and power for working people. It assumes that working people need more power, and that the first way we get it is through our unions. Strong unions are good for their members, for all working people, and for building a more democratic society.

The book is built on six themes:

• Union power *requires* democracy. Unions need active members to be strong, and people won't stay involved for long if they don't have control of the union's program.

• The workplace (not the union hall) is the starting point for union democracy, because the purpose of democratic control in the union is to make it more effective against the boss. If members choose and organize their own job actions, they'll bring that power into union meetings.

• No set of rules can guarantee democracy. When we talk about democracy we mean much more than fair election procedures, for instance, although rules are important tools. We mean a culture of control by the members.

• Racism and sexism are still barriers to union democracy. We can't just remove explicit discrimination and be done; democratic unions consciously and actively strive to include everyone.

- Working people are fit to run our own affairs. We are intelligent, can act cooperatively, and are fully capable of analyzing our situation and crafting the best strategy to improve it. Given real choices we will overcome our prejudices and work for the betterment of all.

- Members have the right to organize around a view of how to run the union. This means more than the right to voice opinions. We have the right to work with others who agree to convince still more to come along. This is the essence of building a reform movement in a union.

From the perspective of the reformer in a corrupt union, it seems that the main barriers to rank and file control are union officials who use undemocratic rules, goon squads, and deals with management to ward off any threats to their perks. Unfortunately, there is no shortage of examples.

But increasingly, as reformers of various degrees and stripes take power in locals and gain more influence in international unions, it is clear that there are other enemies. Sometimes members make tremendous sacrifices to reform their union, only to find that the new leaders they have elected turn out to be almost as dictatorial as the ones they replaced. These new officers may genuinely have the members' interests at heart, but believe the ranks are best served if the leaders maintain control.

And reform-minded leaders often find that it is not so easy to involve members in running the union. They complain that members refuse to participate and prefer to let the servicing rep take care of business.

Sometimes it even seems, paradoxically, that members prefer those who would deny them power in the union—if they think it will get them more power on the job. Thus we often see corrupt and bureaucratic officials gain a following—and get elected—because they talk tough against the employer.

The truth is that the enemies of democracy are not just a bunch of corrupt officials. Democracy is undermined systematically by many forces in our society. These include the power of employers to interfere in unions, the belief that democracy is simply about correct procedures, and the hope that someone else will do all the hard work.

The impetus for this book comes from three sources. First,

reformers in a number of unions who have won local and some national leadership positions want to restructure their unions to make them genuinely democratic (contact information for some of these groups appears in Appendix 6). Second, serious rank and file reformers want to carefully pinpoint what is wrong with their unions so that their call for change is not just a complaint but a plan for a better way.

Third, the election of the current AFL-CIO leadership in 1995 led to an emphasis on organizing and member involvement. But as advocates of the "organizing model" are discovering, seeking to involve members inevitably raises the question of democracy within the union.

Indeed, parts of this book will sound familiar to someone with good training in organizing. "Organizing" in its best sense—helping people work together to achieve what they want—is another way to say "union democracy." Where "organizing" people—whether it's those who already have a union or those who want a new one—does not put them in charge of their own activity, it's not democratic, nor is it powerful.

We have three aims:

> To make the case that democracy is essential to the power of the union. Democracy is not simply a moral question but the key to unions' ability to meet today's challenges from management and government alike.
>
> To lay out guidelines activists can use to create and maintain a democratic union environment.
>
> To use these guidelines to sort through some tough questions about democratic procedure. How do we get members involved? How do we conduct elections? How do we handle dissent?

The answers are not obvious. What seems democratic to a dissident in a local union—such as filling all positions by election rather than appointment—may not look so appealing or democratic to the reformer who has just won a close election and wants to sweep out the corruption.

There are no universal right answers on most of these questions. At the same time, the similarities among modern American unions and the problems they face make some answers pretty common. Instead of providing a manual of procedures with yes/no positions, we try to provide some analytic tools so that unionists can choose what is most appropriate for their situation.

Two subjects are not goals of this book, although they certainly fall under the heading of union democracy. It is not our aim to compile a list of atrocities against democracy. Where we can learn something from discussing a bad union practice we do so; many egregious examples are left out. This is also not a book about the legal rights of union members. Assuring legal rights is an important tool for democracy, but is far from the whole solution. An excellent resource on legal rights is the Association for Union Democracy (see Appendix 6 for more information).

The material for this book comes from many sources. Many unions have long histories of struggling with the question of internal democracy; we draw most heavily on recent experiences within the Teamsters. In the last decade the struggle in that union has taught us the most lessons about winning rank and file democracy, although clearly the Teamsters still have a long way to go.

Union Abbreviations in This Book

AFSCME	American Federation of State, County and Municipal Employees
AFT	American Federation of Teachers
BMWE	Brotherhood of Maintenance of Way Employees (now part of the Teamsters)
CAW	Canadian Auto Workers
CWA	Communications Workers of America
HERE	Hotel Employees and Restaurant Employees (now part of UNITE HERE)
IAM	International Association of Machinists
IBEW	International Brotherhood of Electrical Workers
IBT	International Brotherhood of Teamsters
LIUNA	Laborers' International Union of North America
NALC	National Association of Letter Carriers
NEA	National Education Association
OCAW	Oil, Chemical and Atomic Workers (now part of the United Steelworkers)
SEIU	Service Employees International Union
TWU	Transport Workers Union
UAW	United Auto Workers
UE	United Electrical Workers
UFCW	United Food and Commercial Workers
UMW	United Mine Workers
USW	United Steelworkers

One of our most important sources is the experience of the reform caucus Teamsters for a Democratic Union. Formed in 1976 out of a struggle against a poor contract in the freight industry, the organization grew from a tiny group of rank and filers to a large and influential movement. Much of its success is owed to TDU's own form of membership control. Because we refer to TDU and the Teamsters so frequently throughout this book, we have included a history and description of TDU below.

Many of our ideas come directly from other organized reform groups, particularly New Directions in the UAW, (another) New Directions in the Transport Workers Local 100, and REAP in the UFCW. Our monthly publication, *Labor Notes,* has covered reform movements in a number of U.S. and Canadian unions and a few in other countries such as Mexico, Brazil, and Germany. Others have written thoughtfully on union democracy. In particular, we have learned from the work of Herman Benson, Steve Early, and Michael Eisenscher.

Our first three chapters lay out ideas basic to understanding the potential power of union democracy, and the roadblocks to fulfilling this potential. Later chapters look at how to put these ideas into practice. The appendixes focus mostly on holding good meetings (a necessary but not sufficient aspect of union democracy); Appendix 5 suggests some pointers on bylaws.

The reader will notice that we've written the book for two different audiences, and that therefore the assumptions about what's going on in the local union vary from section to section. The two audiences are rank and file reformers working to democratize their unions in the face of opposition from incumbent officials, and reformers who are in office. Thus we've emphasized two kinds of action: ways for members to organize to stop poor practices, hold leaders accountable, and force their views on a reluctant officialdom, and ways for officials to get the members involved in building strong unions.

Like any Labor Notes book, we consider this one a work-in-progress. The authors, the Labor Notes staff and Policy Committee, and other leaders in our network fully expect to learn more about union democracy as unionists comment on this book, and as they forge ahead on the nitty-gritty of building democracy. New ideas and new stories can be expected in the pages of *Labor Notes.* Please send us yours.

What Is Teamsters
for a Democratic Union?

TDU is a movement of Teamsters dedicated to reforming their union. Teamster spouses and retirees, and members in both the United States and Canada, are welcome as members. TDU is funded by its members' dues of $35 per year—about the same as a month's union dues for most—and by their donations. TDU has a sister organization, the Teamster Rank and File Education and Legal Defense Foundation, that carries on education and legal work only. TRF receives foundation grants and non-Teamster donations.

TDU got its start in the 1970s among Teamsters pushing for a stronger national freight contract. Their immediate goal was to show that the union could get better agreements if members voted down bad contracts and were willing to strike. Since top officials were trying to sell the contracts, TDUers saw officials' lack of accountability as a major impediment to taking on the employers. Starting from a few dozen truck drivers and dock workers spreading information about bargaining demands, TDU grew to include several thousand members in the mid-nineties, from every Teamster jurisdiction.

From its founding in 1976 until 1989, TDU's main emphasis was on contracts—pushing bargainers and, between negotiations, working on grievances. By the mid-eighties TDU was still small, but had enough influence to convince a majority to vote "no" on concessionary contracts in the freight industry, at UPS, and for carhaulers (the truck drivers who move new cars from the factory or seaport to the dealer's lot).

At the same time, TDUers listened to members talk about how their officials were selling them out. TDU agitated for the right to vote directly for top officials, to help keep them accountable. The Teamsters, like most U.S. unions, elected top officers at conventions. Unlike most, the Teamsters convention was almost entirely composed of *ex officio* delegates—local officials who automatically became delegates by virtue of their office, with no chance for rank and filers to vote for delegates. The effect was a closed system of local and international officers helping each other maintain power—without having to consult the ranks.

In 1989, the system was knocked open. The Justice Department pressured old guard officials to allow a rank and file vote for top officers, with candidates nominated at a convention where all delegates had to be elected for that purpose. TDU backed a local president not of their ranks, Ron Carey, who had been outspoken nationally on UPS contracts. With TDU's network of trained activists, Carey won the election in 1991. The Teamsters union began to change, although the many old guard officials still firmly embedded at regional and local levels resisted fiercely.

TDU worked with the Carey administration, supporting it against the old guard while pushing it farther on reforms. TDUers continued all kinds of organizing within the union, including running for local office; the fight for democracy was far from finished. In 1997 an election scandal threatened reform efforts. Ron Carey, in his successful 1996 reelection campaign, had hired consultants who carried out an illegal contribution-swap scheme. The government barred Carey from the rerun election. But TDUers understood what Carey himself had said: "It's not about one man."

Though angered at the government's removal of Carey, TDUers pushed on. They organized to back a new slate of candidates, led by Tom Leedham. Leedham, as a local president and head of the union's 400,000-member Warehouse Division, was a solid practitioner of rank and file power through democracy. The Leedham slate did remarkably well in December 1998: after campaigning only six months—compared to Hoffa's four-year effort—and outspent seven to one, they garnered about 39 percent of the vote. The reform slate won a majority among members of those locals that included a sizable number of people covered by national contracts. This was the group most affected by the policies of the international, and the group most knowledgeable about international union affairs. As in 1991 and 1996, the best reform vote came from the areas and locals where TDU was strongest.

TDU Acts Locally

Because TDU dealt with national contract issues—for freight workers, UPSers, and many other Teamsters—it took on a national structure from the beginning. For instance, TDU held national conventions when the organization was still small, and distributed centrally-produced national "TDU contract bulletins." But most of TDU's activity was and is carried out at the local level.

Local activists distribute TDU information and bulletins and do much more. They are essential organizers: talking up the issues among members, hearing what they think, and communicating responses and concerns back to the national office. Based on this local organizing, they discuss strategy for the next steps.

Local activists work to build a TDU chapter in their area. In some cities the chapter will include members from several different Teamster locals; in some places there is only one Teamster local, or only one with an active TDU membership. Chapter members determine their own structure, finances, and priorities. If the chapter is new or not very strong, its members may do little more than pass out TDU's newspaper, *Convoy Dispatch,* to co-workers and sponsor an occasional meeting with a guest speaker from TDU headquarters. A more active chapter will have a leadership body, meetings, campaigns around local and national issues, and methods of raising money.

Naturally, each chapter's strength and activity will vary over time depending on many factors—a major one being the energy and effectiveness of its volunteer leaders. Within each chapter certain local unions may take center stage at different times. TDU's national leadership and staff, and the national newspaper, provide these groups a picture of how they fit into the overall scene: are their bylaws proposals similar to reforms that have worked in other locals? Are their co-workers upset about the same workplace problems as Teamsters across the country? What responses are being tried elsewhere?

Like reformers in other unions, TDU activists in some locals must do double duty: they take over much of the work abandoned by lazy or corrupt officials—member education, organizing around grievances, determining priorities for bargaining—while at the same time pushing officials to change their ways or be moved aside.

Here's how those activities might fit together. Maybe someone notices that a TDU member has a lot of contract information and asks about a particular problem. The TDU member helps this co-worker get more information from the national office, if needed, and helps file a grievance—which the local officials sit on. Meanwhile, TDU members are asking around to see if the problem is widespread and finding out that many people are concerned about it. They plan and carry out a show of solidarity, like taking turns dropping by the supervisor's office to quote the contract. After about a day of this, the business agent magically appears and the grievance is won.

Then perhaps one of the chapter members writes a story about the win for the *Convoy,* and the chapter orders extra copies of that issue. Many of the people who helped pressure the boss sign up for TDU; one of them has friends in a different company where conditions have really deteriorated since the last contract, and they start asking questions too. Eventually, the group decides to run one of its number for steward.

When they run to take over the local, TDUers often form coalition slates with independent forces. When they win, they can look to the national TDU office for help in setting up their new administration. As more TDUers have won office, the organization has held special meetings for reform officers.

You will find much more information about TDU in the chapters that follow. To contact TDU, see Appendix 6.

DIGNITY
for
PATIENTS
&
Workers
SEIU
Dignit
98
DEMAND
NURSING HOME
STAFFING BILL
4176

1. Democracy Is Power

If our real goal is strong unions—powerful ones—why bother with democracy? Because we have to. Let's look at power and democracy.

We learned in Civics class where the original word *democracy* came from. In Greek, it's *demos*—the people, *kratein*—to rule. The people rule. All the procedures and protections that we usually associate with democracy—elections, rights to debate, a free press, for example—are simply means to achieve the power of the people.

The procedures (the means) are often confused with democracy itself (the goal), for two reasons. First, the procedures are usually necessary to reach the goal of democracy. The more complicated our society, the more we need division of labor, representatives, leaders, experts, and rules for how to make decisions. Second, it's in the interest of those who don't want the people to rule that we get distracted from the goal and hung up on the procedures instead. We will talk more about this later.

Where do unions fit in?

To begin with, unions exist to give workers power in society, where the bulk of the economic and political power is held by those few who control the corporations. When unions make working people more powerful, they are imposing some democracy on a society which otherwise is not very democratic at all.

The basic reason working people organize unions is for power over pay and conditions in the workplace; that is the most important place where members measure the union's strength, and also where we measure union democracy. No matter what happens at meetings or conventions, the union will not be democratic unless members control its actions on workplace issues.

That's why union reform efforts are strongest when their message is, "We need to fix the union so it can win changes the members need at work." If members think a bylaws change will make it easier to win grievances, they have a good reason to come to a meeting to vote on it. If an opposition slate has a better idea on how to deal with forced overtime, it may seem worth the effort to campaign for that slate. Union democracy is about power in the workplace.

Most union members would agree that the United States could use a healthy dose of democracy, especially in the workplace. But that does not automatically mean that democracy is the best method for running a union. If there were a non-democratic way to run

Democracy and Corporations Go Together Like Pacifism and Ice Hockey

Unions promote democracy in two ways. First, to the extent that unions—even bureaucratic ones—offer a counterforce to the power of corporations, they play a crucial role in democratizing society.

Second, unions themselves are held to democratic standards, if imperfectly so—by their own principles, by the expectations of society, and by law. Members have avenues for reforming their unions.

Compare the expectation of democratic rights, even in a highly bureaucratic union, to your rights on the job. The corporation makes not even a pretense of democracy, or protection of anyone's rights except the owners' and managers'. In a nonunion workplace, you can devote your most productive years to serving a corporation and then be fired for speaking your mind, or for not appearing enthusiastic, or for any reason at all except the few specifically prohibited by law.

If the standard to which we hold unions is democratic rights, the standard the society holds for corporations is bottom-line profits. By their nature, all unions contribute far more to the level of democracy in our world than does any corporation.

unions that gave workers more power in society and against the boss, then members would have to consider it.

In fact, there are many people—members as well as leaders— who believe that democracy actually weakens the union. They say it's a luxury that only gets in the way of unity and swift action. Few leaders will say this in front of the members, of course. In the Teamsters, for example, officials who had tried for years to keep members from having the right to vote for their president gave convention speeches in favor of it when the election was imminent. But behind closed doors, you would hear some union staffers or officers assert, "Members aren't interested in democracy; they're interested in results. We'll get good results if we the leaders just come up with the right plan."

Or they may simply leave democracy out. A clear example of the "militancy without democracy" point of view appeared in a spring 1996 article by Stephen Lerner, published by the Boston Review. Lerner was architect of the SEIU's Justice for Janitors campaign under John Sweeney, and then became an AFL-CIO staff

Even a Little Democracy Counts

The 1987 and 1990 UPS contracts were bargained under similar conditions: the same old guard union leadership and the same financially healthy company. Both contracts were negotiated without strikes and without union-sponsored contract campaigns. But the 1990 settlement was substantially better for UPS Teamsters.

The difference was the amount of member control. In 1989 the government forced the union to schedule a membership vote on international officers, who control national bargaining with UPS. The election campaign was well under way in 1990 when old guard officials announced they'd bargained a much better pay package at UPS than the one they had gladly accepted in 1987.

As Ken Paff, national organizer of TDU, put it, "The officials couldn't say anymore to the members, 'We don't care.' They had to care."

Officials had to care because there was widespread dissatisfaction with the 1987 settlement and this time around, even a little discontent could cost bargainers their jobs. That little bit of democracy was worth an extra $1.23 an hour for UPS Teamsters.

member. Lerner rightly notes that unions can only inspire workers if we abandon "partnership" with corporations. Instead we need to show that we can take on and beat aggressive employers. He proposes an action program for the labor movement, calling for mobilizing the most active one percent of union members into "an army ready to risk arrest...to bring whole cities to a standstill." Certainly such action is needed.

But one plank was missing: Lerner said not a word about rank and file initiative or control of these militant actions. Quite the contrary; Lerner clearly means officials and staff when he says "we" should build campaigns that "give our members reason to be involved." Workers are to be "activated," in Lerner's word—a cannon fodder version of organizing. In this view, member control is not relevant to rebuilding unions.

But far from being a distraction, internal democracy is key to union power.

First, a union will act in the interests of members only if those members control the union. If members do not control their union, then others tend to run it in their own interests—management, the mob, or officials seeking to preserve their easy job and comfortable lifestyle if not line their own pockets; the opportunities are just too rich to be passed up. Even a leader with a personal commitment to the members' interests, but who lacks serious input from them, is vulnerable to the other interests just mentioned.

Second, the power of the union lies in the participation of its members, and it requires democracy to make members want to be involved. A union that tries to function without member involvement becomes weak no matter how well intentioned its officers. Officers seeking participation without asking what the members want to accomplish will be frustrated.

A union run by the members is also more likely to exercise its power. When the members run the union, they have chances to measure their collective strength against the boss, and gain the confidence to use it. When members, for instance, see that a cartoon they've posted on the union bulletin board really shakes up the supervisor, they start thinking about other ways to push that boss's discomfort into positive changes (and they think up more cartoon ideas). Yet many unions keep their bulletin boards behind locked glass.

When members are in the habit of using their heads to figure out the problems of running the union—handling disagreements among themselves, setting priorities for scarce resources, and learning each other's concerns—they have more effective ideas for dealing with management's assaults as well. Conversely, if the rank and file can't even control their local union, how are they going to "control" some aspect of a big corporation? Who'd dare to try?

Does democracy make the union more powerful in every instance? Democratic rule allows, even guarantees, that members will make mistakes—even serious ones. For example, leaders may worry that members will believe management's fear campaign and want to give concessions that will undercut another local. Such concerns are real, but are not valid arguments against democracy.

First, there is no evidence that any system other than democracy is less prone to mistakes. Indeed, we have ample evidence that the self-proclaimed experts are fooled at least as often as the members. One example: throughout the 1980s and 1990s, "experts" and leaders signed on to a string of labor-management cooperation fads. When members were cynical about the "flavor of the month" new program and reluctant to give up union rights, leaders chalked it up to "thinking inside the box" and fear of change. As it turned out, the members were right and the experts were wrong. Any reader from an undemocratic union will have his or her own examples of strategic mistakes by officials that most members could have avoided.

Second, members have the right to make their own mistakes; they deserve to decide for themselves how best to improve their lives and their children's lives.

Third, as members learn from and correct their mistakes as a group, they're better able to avoid repeating them. An individual "dictator" seldom has a clear view of his own failed policies—and he has a stake in not admitting them.

Democracy with its mistakes and inefficiencies works better than any other arrangement. See the boxes on the Machinists at Boeing and the Teamsters at UPS for examples.

A union that operates purely top-down may appear strong, or at least united, if members are willing to follow orders. But if members lose faith in their commanders, and have no other way to make decisions or to exercise collective power, they'll end up acting as individuals instead. The results can be disastrous: members scabbing, or

engaging in militant but foolhardy individual acts, or most likely
abandoning the cause. This is one of the reasons (not a justification)
that there were members who scabbed during the UAW's strike at
Caterpillar in the 1990s: members weren't consulted on strategy at
any point, and had no collective way to try to turn around what

Machinists' 'Right To Review' Leads to Victory

by Carl Biers

At the Boeing Company a fight for democratic reform in union
practices led to victory over management. In 1995, officials of the
Machinists local lodges (local unions) at Boeing agreed to a demand
put forward by reform caucuses in Seattle and Wichita. As contract
negotiations approached, officials announced that for the first time,
members would have three days to review the tentative contract
before voting on it.

The reform caucuses had demanded this window because of
their experience three years earlier. Seattle members had voted on a
deal only moments after it was presented to them at a mass meeting.
Later, they discovered that the agreement they had voted on was
incomplete; officials continued to negotiate in secret over several
unresolved issues. When the contract was finally distributed, four
months after the ratification meeting, it contained language that
members had never voted on.

In 1995, the ranks used the three-day period to demonstrate
their unity and opposition to the contract with marches and rallies—
some led by rank and file activists, some by union officials who
could see which way the wind was blowing, and others erupting
spontaneously. One group marched through the huge Everett,
Washington complex, banging on their tool boxes as they went. A
group in Wichita occupied the plant for two days.

Thirty thousand members overwhelmingly rejected an agreement that would have loosened protections on contracting out and
required workers to pay a portion of health insurance premiums.
Instead, workers embarked on a militant strike. After six weeks on
the picket line, they voted by 61 percent to reject yet another offer,
this one endorsed unanimously by union officers at all levels.
Finally, after ten weeks on the picket line, workers returned to their
plants with an agreement that maintained tighter restrictions on sub-
contracting, added no co-pays on insurance, and included substantial

looked like a losing operation.

Confidence in leaders can come either from a history of those leaders' winning regular gains, or from the ongoing interchange between leaders and members that we call democracy. Since these

---

wage increases and a signing bonus.

In rejecting their leadership's recommendations, Machinists handed the labor movement its best victory of the 1990s to that point. But the victory might never have happened if the membership had not had the opportunity to review the contract. The three days proved to be a crucial period for members to show the company, union officers, and themselves that they were prepared to strike.

A pre-vote review period had been a demand of reformers since the mid-1980s, but caucus organizing began in earnest in both cities in the early 1990s. In 1992, the Seattle area caucus, known as the New Crew, ran for office in the first widely contested elections in the lodge's history. They won several offices and managed to pass a motion in support of contract review at one lodge meeting. Meanwhile, in Wichita, Unionists for Democratic Change, running on a similar platform, won spots on the executive board of Local Lodge 834.

Reformers also challenged another undemocratic practice, a rule designed to keep the union in the hands of incumbents. As in most local unions, attendance at union meetings was low. A bylaw requiring attendance at six of the previous twelve meetings in order to be eligible to run for office disqualified 98 percent of the members of most lodges. In 1992, with the assistance of the Association for Union Democracy, insurgents complained to the Department of Labor that the rule had disqualified some candidates.

Shortly before negotiations with Boeing began in 1995, the DOL announced new regulations invalidating most uses of meeting attendance rules. Faced with the threat of a snowballing insurgency, and without the meeting attendance rule to insulate them from challenges, the incumbents decided to adopt one of their opposition's most popular proposals—the three-day waiting period.

The Boeing story shows how, even without control of the union, caucuses won a key reform that made possible a big labor victory.

[Carl Biers is executive director of the Association for Union Democracy.]

days significant improvements are near impossible to come by without a mobilized membership are near impossible to come by, unions had best rebuild democracy.

When Members "Get It Wrong"

One of the most demoralizing experiences for reformers is for members to vote against reform candidates or to reject referenda aimed at giving members greater rights. Why do members "get it wrong" and vote against their own rights and interests? The very powerful forces that unions must contend with, which operate inside the union as well as outside it, help explain why members sometimes expect to gain more power—better jobs or pay, more job security—

Taking on Big Brown

The clearest example of union reform leading to union power is the national UPS strike of August 1997. Although the Teamsters were not a thoroughly rank and file-run union, five years earlier members had bucked the union's hierarchy and elected a new reform leadership. Changes at the top of the union combined with 20 years of education by TDU made the difference between beating UPS and not taking on the company at all. (For a description of TDU see the Introduction.)

TDU members at UPS had organized for years against productivity harassment and for including part-timers' issues in union demands. Their discussion of working conditions over the years prepared UPSers to see through the company's rhetoric on 1997 bargaining. TDUers then became many of the key frontline warriors to organize the union campaign and strike, even where old guard leaders dragged their feet.

The Teamsters' contract campaign began in 1996. That year, the union surveyed UPS members about bargaining issues, reported the results, and announced contract goals based directly on survey responses. This contrasted with the more usual practice of not setting specific goals for fear of raising members' expectations too high. (The UAW Bargaining Convention, for example, passes a resolution every three years for "a substantial wage increase.")

In announcing their goal of 10,000 new full-time jobs, union leaders showed that it would be up to the members, later, to decide whether any proposed agreement came close enough to that goal; the by some method other than union democracy.

The most powerful force a union faces is usually the employer. Management starts with power simply because of an economic and legal system that assumes management rights unless otherwise specified. Whatever the issues members are concerned about, it is the employer who gets to set the terms of the debate. It is management who decides whether the business will stay open or whether the agency will be privatized, what products will be made, in what places, by whom, and with what processes. Often the union is in the position of reacting to management initiatives.

Management operates inside the union, too, by its power to divide workers by favoring one group or individual over another,

---

bargainers would not be able to say "really we were shooting for 1,000 new full-time jobs." (Leaders did lower the goal from 15,000 jobs to 10,000 during pre-strike negotiations.)

In framing the issues, union leaders paired the full-time jobs question with the demand to stop contracting out; that way, all major sections of the workforce were involved in the struggle. Leaders trusted members to see the importance of the issues, and to stay unified if the company offered something (like pension improvements) that benefited only full-timers. That trust was confirmed later when the members stuck together on the picket lines and became the best spokespeople to local news media on the strike issues.

International officials were also clear they needed rank and file involvement to succeed. Where local officials were slow to distribute campaign information or materials like buttons or whistles, the international sent them directly to rank and file activists. Again, top officials trusted the members; they could not expect to control from Washington how materials were used.

UPS management devotes considerable attention to winning workers' loyalty, and before 1992 the international union had not challenged them in this arena at all. Management fully expected that within a week or so, Teamsters would start crossing the lines and the strike would be broken. But the months of preparation paid off; the strike was solid, and the victory was the biggest the labor movement had seen in many years.

The victory was possible because so many UPS workers felt that the struggle belonged to them.

whether it's through distribution of overtime or race discrimination. By offering better conditions and advancement to those who show their "loyalty," management can always find people willing to carry out its bidding in union affairs.

Management also exercises its power directly on the union structure. It's common for management to let it be known which candidate for union office they'd prefer to "work with." In some unions, it is traditional that the best route into management is to become a steward first. Or management can set up a system of thinly disguised but legal payoffs: jointness junkets and ease of getting overtime pay keep some officials addicted to their positions. Leaders

Members Vote to 'Let George Do It'

The June 1997 local union elections at the NUMMI plant in Fremont, California show how members' view of business unionism can guide their actions. The business union-oriented Administration Caucus retook the United Auto Workers Local 2244 top offices from reformers in the People's Caucus. In a key vote, former Shop Chair George Nano ousted People's Caucus leader Richard Aguilar from that position.

The election had broad significance because the NUMMI plant has been the first and foremost model of lean production, team concept, and Japanese methods in the United States. Created as a joint venture of GM and Toyota, and operated by Toyota, the plant regularly hosts delegations from workplaces around the world. Yet a brief strike at the plant in 1994, and the company's many anti-worker policies, gave the lie to many of the myths of labor-management cooperation.

Until shortly before the 1997 election, the People's Caucus had confidently expected victory. The local executive board dominated by the Administration Caucus was responsible for chaotic financial practices that finally resulted in trusteeship. Aguilar, on the other hand, had been an aggressive, hard-working shop chair. Whereas grievances had been systematically discouraged under Nano in favor of joint problem solving, Aguilar set in motion training programs for all committee people of any caucus on how to pursue grievances. He was generally regarded as someone who was fair and put the membership first.

Why did the People's Caucus lose the top spots? People's Caucus members and others have suggested a variety of reasons, can choose to base their power on the company's power rather than the rank and file's. Union leaders offer a cooperative relationship with the company, helping to run the workplace and discipline the workforce. In exchange, the company offers its power to help union leaders keep their positions by rewarding friends, punishing enemies, and occasionally making the officials look good.

Looking to management and its allies for protection may seem to offer an easier, safer course than democratic unionism.

Take the case of SEIU Local 32B-32J, which represents janitors, doormen, and elevator operators in New York City. The president of

---

some special to the circumstances: some say the People's Caucus started its campaign late, over-confident, and poorly organized. But mainly the members were lured by the business model of unionism. Nano was able to appeal to the illusions that members often have about unions and politics alike: leaders deliver the goods. If you don't like what you're getting, fire the bunch. Then go home and wait. "Are you a new-hire who doesn't like the two-tier negotiated in the last contract? Don't ask how you should organize to change it; just vote for me."

It was the membership belief in this service model that allowed Nano to pin the blame for unpopular contract provisions on Aguilar, despite the fact that Aguilar had opposed them and was in the minority on the bargaining committee.

The People's Caucus itself failed to counter the business union message. Many of their leaders thought they could use the same "We-do-it-all-for-you" approach as Nano. It's not that People's Caucus members were against membership mobilization. But it was never a part of their UAW training and consciousness. They underestimated the anger the members had with the day-to-day operation of the NUMMI system and did not recognize that clean and fair grievance administration was not enough. Members wanted something done.

Because the People's Caucus did not have the cooperation of either the UAW international or the company, the good service campaign just bolstered the Administration Caucus's claims that it could get more; they were the ones with connections to powerful people. The only power the People's Caucus had was its base in the membership. The more effective, though difficult, strategy would have been a campaign that emphasized membership initiative and action.

the local, Gus Bevona, makes multiple salaries totaling about half a million dollars, plus considerable expenses and perks. In 1997, reformers in the local called for a referendum on cutting officers' salaries (Bevona would have had to get by on $122,000 a year), and on electing rather than appointing the business agents who are supposed to handle daily representation duties.

The reformers lost 55-45 percent (they needed two-thirds) but went to court because of election irregularities. The judge ordered a new election, noting that members had to mark ballots in view of union officials who were wearing "Vote No" stickers; ballots were in English only (many members speak only Spanish); there was only one voting place in the city, with limited hours; and the ballot carried a message from the leadership urging a no vote.

The reformers welcomed the ruling, convinced that with a fair vote—to be conducted by an outside agency—they would surely win. But when the vote was held in February 1998, Bevona won by 70 percent. To be sure, there were election irregularities, including an enormous amount of official campaigning on union time. But probably more important was Bevona's campaign. His machine created a climate of fear—on both a general level (the union, jobs, and pensions will be destroyed) and on a personal level (support the reformers and your business agent may forget about you). The Bevona machine, by its own power and by its close relationship with the employers, was able to make such fears credible.[1]

If you spoke to Gus Bevona about this campaign, he would probably express a conception of unionism that justifies his pay and power. Members too adopt views on how unions work that become powerful supports for the status quo and barriers to democratic reform. We now turn to consider these conceptions. We'll look at different models of unionism, the belief in the "powerful provider," and the smokescreen around democracy.

The Business Model of Unionism

Most Americans unions, local and international, operate as though they were a business providing services to customers. The customers are the members and the employers. In this view, the union is the officers and staff. They provide services for members, including grievance handling, contract bargaining, and various social services; that's why staffers often have titles like "servicing rep" or "business agent." Paying dues to the union is like hiring a lawyer. The lawyer is the expert and you turn your case over to her. She tells you what to do and what your choices are.

In the boom years after World War II, business-model unions were able to deliver wage increases without much activity on the part of the rank and file. Nearly every contract contained substantial improvements. Management could pass on increased costs to consumers; they were ready to deal.

But the basis for such deals fell apart in the 1970s. Competition from now-rebuilt factories in other countries meant profits could be maintained only by reducing costs, including labor costs. Although

Looking for the Powerful Provider

The 1998 election for president of the Teamsters, where James Hoffa "Junior" won 55 percent of the vote, is an example of the appeal of the "powerful provider," the strong leader who will do it for the members. Invoking his father's name and using the slogan "Restore the Power," Hoffa called up an image of the strong man pounding on the table and causing the bosses to shrink back in terror.

TDU, on the other hand, when the group campaigned for reformer Tom Leedham, didn't promise immediate success against the employers' offensive. They reminded members that victory would require lots of hard work.

Hoffa offered easy results: take one Hoffa, mix with union office, and get instant Teamster power. The members didn't have to do anything difficult, take chances, or use their own valuable time. All they had to do was mark the ballot for tough guy Jimmy.

Given Hoffa's other advantages, including a mesmerized press, a huge campaign budget, and a three-year head start on the campaign (Hoffa ran and lost against Ron Carey in the overturned 1996 election), it is a victory for the rank and file model of unionism that he won only 55 percent of the vote. Apparently over the years many members had come to learn that the way to power was not through blowhard leaders.

Hoffa expounded again on his theory of union power after the UPS strike when he told the press, "You want a union with a lot of money in the bank, and a strong leader. That's what gets an employer's attention."[2]

recently some union officials have begun to discuss new strategies to deal with the vastly changed situation, most still rely on the business model whose success ran out decades ago.

The business model precludes democracy by denying knowledge to all but the experts. Members don't have the opportunity to learn about winning grievances, bargaining, or figuring out strategy, and the idea that they need servicing becomes self-fulfilling. As contracts become more and more complicated, the existence of experts is justified.

The question of expertise is then used against any group of members that questions officials' strategy. A recurring theme in incumbents' campaign literature, for instance, is the checklist on expertise, noting that the rank and file challengers have "never bargained a contract, never prepared an arbitration case..." Of course not! Only the officers are involved in those processes.

The business model is not just the product of controlling union officials. It serves the interests of management and others who seek a compliant, "business-like" union. Instead of dealing with various, often angry, rank and filers, management would rather deal with someone who dresses and talks much like themselves, someone who has far less at stake in a decision on working conditions—a "business agent."

Of course, the business model as described here is the best version, where leaders actually do try to deliver for the dues-payers. Worse is the "no-service" model, where office holders see the union as a means to enrich themselves, a barony to be handed down to sons and nephews. With high-paying jobs at stake, these autocrats will use any tactics to retain their perks. They may use undemocratic rules to prevent members from running for office. They may ask management to fire members who speak out at union meetings, or retaliate against them at the hiring hall. They may hire detectives to follow dissidents. In such unions, the rank and file's tendency is toward cynicism and passivity; it's remarkable that some do form caucuses and run for office under these circumstances.

Most local unions are not this bad, of course. But even where leaders are not corrupt, where members do seem to have every opportunity to take control through honest elections, it's still not common for a sizable group of rank and filers to get together and say, "Let's take back our union and run it ourselves." Why?

The business model has definite attractions. Who wouldn't prefer to "leave the driving to us," as Greyhound used to advertise? Union members have demands on their time, from kids to church to overtime. Why go through all the headaches of meetings, debates, campaigning, all the frustrations of trying to convince others to be active, all the possible repercussions from management, if the local president can deliver the goods instead? It's comforting to think that all you need for a strong union is a strong leader who can take care of you.

Members thus can easily get stuck between a rational desire to be "serviced" and the frustration that comes when their hired leaders don't deliver, as happens more and more often. And if finally new leaders are elected who do want members to take responsibility, they are frustrated when members resist getting active. Our entire culture has taught them that it's the officers' job, not the members'.

Almost everything in our society teaches the message that we *can't* do it ourselves, anyway. In particular, the relationship between boss and worker starts, from the moment of hiring, by establishing that the boss has power and the worker has none: the worker needs a job to live; the employer can pick and choose whom to hire. Much of the new technology and the de-skilling of jobs leave the worker with less power than before. Advertising reinforces the idea that our only "power" in the world is to acquire more stuff (but we get to choose which brand). In the face of all these messages, it's no wonder that many union members don't even try to take back their unions.

The Organizing Model

In the last few years, many union activists have talked about replacing the "servicing model" of unionism with the "organizing model." Under this method of functioning, members are involved and active on their own behalf. For example, rather than a steward simply writing up a member's grievance, arguing it out with management behind closed doors, and reporting the results six months later, the organizing model would have him talk to lots of members about the issue and get them to sign on, making it a group grievance. If management is stubborn they pull an action of some kind, such as all wearing stickers on the same day. If necessary they escalate to actions that disrupt the work flow, like all visiting the boss's office together. They're in motion; they're organized.

The organizing model is a big step forward from the servicing model, but it can have limitations. In practice, some union leaders encourage member *involvement* without member *control.* They expect to turn member involvement on and off like a faucet. That way, leaders can keep tighter control of a possibly volatile situation. When the rank and file await their marching orders from clever staffers or officials, there's less likelihood they'll undertake tactics that step outside conventional boundaries, or threaten deals made elsewhere.

An example was the "mobilization" for the Detroit newspaper strike. In the strike's early days, in September 1995, local leaders called a rally and march on the newspapers' printing plant. Members and supporters, feeling a sense of strength, decided to stay overnight at the plant gates to block scab trucks from exiting with the important Sunday edition. When the companies obtained an injunction against picketing, leaders quickly turned the mobilizing faucet off and ordered members away from the gates. They held no meetings

An 'Organizing Model' that Falls Short

When unionists talk about discarding the "servicing model" of unionism and building an "organizing model," sometimes the wires get crossed because "organizing" means two different things.

For some, the organizing model means member mobilization. For others, the organizing model means that the union should change priorities to put more resources into recruiting new members. A large percentage of the budget should go to the Organizing Department, and staff resources spent on "servicing" the already organized should be decreased.

In this second sense, the "organizing model" is not enough. It's true that protecting working conditions for the already organized depends on spreading unionism. But the most effective organizing tool is a winning union—a union its members can brag about. As John Sweeney told the 1997 AFL-CIO convention, "You could make a million house calls and run a thousand television commercials and stage a hundred strawberry rallies and still not come close to doing what the UPS strike did for organizing."

After the 1997 UPS strike, more UPS workers than ever contacted the Teamsters Organizing Department to volunteer for the to discuss the decision, or even other tactics. Instead, they tried to turn members' energy toward a much tamer tactic—leafleting for a boycott of the newspapers' advertisers. Denied the opportunity to choose or even discuss strike strategy, members' participation dropped.

Top-down mobilizing tends to be inflexible, to say, "Here are the steps. Follow them." Now that various unions have involved members in contract campaigns, there tends to be a formula for how to carry them out. The steps are predetermined and members are not involved in making decisions on when or how to act. If the manual says "petition day comes before sticker day," that's the way it's got to be.

Members are often enthusiastic when first invited to get involved in organizing model-type actions. But they may have their own ideas about effective tactics or timing. If they're not allowed some say in the new actions, they'll eventually vote with their feet. If enough members are turned off this way, the actions fail. In the

drive at Fed Ex. The best organizers are empowered union members; that means bringing in new members has to be combined with winning better conditions for current ones.

Another example is the organizing done by UAW Local 3000, based at a Mazda-Ford joint venture in Flat Rock, Michigan. These assembly plant workers helped organize four smaller parts plants that supplied Mazda. The local recruited members to work on the campaigns and invited workers from the targeted plants to union awareness classes. Mazda workers made home visits and leafleted the plants: "Have no fear. We are three thousand members strong! Come join us." A week before one election, a 150-car caravan traveled 50 miles past the home of the plant manager on the way to a union rally.

The Mazda workers joined in enthusiastically to recruit their lower-paid sisters and brothers because they had experienced power in their own local. Earlier, a reform slate had won office against officials who were management's partner in implementing "lean production" when the plant opened. Many Local 3000 members had never belonged to a union before, but after electing reformers they organized an aggressive contract campaign and a spontaneous protest against an unfair attendance policy. The union was theirs, and they were glad to invite others to be part of it.

long term, top-down mobilizing does not develop new leaders. Nor is it the best way to get members to volunteer to organize new workplaces; how inspired can you be about your union if you have no say in it yourself?

Enthusiasm for the union is also key to building solidarity beyond the membership; potential supporters are mostly inspired by person-to-person contact and seeing that the people involved are active and making even greater sacrifices. But if the members of a striking union participate only as troops following marching orders, they're unlikely to inspire others; their solidarity does not become infectious. Some of the best-known labor solidarity efforts have depended on "road warriors": rank and filers who took up their cause as a full-time job and traveled to spread the word about Local P-9 at Hormel, Pittston, the Staley lockout, Ravenswood, the Diamond Walnut strike.

If democracy helps build member involvement, why not? Officials who want the ranks involved as troops often see rank and file *leadership* as a risk. Members may gain skills and confidence; they may demand even more say-so. Members who take initiative may run for office or in other ways get out of control. They may, for instance, organize a job action about working conditions the week after union and management officials agree to a cooperation program.

The case of the janitors of SEIU Local 399 in Los Angeles is an example of the "faucet" approach to mobilization. When SEIU staff were organizing these mostly Latino immigrant cleaners for union recognition, they conducted a whole range of militant actions. Janitors staged civil disobedience to disrupt business as usual in luxury office buildings and were beaten by the police. Finally they won a union and a contract.

Then they found themselves in a 25,000-member citywide SEIU local run very much in the old style. Suddenly it was business-as-usual unionism. In response, the janitors joined with health care workers to organize a dissident slate called the Multiracial Alliance for the local's first contested election ever; they won every seat except the presidency (which they did not challenge). The old president refused to cooperate, there was some tumult—and the SEIU's president, John Sweeney, threw the local into trusteeship. The rank and filers had violated the understanding that their militant organizing was to stop when the staffers turned off the faucet.

Since the term "organizing model" can mean either a top-down version or a bottom-up one, we won't use that term in this book. When we want to talk about getting in the boss's face, and members having the chance to shape whether, how, and when to do that, we'll talk about "democracy" and "rank and file power."

Our constant emphasis on the rank and file does not mean that we're against strong leaders. On the contrary, democracy makes leaders stronger—they look over their shoulder, and they've got someone behind them. We're describing a healthy relationship between leaders and the ranks, not a way for the ranks to eliminate

---

With a Flick of the Faucet...

One sign of top-down mobilizing is quick about-faces in basic strategy. SEIU's Justice for Janitors campaign in Washington, D.C. switched from militancy to "cooperation" with building owners with the writing of one open letter. Justice for Janitors campaigns have mobilized tens of thousands of building cleaners in various cities to demand union recognition. A partially successful ten-year campaign in Washington included sit-ins and blocking bridges. In early 1997, SEIU President Andy Stern decided to turn off the faucet: he sent a letter to building owners pledging to stop "strikes, picketing and similar activities" in return for the hope that owners would pressure the contractors who directly employ the janitors.

Before, the building owners were considered part of the management team that benefits from holding down pay and working conditions. Now, the union was proposing to the owners a partnership, and saying to all those janitors who helped stage protests, "You may now go home."

There is nothing wrong with unions changing strategies, and union leaders should be able to make occasional quick, perhaps drastic, tactical shifts. But each time such a top-down shift is made, there's a cost to members' confidence in their leaders. If union officials have not already proven they'll seek full democratic decision-making wherever possible, or if officials chart a course that most rank and filers would have opposed given the chance, the cost will be high. In the janitors' case, it seems unlikely that many of them changed their minds about the building owners in May 1997 just because Stern wrote his letter; we expect they'll be disheartened and less willing to participate the next time.

leadership. In fact, as we discuss in Chapter 2, the relationship between an empowered membership and a strong leadership is a central part of union democracy.

Democracy and the New AFL-CIO

Since 1995 the AFL-CIO has seen big changes at the top levels. The election of new, energetic leaders was a boost to unions' image. John Sweeney's New Voice team, and thousands of lower-level officers, staff, and activists in various unions, are calling for rebuilding labor by organizing the unorganized and making political action count. In many places, they're calling on members to get involved in these projects. What the New Voice team is not calling for, though, is a new, more democratic way of running our unions.

A Little Mobilization

To their credit, the new AFL-CIO leaders encourage membership mobilization on several fronts. They encourage affiliates to train members as volunteer organizers; they envision "street heat" teams to carry out cross-union solidarity actions; and they propose a "permanent base of at least 100 union activists in each Congressional district" to augment the work of paid lobbyists on Capitol Hill.

But there's mobilization and there's mobilization. Without a big increase in democracy, the faucet model is the only way the labor movement can mobilize people.

One sign of faucet-style mobilizing is large numbers of staffers with their hands on the tap. Both as president of the Service Employees International Union and at the AFL-CIO, Sweeney has dealt with just about any issue by hiring more staff: the 50 new state AFL-CIO directors plus four new regional directors and their assistants hired in 1996-97 are one example.

Choosing Sides

One of the big reasons for top-down mobilizing is a need to control where and when mobilization is to be used. Often top-down mobilizers advocate militant tactics, up to and including civil disobedience, for organizing the unorganized. But such tactics are seldom encouraged when established unions confront management.

This is because the leaders of most international unions—along with the AFL-CIO leadership—are committed to labor-management cooperation. As Sweeney told the 1997 AFL-CIO convention, "One of our paramount goals is to help the companies we work for succeed, to work with our employers to creatively increase productivity and quality and to help American companies compete effectively in the new world economy and create new jobs and new wealth for our families and our communities to share."

Under this win-win scenario, union members benefit without cutting into profits. The problem, of course, is that companies continue to cut jobs, bust unions, and contract out work even when the union is thoroughly cooperative. They're searching for even more profits, and they're not planning to share.

If you're a labor leader who believes in cooperation, though, you have only one criterion for deciding who's a bad employer, to be mobilized against, and a good employer, who deserves cooperation. The employers who allow unions to exist in their facilities are the good ones. We only get militant toward employers that don't recognize the union.

This charting of good employers and bad employers can get pretty confusing. Companies are often switched from one category to the other without any noticeable change in workers' pay and conditions. That's why the cooperators and the top-down mobilizers don't trust the members to decide their own strategy. The question is too subtle to leave in the hands of anyone but top staff.

The AFL-CIO's commitment to labor-management cooperation, and the good employer/bad employer distinction, is illustrated by the partnership with Kaiser Permanente, a health maintenance organization. This arrangement was signed in 1997 by the federation and the affiliated unions (SEIU, AFSCME, and others) that represent Kaiser workers.

Under the agreement, Kaiser gets the AFL-CIO's commitment to aggressively market Kaiser to unions as a health plan; in late 1997, SEIU launched its "I Choose Union Healthcare" campaign as part of fulfilling this promise. What the unions get is recognition on the basis of a card check at any newly-organized Kaiser facilities. Plus, union officials will sit on joint partnership committees for nonbinding discussion of future changes in Kaiser's operations.

The AFL-CIO initiated the partnership at a time when Kaiser was systematically cutting jobs, speeding up employees, demanding pay cuts, and planning to close facilities and contract out major operations. Kaiser workers have charged that quality of care is being hurt badly, and federal investigators have cited serious deficiencies. But because the AFL-CIO unions are now bound to market Kaiser, they will have to keep their mouths shut about problems with the quality of care. They will lose an important weapon in their fight against these conditions—the possibility of drawing on public support.

What unions gain is a chance to organize Kaiser workers without employer resistance. Kaiser joins the ranks of "good" employers.

Cooperation is a mistaken strategy, and it tends to distance union officials from the members since those officials must always be sensitive to management's needs. In theory, members could choose cooperative strategies; democracy doesn't guarantee good choices. In reality, though, most union members exposed to cooperation programs quickly find that management's "actions speak louder than words" (this was the Teamsters' slogan about UPS's team concept program in the months before the 1997 strike). Workers in partnership programs find the employer is still trying to squeeze more work out of fewer people, and they are understandably angry.

When union officials are committed to cooperation, rank and file anger must be repressed to maintain good relations. Seldom are the ranks involved in deciding when, and over what issues, to end a joint program. Officials who favor cooperation believe the members would end it with little provocation, and they're probably right. That's why it's important to officials that they keep control of that decision.

In many ways, the AFL-CIO's plans for revitalizing labor are very ambitious; in other ways, they continue the same old policies. But even the AFL-CIO's version of revitalization will not go far without democracy, without rank and filers organizing themselves. The massive scale of organizing now proposed, for instance, can't happen under staff control, if only because of the numbers; members must be out there telling their stories, sometimes acting on their own initiative. And members will have the stories to tell only if we increase union strength through democracy.

The Smokescreen Around Democracy and Power

One of the reasons members don't take control of their unions is that they don't equate democracy with power. Why not? Partly because corrupt union leaders, and even more so corporations, have an interest in maintaining a smokescreen around democracy and power. Members are led to see themselves as dependent on their elected officials, and to see democracy only as a question of mechanics.

The confusion begins with what schools teach and the media reinforces. Ideas about power are not what we're taught in school. We're taught that democracy means simply the right to make a free choice between two candidates, with no stuffing of the ballot box.

Likewise a union is said to be democratic if it has conventions, elections, votes on contracts. But conventions usually act as rubber stamps for top officials, elections may be organized to exclude most of the members as candidates, and contract votes are often taken without providing a true and thorough description of the terms.

In other words, these forms and procedures don't guarantee rank and file power in the union. Certainly conventions, elections, and contract votes are necessary steps, but democracy depends on an on-going process of involving the ranks in knowing and grappling with the real issues facing the union—a process that's not automatic every time a member is handed a ballot. Holding delegate elections where candidates don't discuss the big choices facing the union, for example, is a smokescreen for backroom decisions on those choices.

Another smokescreen is the confusing ideas we've been taught about power—that it means strong-man, individual power, and power over others. School conditioned us to look at history in terms of great people taking heroic actions. Didn't Lincoln free the slaves? Didn't Walter Reuther build the UAW? Didn't Ron Carey win the UPS strike?

Even within the union, power is seen as power to appoint, power to punish your enemies, the power of your machine. Thus power becomes identified with intense personal competition.

Perhaps because of this strong identity between power and personal competition, or perhaps because they've been on the receiving end of dictatorial power in the union, some union members try to give their leaders as little power as possible. In practice, this usually backfires: formal, above-the-table power is replaced by backdoor and informal power, which is less accountable. The answer is not to try to abolish power but to counter personal power with cooperative power.

You will recognize the style of personal, *non*-cooperative power shown below from the way corporations, armies, and other non-democratic institutions function. Unfortunately, this mode is also reflected in how powerful people act in non-democratic unions. Individually and as a group, we have more to gain from cooperating to build our power.

Cooperative power operates differently.

Two Kinds of Power

Union Official Controls Others	Members Cooperate to Wield Power
Control over other people	Control over the problems imposed by the external world
Control over information	Spread information widely
Keep people ignorant	Educate people
Pit people against each other	Identify common interests
One moves up at expense of others	People move up by building others up
Members' involvement is passive: they follow orders	Members actively involved: they contribute ideas and decide direction
Hierarchy controlled from top down	Hierarchy controlled from bottom up
Whoever has the most toys wins	Service, not wealth, is recognized

The power of cooperation is the true power of a union, and the power of the rank and file within a union. This is the power that can explore Mars, create a precision basketball team, or make kids happy at a holiday party. It is a power that is potentially equal to the largest fortunes and the most destructive weapons. It is also the power that transforms the people who use it.

This kind of power brings along with it a different set of personal values and ways that people organize themselves. It is not a new discovery. It has been a theme of solidarity unionism for more than a century. Democracy and cooperative power go hand in hand. Unless many members do this work, the union can't succeed.

Reform and the Workplace

Again, the fundamental purpose of the union is power in the workplace. And since democracy and power are so intertwined, democracy also has to be rooted in the workplace; that's where it makes a difference.

Thus successful pro-democracy union reform efforts are essentially campaigns for workplace changes that the members need; if officials or bylaws get in the way, then they may need to be changed. For example a central organizing tool of Teamsters for a Democratic Union is to organize members for contract demands. (TDU started out as Teamsters for a Decent Contract.) TDU activists often become known as the people who can help with a grievance if the business agent is ignoring it.

When reformers take on workplace issues, officials may decide their methods are more effective and seek coalition with them. Or officials may try to protect their own positions at the expense of winning improvements from the company, thus revealing their own priorities. In any case, few members will work to change bylaws or elect new leaders unless they're convinced it will improve the way the union addresses their problems at work.

Thus, whether we're talking about the elected leaders of a statewide local considering how to make a stewards system work, or about a couple of coworkers at a kitchen table planning how to get a steward replaced, their success or failure in building democracy will be measured in power on the job.

Notes

1. Steven Greenhouse, "Judge Orders New Union Vote," *New York Times,* December 16, 1997; Steven Greenhouse, "Union Big Triumphs in Referendum over own Salary," *New York Times,* February 6, 1998; and Michael Hirsch, "Dissident Building Service Workers Win Supervision of By-Laws Vote," *Labor Notes,* February 1998, p. 5.

2. Dirk Johnson, "Hoffa on the March Again in Quest for Teamsters' Presidency," *New York Times,* September 4, 1997.

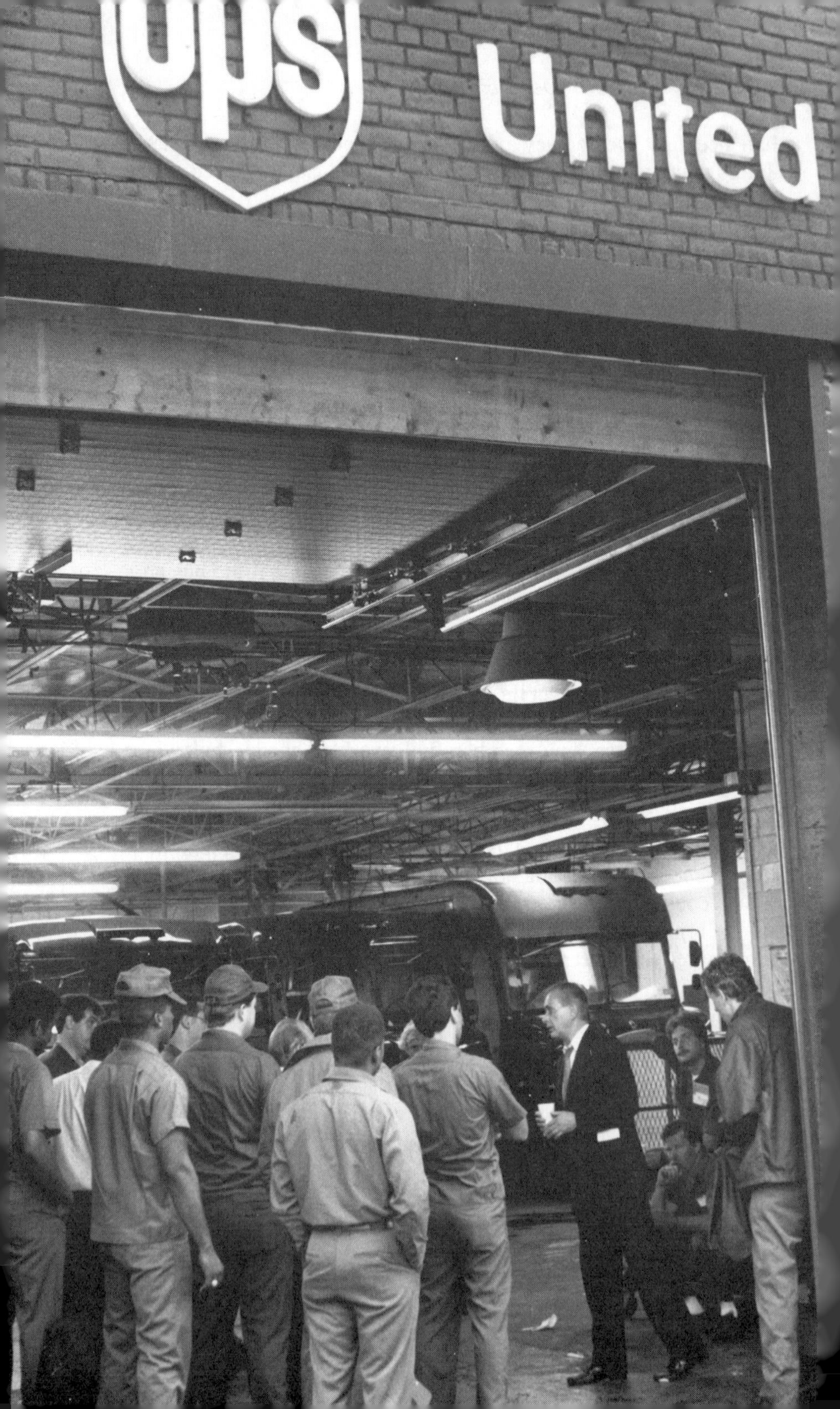
ups
United

2. A Culture of Democracy

We start from the basic notion that democracy is the people ruling. How do we make it happen in our unions? One thing is certain: you can't implement democracy simply by adopting a list of rules. Many unions use bylaws that look very democratic, but it doesn't take long for members to catch on that they hold little power. In other cases, despite using procedures that are essentially undemocratic (such as Robert's Rules of Order) the members know it is their union. The culture of democracy is alive and well.

How do we build such a culture? How do we build it in a world where people have so many different interests, skills, and competing demands on their time? In this chapter we'll describe what a democratic union looks like. Be aware that we're proposing a level of democracy that doesn't much exist in this world, in unions or beyond; so the benchmarks here will be imperfectly met in even the best unions.

Benchmarks of Union Democracy

- The members look to the union for power in dealing with the employer, the community, other unions, politicians.

- The members decide how the union deals with these forces.

- "The union" is "we," not "they."

- The issues facing the union and options for action are discussed openly:

  Mechanisms exist for issues to be voiced.

  Decisions are made openly, in the forums established for that purpose (such as executive board meetings or membership meetings).

  Expression of dissenting views, and organizing to promote them, are encouraged rather than punished.

- Leaders and followers are strongly linked.

  Leaders act in the interests of members.

  Members easily organize themselves, without waiting for marching orders.

  Members move easily into activist and leadership positions.

  Leaders encourage participation and help new leaders to develop, and there are many sources of leadership.

  The members trust the leaders and the leaders trust the members.

In other words, democracy is member power, participation, and a certain relationship between leaders and the ranks. Democracy is about power over the things that matter. Motions and votes and other procedures are valuable if they contribute to this bottom line.

The primary place to check for these benchmarks is in the workplace: how are job issues, grievances, and contract terms handled? If the union is functioning democratically there, it will be easier to carry that culture into other areas such as union meetings and elections, or other decisions such as how much money to budget for organizing.

Make Workplace Culture a Union Culture

Union democracy at the workplace level means that unionism is part of what people do at work day in and day out. It needs to be taught, in this individualistic society, but a union culture means that it becomes second nature for members to take a stand for solidarity when they see the need:

- A member sees management abusing another worker and tells the manager that the union does not tolerate that kind of behavior.

- A member sees a fellow worker engaging in sexual harassment and explains why it must stop immediately.

- A member meets a nonunion worker and works to recruit her to the union.

In other words, in this culture solidarity is the norm and the expectation: members don't feel they have to justify activities that contribute to solidarity, they would feel pressed to justify the exceptions. And members don't sit back and wait for a union rep to take care of problems. They take the initiative, whether it's on a grievance, on a problem not covered by the contract, or on organizing a response to a new management scheme or program.

Leaders and activists can help develop a union culture on the job through simple organizing techniques. The most basic element is making the workplace the place where union issues are discussed. Since most union members seldom attend meetings, the broadest, and often the most honest and imaginative, discussions about union strategies happen informally at work—on breaks or at lunch, or waiting for the copier. The union should not only defend members' right to express various points of view in the workplace, it should encourage the means. It should insist on members' right to distribute their own leaflets and to post any kind of union-related material they wish on accessible bulletin boards. One sign of an authoritarian atmosphere is a policy prohibiting workers from posting their own notices without management approval. Often even union bulletin boards are under lock and allow only "official" union publications, initialed by an officer.

Good discussion depends on good information. Is union literature circulated in the workplace, rather than just mailed to members' homes? Are contracts, including all letters of understanding, made available? Do members have easy access to the status of all grievances in progress or recently decided? One of the most important sources of information is other unions dealing with similar circumstances or the same company. Are members encouraged to contact other locals on their own, or do officers make this as difficult as possible (see the box)?

One key to making union culture central to the workplace is recognizing natural work groups. Every good organizer understands the idea of "mapping" the informal communications patterns in the workplace.[1] Leaders can find out who the natural leaders are and make sure they are part of the union information system in both directions (getting information out and gathering feedback). Officers can show up at the workplace on a regular basis for informal but organized discussions with the members; in between, stewards should report what co-workers are saying about their concerns.

Modern management techniques such as quality task forces and work teams lend urgency to the idea of making the workplace culture a union culture.[2] Management designs these programs to gradually strip members of their union identity and promote identification with the "company team" instead. They try to institute their own brand of workplace culture, with "champions," "change agents," and "consensus." Often the programs go under the guise of "workplace democracy," as management makes a point of gathering "input" from workers. Participation programs include their own layer of facilitators or team leaders, a group of union members who are paid to help the program succeed. That is, their job is to promote the idea among co-workers that the company's interests are their own.

At the Saturn plant in Spring Hill, Tennessee, for instance—one of the best-known team concept programs—hundreds of members are appointed to help run the program, out of 7,200 total workers.

Postal Union Says 'No Addresses'

Control of information—especially information that would allow members to be in direct contact with each other—is often seen as key to officials' grip on their positions. Rank and file delegates at the National Association of Letter Carriers' 1996 convention proposed what would seem a common sense resolution to help local branches (local unions) learn from each other:

> Resolved, that the National Headquarters of the NALC publish annually a directory of all NALC branches. This directory shall consist of the mailing address of each branch. Branches may reserve the right to refuse publication for their branch address in the said directory.

The national executive board opposed the resolution, but it passed. Late in 1996 the national office sent branches a notice requiring that they specifically notify the national office if they wanted to be included in the directory. By the simple technique of changing the implementation from "opting out" to "opting in," and depending on the tendency for projects that are not pushed to be buried, the national officials tried to sabotage the project. Even still, the final publication included addresses for nearly two-thirds of the NALC's 3,000 branches (and none for the NALC state associations).[3]

The appointees work mostly straight day shifts while the rest of the plant works grueling alternating shifts; the appointees lose contact with life on the assembly line and have an investment in keeping the program going.

It falls to the union (or reformers within) to champion real workplace democracy. Workers' best chance for any say over working conditions is a contract and members' initiative to enforce it on the shop floor. Meanwhile, they can do their best to besiege the teams with union culture and values. First, the union should organize open debate on the impact of the teams, both at the hall and on the shop floor, to replace the backbiting and resentment that so often poison relations among members. Second, the union should insist that positions such as team leader be elected so that any who become too enamored of the corporate line can be replaced. Third, unions should train members that they are representing the union—not simply their own individual ideas—whenever they meet with management in task forces or teams. Members should make a habit of calling timeout for a union caucus at these meetings, and then deal with management in a united way. Thus solutions to workplace problems get hashed out with other union members, not through brainstorming with the labor-management quality team.

Discuss the Real Issues

The value of open debate ought to be non-controversial. It's the best way for a group of people to put their heads together to find the best possible solutions. In practice, lack of democracy begins with lack of real discussion. For instance, many officials don't involve members in winning a new contract: members don't help formulate demands or bargaining strategy. And when they vote on ratification, they have to make a decision based on a pep-talk, without seeing the actual contract. That's why many successful union democracy efforts started as rank and file-organized contract campaigns (see the TDU section of the introduction and a Machinists example in Chapter 1). Members wanted to discuss their contract concerns and the leadership wasn't listening. The issues that affect work life most—work reorganization and rapid technological change—need to be discussed in the break rooms as well as at local meetings. If the ranks aren't involved in forming strategies on these questions, it doesn't matter how brilliant are the policies developed at higher levels.

Freedom of discussion is far more than the right to speak at a union meeting. If members with different points of view are intimidated or insulted, discussion doesn't get far. Attendees can tell whether questions and criticism are considered normal or offensive, and most people won't bother to raise concerns if it will annoy the gathered body. The columns of union newspapers contain many examples of official derision of opposing views.

Another way to limit debate is by simply filling meeting time with boring reports. Or officers can informally squelch debate by making it clear that they deal with the real issues elsewhere, behind closed doors. Then speaking up at membership meetings or talking about union strategy over coffee break may be tolerated, but irrelevant. Again, few people will bother.

Some top-down officers will allow debate as long as members speak as individuals, but not as an organized group. But the right to form a caucus or committee dedicated to some viewpoint is a key part of the right to express that viewpoint. At the 1996 SEIU convention, for example, a caucus of reform delegates brought several proposals, including one to eliminate multiple salaries for international officers. President Andy Stern allowed a limited debate on the multiple salaries proposal. But at the same time he told leaders of the reform caucus that they could join his (unopposed) slate for international executive board only if they disbanded the caucus. They were not asked to stop speaking out as individuals on multiple salaries or other reform issues, just to stop organizing on that basis.

Maintaining free discussion turns out to be difficult in practice. A harsh tone can cause hard feelings. It's often hard to get a roomful of people to concentrate on the same issue at the same time; what some feel is an exercise of their right to free discussion may be seen by others as talking too long. (Information on leading a good meeting is in Appendix 2.)

Who's a Leader?

Union reformers hold divergent views of leadership. Some think their union will be healthy if they can just get a new set—the right set—of leaders. Others—after decades of experience with incompetent or corrupt officers—see the problem as the idea of leadership itself. In this view the best way to democratize the union is to do away with leaders' power, or at least limit it with more checks and balances.

We see leadership differently—as a needed tool in a complicated world. Leaders help us make sense of things we do not understand ourselves. Union leaders need a combination of knowledge and vision, applied to the members' concerns. Good leaders have proposals to solve problems, and the guts to see them through. A democratic union culture requires more leaders, not fewer; stronger leaders, not weaker ones.

Leadership is far more than just elected positions. You may look to your steward or your local union president, but many other people, publications, or institutions also help us understand the complex world. Some may look to the President or their Senator, to Oprah Winfrey, Jesse Jackson, or Rush Limbaugh for getting a handle on what is important. But leaders can also include the buddy who understands computers, the economics columnist in the newspaper, teachers, religious leaders, or the woman in the next department who seems to know how to handle the boss. These are all types of leaders, possessing some combination of expertise, personal character, and a viewpoint close to our own.

Most people serve as both leader and follower. The union president might look to one rank and file member as his leader on technology and to another on city politics. The most important leader on health and safety questions in the local may be a steward. Someone may be the informal leader of her work group as well as a loyal follower of the local president. In every workplace there are informal

What Does a Leader Do?

Teamster activist Joe Fahey asks a simple question to start a discussion about members taking leadership. He asks for people to throw out one- or two-word descriptions of things a good leader does. Here are some typical responses:

Works	Provides direction	Motivates others
Fights	Reacts to events	Brings together
Guides	Negotiates	Promotes others
Campaigns	Facilitates	Models behavior
Clarifies issues	Takes heat	Cares
Supports others	Informs others	Takes chances
Investigates issues	Educates others	

groups—maybe people who hang out together on lunch breaks or bowl together after work. And these groups have their own leaders. Any strong union organization takes these informal leaders into account in distributing and collecting information, in mobilizing the members, and in looking for new leaders for elected positions.

People also move in and out of leadership, sometimes quickly

A Top-Down Decision May Be Best

In a surprise move in 1994, UPS changed its longstanding weight limitation for packages: package sorters and drivers would now be required to lift 150 pounds, not just 70. In response, Teamsters President Ron Carey called, on short notice, a national strike to force the company to bargain the issue. In one day UPS folded. Although many old guard local officers told their members not to strike, the action did force UPS to the table. Negotiations led to the right to get help from another Teamster to handle any package over 70 pounds.

The decision to strike was made at the top of the union with no discussion or vote by the ranks. Was the decision democratic? By itself, the decision was neither democratic nor undemocratic. It *was* part of an increasingly democratic relationship between Teamster leaders and members.

First, the strike could not have succeeded without widespread membership support. Indeed, in every local where the officers supported the strike call, the members overwhelmingly stood up to management's threats (often relayed by the old guard) and walked out. Teamster leaders had to be in close enough touch with the members to be confident they'd support the action in large numbers. Second, the top leaders knew that the members could and would hold leaders accountable for the results of the strike: there would be a national election soon with viable candidates in opposition.

The decision involved risks. The contract had a no-strike clause. It was very possible that courts would rule the strike a contract violation. It was technically possible (though unlikely) that striking members could be fired; the union could possibly be sued for massive amounts of money.

Given the possible severe consequences of defeat for the members and the union treasury, shouldn't there have been a discussion in the union and a vote before action was taken? Indeed, if there had (as when someone asserts himself on a particular issue at a meeting), sometimes over a long time. Most people are fully capable of increasing their leadership ability through work, study, or experience. The frequency with which members develop their expertise and use it to take on leadership roles is a sign of the health of a union's democracy.

been an initial poll, chances are that many, perhaps even most members would have opposed walking out. A good portion of the membership was still cynical about the union and unionism. Old guard officials would have campaigned hard against taking any action. So a strike vote might not have passed.

There are good reasons to have waged an internal campaign prior to taking action—a more united membership, clear on the issues and strategy, would be better able to stand up to management threats.

On the other hand, there were good reasons to act immediately. UPS was vulnerable because it did not have plans and resources in place for a massive strike. A long internal preparation period would guarantee that UPS would also prepare, and an important union advantage would be lost. The sudden policy change made the issue clear and hot now. Waiting would mean that UPS would be able to carry out its oft-used divide and conquer strategy. The policy would be implemented differently at different centers, and it would be harder to establish an obvious point to take action. Finally, the company policy was a direct threat to worker safety. The union needed a strong and immediate response,

Teamster leaders had to weigh all the pros and cons of immediate action versus a campaign to involve the members in making strategy. This single top-down decision couldn't by itself destroy a democratic relationship between leaders and members. In fact, a top-down decision could even bolster democracy.

For instance, it's logical to think that the union may have been strengthened in two ways. For one, UPS members, including those who did not strike, got the message that more militance against the company is possible and useful. Second, the old guard's ability to scare some members out of striking may have reinforced for international leaders the need to have the ranks solidly on board before a major action. Before the 1997 UPS contract deadline, top Teamster officials certainly did work hard to make this unity happen.

How Far Out Front Should Leaders Be?

We need for union leaders to point the direction and step out front—not just carry out members' instructions. At the same time, we require leaders to listen to members about strategy and direction, and often, in fact, to carry out members' instructions. For democracy, leaders must strike a balance between leading the way based on their own knowledge and vision, and taking direction from members. It's not always easy to know how to do that.

Consider, for example, the Service Employees International Union's Committee on the Future. John Sweeney as SEIU president convened this committee in 1992 to study the union's situation and make recommendations for its future course. The group of local and international officials conducted surveys, held meetings at 70 work sites, and consulted with outside experts over a four-year period. The committee published a refreshingly honest report on their findings in early 1996.

Of course, Sweeney and other SEIU leaders already knew what they thought the union needed. Sweeney had been talking for years about the need for more organizing, a theme he carried into the AFL-CIO leadership. The Committee on the Future found, however, that the members distrusted new organizing as a solution to their problems at work; the union already did not seem effective on the job, so members were uneasy about removing resources from servicing.

As Sweeney's successor Andy Stern took the union's helm in 1996, the Committee on the Future recommended, and the convention adopted, a new program to shift resources into organizing— even though the members had said that was not what they wanted.

Was Andy Stern and the SEIU leadership stepping out front, appropriately, on a program that many believe is vital to the union's survival? Or was the SEIU leadership, confident in their superior analysis, ignoring the members' right to make decisions on the future of their own union?

Judging by the relationship between SEIU leaders and the ranks, we would say both are true. The need for new organizing is clear and immediate; leaders should take the lead in showing how it can be done.

But in SEIU, alternative leadership is not encouraged to articulate a different vision for the future. At the same 1996 convention that adopted the Committee on the Future report, a group of local officers that had been organizing for more democracy was dismantled, through a combination of threats and rewards; alternative leadership and vision were removed.

Did the Committee on the Future process help involve members in their union by giving them a feeling of control? More likely, for those that participated by completing a survey or speaking to the committee, the outcome seemed like a foregone conclusion and their participation of little use.

Was the committee's research on members' views part on an ongoing exchange of views between leaders and members? In the SEIU, like most large unions, communication between the members and leaders at any level is weak—composed mostly of newsletters composed by staff and occasional votes taken among the members. That was one reason the Committee on the Future's series of meetings with members was remarkable: it was an exception.

Now that the program has been adopted, do the ranks have a reasonable chance to judge its effectiveness and adjust the policies later, or elect new international leaders who will? The SEIU's convention system and culture of top-down leadership and staff control make that nearly impossible in the foreseeable future.

Has the SEIU leadership built up trust among the members by acting democratically on members' concerns over the years? Such trust, earned over time, allows leaders to step farther out front and still have members follow. But one of the Committee on the Future's findings was that members want more voice on the job and in their union—a sign that their trust of leaders is not strong.

The SEIU leadership did give a nod to members' desire for democracy by including "expanding members' voice" among their stated goals; the international magazine has occasionally since 1996 highlighted locals that are training members to take over more of their grievance handling.

Since the new organizing program cannot succeed without members' approval—that is, volunteering their time as organizers—members do have some control. But without an ongoing debate over the strategy, SEIU risks that members will continue to feel the leadership's program has little to do with them.

Leaders Should Lead

Union leaders are not just a statistical sample of the membership. Since they are more active in the union than the average member, they are likely to be more knowledgeable about issues facing the union and to spend more time thinking about strategies. These differences mean that leaders have different points of view than the members on many questions. (Here we're not talking about the leader who is out of touch because she's adopted a management point of view or lifestyle, but the good leader who's had more experience and a chance for a broader view than most of the rank and file.) What should be the relationship between what leaders do and the positions held by the members? It is not leadership simply to announce the results of a membership opinion poll, or to do the political equivalent. For members to have real alternatives, leaders must actually lead. They must step out front to argue for what they believe is the best plan of action even if the members do not currently agree. Those who disagree should step forward and offer a different plan.

When leaders step out front in a democratic union, it works because there's a feedback loop: a chance for members to reverse policies and/or throw out leaders who have led in the wrong direction.

In a democratic culture, good leaders will, whenever possible, seek to win over the membership before committing the union and its resources externally. It will put forward its program boldly and clearly and rely on discussion, opposition, educational programs, resolutions, and internal campaigns to achieve membership support. The process of debate helps refine and improve the plan. Further, as we argued in Chapter 1, the union's power to implement the plan depends in large part on the membership having a clear understanding and strong commitment to it—results that don't come from sneaking something through or keeping it only among the top leaders. To prepare for the 1997 UPS strike, for example, the Teamsters international waged a contract campaign so that members would be on the program to make the strike and related job actions as effective as possible.

Another example can be seen in the support that the Oil, Chemical and Atomic Workers union gave to the formation of the Labor Party. For many years a few leaders of the OCAW believed that the formation of a Labor Party was essential if the labor movement was ever to break out of its dependent relationship to corporate politicians. There was no spontaneous demand for a Labor Party from the OCAW members, who were probably not much different from other unionists on political views. As a relatively democratic union, the leadership understood that putting big resources into the Labor Party required winning over the members. And they did. Not every member, of course, and for many others their support is minimal and passive. But a significant number of OCAW secondary leaders became Labor Party activists, and the convention regularly voted continued support for the project.

It is not always possible for leaders to take a discussion to the membership before acting (see the box on "A Top-Down Decision"). Decisions here become a real test of leadership. Circumstances may require that union leaders step out and commit themselves and the union on an issue that may not yet have full support among the members. Yet waiting can also have enormous consequences. "No action" is also an action. It is one of the jobs of leaders—one of the reasons we elected them—to make these kinds of judgments and to have sufficient knowledge of and confidence in the members to expect that they will likely agree with the action once it is explained. In a democratic situation a leader also takes the consequences if she misjudges.

Linking Members and Leaders

In a healthy relationship between leaders and members, there's a flow of people, information, and influence, back and forth.

1. Leaders need active members, and that gives members some control over leaders.

Conscientious leaders need "the consent of the governed." They can't lead well if the members don't agree to follow, that is, to participate in the union's affairs. Although some officers think they can or must handle everything themselves, management usually knows whether leaders have anyone behind them. Because leaders need followers to accomplish anything, they have to respond, at least to some degree, to what members want. (Of course many union leaders don't want to accomplish anything beyond a better golf game; this doesn't apply to them.)

This "consent of the governed" connection between leaders and ranks is very clear in the organizing phase of a union. In-plant leaders have to work very hard to respond to potential members' interests and thereby convince them to join. The net result is a highly democratic atmosphere, even if security considerations limit the usual democratic procedures such as election of officers or votes on policy.

A similar situation exists in "right-to-work" states, where belonging to the union is voluntary. Leaders who want to maintain membership numbers have to pay constant attention to recruiting

Does Dues Check-off Harm Democracy?

Before unions got employers to deduct dues from paychecks (the "check-off" system), they had to work hard for the money. In industrial unions, dues collection was one of the main jobs of stewards. Unions that wanted a healthy treasury made sure that the steward was someone strong and respected by the people in her department. This meant in turn that the higher levels of union leadership had to respond to stewards. If members were unhappy it would be harder to collect dues and leaders would hear about it in two powerful ways: the treasury would go down and the stewards would be giving them an earful.

There is no question that the introduction of dues check-off happened right alongside the rapid destruction of the shop-floor steward system in major production industries in the late 1940s and early 1950s. But it's debatable what caused what.[4] Some argue that the bedrock of the steward system and indeed of democracy in the union was the dues collection arrangement.

Given the current bureaucratization of the labor movement, we'd better take this point seriously. The loss of the steward system was probably the biggest single marker of the rise of business-unionism. But before we demand that unions give up dues check-off, consider the alternative arguments:

1. If shop floor leaders spend a big chunk of their time collecting and keeping track of dues, where is the time to organize the members, challenge the boss, do solidarity work with other unions, or organize the unorganized?

2. Doesn't the regular and dispersed handling of so much cash open the way for corruption, fronting for gambling, and mob activity? The numbers racket also depends on regular collections, but no one confuses it with a democratic organization.

new members and retaining current ones, and thus stay in good touch with what workers want. Some believe this situation contributes to a more active membership and healthier internal life than in unions that can require workers to join. (Nonetheless, an open shop is not a good way to strengthen members' control over leaders. An active membership doesn't count for much if too few of the workers in the bargaining unit sign up. Quitting the union may be an immediate tool for showing displeasure with the leaders, but using

3. Wouldn't using dues collection to make the union responsive make it responsive mainly to the people who are least committed to the union? After all, solid union members will always pay quickly. The dues collector mainly has to spend time cajoling the people who are not certain the union is worth it.

4. Should the main qualification for steward be the person who can best collect dues?

5. Doesn't this system hurt the union at the time it is most vulnerable? Tough times when there is high unemployment, layoffs are likely, and people are more inclined to save a little extra by skipping union dues is just the time the union does not need to be hurting financially or dealing even more with dues collection problems. In fact, employers sometimes cut off dues check-off at strategic times to weaken union resistance, as the HMO Kaiser Permanente did during a 16-month contract battle with the California Nurses Association in 1997-98. (The CNA reports that 80 percent of its Kaiser members paid dues anyway.)

6. Doesn't the very idea that people should choose to be in or out of the union on a monthly basis depending on how they feel the union is doing encourage the individualist and consumerist approach that underlies the service model of unionism? On this model, people could decide whether to pay dues or not based on whether they personally received services they felt were worth the money.

7. Was it really dues check-off that caused destruction of the steward system? Or were these two parts of a deal—the general labor-business accord that increased management's control over the shop floor (weakening stewards) in exchange for providing some institutional security for unions (reliable dues collection)?

that tool weakens the union. And in an open shop the boss can count on certain workers to scab and can mark the union members for retribution. If we measure democracy in terms of members' power to use the union against the boss, an open shop isn't a very democratic situation.)

Members have the most control over leaders when they're in a struggle with management. If they want a good contract, leaders need members to come out to rallies, picket, carry on an in-plant campaign—but all these are voluntary acts that members aren't likely to take on if they don't think their leaders are acting in their interests. That's why so many contract campaigns start out with surveys to determine members' priorities.

2. Membership input should be based on good information.

We cannot expect leaders to act in members' interests unless they know what members need and want. And members can't make good decisions without good information. Elections and surveys gather input, but they are only snapshots at particular moments, they tend to provide limited choices, and they often detect only the most intense and widespread views.

More immediate forms of feedback are required: discussions at meetings, letters columns in newsletters, open-door policies at union offices, e-mail and message centers, meetings with intermediate-level leaders, workplace walk-arounds, "working" leadership, and social activities. Officers who spend time on the job site, not just down at the union hall, have a big advantage.

To get good input, leaders must provide good output, through union publications, regular meetings, and formal and informal networks. Telephone trees, web sites, and e-mail are important for fast-moving events.

Here's an example of bad information: because they think the members are not smart enough or can't be trusted with the truth, leaders publish a "summary" of a proposed contract with only the good points highlighted. Leaders may believe that proclaiming every contract a victory will be better for morale in the long run. (Or they do it to save their own jobs.) But members usually see through such declarations. Calling a defeat a victory simply cuts off discussion, and the chance to learn from experience—why the defeat happened and how to keep it from happening again. Ironically, open discussion could actually help officials stay in office by making it clear that it was company power, not leadership incompetence, that caused the loss.

3. Moving into leadership should be fairly easy.

A healthy union strives to expand and replenish leadership. It rejects the notion that training new leaders means "you're training your own opposition." When new people move into activity they bring the members' most current concerns. The union can make becoming a leader as easy and attractive as possible with a mentoring system and a committee structure that is open for participation. The union should encourage college labor studies courses; members can learn a lot more about being a leader through action groups like Jobs with Justice or the Labor Party. In a democratic union, members have the chance to change their leaders. Even if they don't contest every election, there are always alternatives: people with skills and confidence who can voice competing views. Opposition caucuses are the most important source of alternative leaders, and successful caucus leaders consciously train members in the same skills a good union leader needs.

Does Leadership Power Always Corrupt?

In unions and politics, and indeed from athletic clubs to PTAs, there are plenty of examples of leaders who betray those who elected them by serving themselves at the expense of their members. Some social scientists say that leadership in any kind of organization leads directly to betrayal. "Power corrupts," the saying goes. Yet we cannot imagine a society without organization and leaders. Put these "facts" together, and we are doomed to betrayal every time.

The belief that betrayal is inevitable breeds massive cynicism and apathy. But it's not true.

There is abundant writing on the pressures that separate leaders from followers and tend to lead to betrayal. The phrase "the iron law of oligarchy" comes from a classic work by Robert Michels, who observed developments in the German Social Democratic party (the mass political party of the German unions) prior to World War I.[5] Michels argued that initially leaders act to aid the movement. But soon, says Michels, leaders tend to become professionals. The organization's structure becomes an end unto itself and not a tool for the members. The leaders become entrenched and manipulate the organization into serving their own special interests.

Modern unions would seem to confirm the iron law.

First, full-time officials have many reasons to hang onto their positions. Typically their income is significantly higher than members'. The working conditions are usually better too: the jobs are more flexible, and the work is clean, safe, and not physically exhausting. Charles Hughes, president of an AFSCME local representing school crossing guards and cafeteria workers who make $10,000-$15,000 a year, makes $241,000 himself: "I think it's justified," says Hughes. "The members of my local have the best fringe benefits for part-time people in the United States of America."[6] Even when the income difference is not so great, leaders develop a strong interest in protecting their jobs from potential rivals.

Second, organization provides officials with ways to maintain

Socialists in the Labor Movement

Historically, in the U.S. as well as the rest of the world, socialists have been important sources of union leadership and alternative leaders. But in recent decades their radical views have been seen as dangerous and almost anyone who challenges union officials with a more militant outlook could expect to be called a "red."

Socialists, with their vision of a new society that included strong trade unions, developed union leaders who were frequently both self-sacrificing and knowledgeable. They provided the activist cadres for difficult union struggles, and were a strong counter to those who viewed union leadership as a ladder to personal gain. Their long-term vision helped carry unions through difficult periods. In one sense socialist thought is the ideology of unionism carried to its logical conclusion: if workers should have more power and control in the workplace, why shouldn't they have full power and control in society as a whole?

The history of such groups reveals a mixed impact on the labor movement in the United States—some bad, but mostly good. Despite their role in the formation of the labor movement, however, McCarthyism and redbaiting caused socialists to be written out of much of labor history.[7]

their privileges: control of patronage jobs, the distribution of paid time off the job for union activity, and grievance handling are potential ways to reward friends and punish enemies. The officials' control of communications—newsletters and stewards networks—also tends to protect their status. Third, plenty of examples seem to confirm Michels' description of the membership as passive and tending to rely too much on leaders.

Nevertheless, Michels' "iron law" is wrong.

The main problem with this "iron law" is that it confuses forces with outcomes. Yes, there will always be forces that tend to cause leaders to go bad, but such forces are not irresistible. Let's look at the Teamsters, again, for an example. The membership elected a reform team of officers in 1991 that vastly improved communications, got member input, weeded out many of the worst officials, and even won a major strike (against UPS). Then a fundraising scandal was uncovered inside reform leader Ron Carey's 1996 reelection

---

In the height of the redbaiting of the 1950s, UAW President Walter Reuther explained how damaging this was to the cause of labor:

> Many years ago in this country, when the bosses wanted to keep the workers from forming a strong union, they tried starting scares of various kinds. One scare the bosses raised was the Catholic against the Protestant. Another scare they used very successfully, was the American born against the foreign born. Then they placed one foreign group against another, like Poles against Germans, and so on.
>
> All that is played out now. It has been worked too often. So now the bosses are trying a new stunt. They are raising a new scare, the red scare. They pay stools to go whispering around that so and so, usually a militant union leader, is a red. They think that will turn the other workers against him. What the bosses really mean however is not that he is really red; they mean they do not like him because he is a loyal dependable union man, a fighter who helps his brothers and sisters and is not afraid of the boss.
>
> So let's all be careful that we don't play the bosses' game by falling for the red scare. Let's stand by our union and fellow unionist. No union man worthy of the name will play the bosses' game. Some may do so through ignorance but those who peddle the red scare and know what they are doing, are dangerous enemies of the union.[8]

That Reuther's actions were not always consistent with these sentiments does not make the principles any less true.

campaign. Wasn't that proof that no matter the progress, corruption is inevitable? Many disgusted rank and filers voiced the sentiment "they're all alike."

Reform suffered a major setback. But the problem was not inevitable. Carey relied on unscrupulous consultants for much of his 1996 campaign, and they hatched the illegal fundraising scheme. If TDU had been bigger—if reform forces had been stronger—they would have been much more the core of the Carey campaign. Corrupt consultants would never have had such influence in the campaign or the union.

What's more, even with this setback, which led to a chance for the old guard to reassert itself, the culture of the Teamsters had changed. No future Teamster international official, reformer or old guard, will dare to bargain major contracts in secret as was the practice until 1992, nor impose contracts voted down by the majority, as happened several times in the 1980s. Teamsters have come to expect a higher level of democracy, and TDU remains active to give voice to that expectation. The net result of the reforms is positive and long-lasting.

In fact, as much as we can cite evidence for the inevitable forces of bureaucratization or corruption, time and again new struggles and new organizations arise to fight for the original union goals. People want decent lives, and that requires continued effort. If TDU didn't exist today, Teamsters would be forming it, just as members of other unions are starting reform groups every year.

The "iron law" is not a neutral theory. It masquerades as objective academic science, telling us that some form of dictatorship is inevitable, and that we are powerless to do anything about it. As such, the "law" becomes a powerful weapon for those who want to keep people cynical and disorganized—the very conditions required for a dictator to rule.

When people give up on struggle and accept the "iron law," it becomes a self-fulfilling prophecy. If dictatorship is inevitable, then you might as well pick the dictator you like best. Michels' own logic led him to be an ardent supporter of Mussolini and Italian fascism.

Guidelines for Rules and Procedures in a Democratic Culture

A dictatorship requires only one rule: whatever the boss wants. A democratic union seeks to involve as many members as possible in decision making, so it needs many more rules and procedures for how this should happen fairly.

Of course, rules and procedures are just the connecting devices between the essential elements of democratic culture: membership information and involvement, real power, and a healthy give-and-take between leaders and members. Rank and file organizing is the key to building these elements.

Look at two unions that were both pressured, by the Justice Department, to change their election procedures: the Teamsters and the Laborers. Both held rank and file, monitored elections for international officers. In the Teamsters, the constitutional changes would not have mattered much if it weren't for the work done by TDU before and after the election. TDU provided what new rules could not: a coordinated movement to define issues, train rank and file leaders, and back up campaigners on their rights. Without this organization, no reformer could have won the first direct election in the Teamsters in 1991; and if a reformer had won without this network of rank and file activists, he could not have led the union, most of whose 600 locals were still governed by supporters of the old guard. In the Laborers, no strong rank and file organization existed, incumbents were reelected, and little changed (see box).

When evaluating the union's rules, remember that different circumstances call for different procedures; democracy takes many forms. Holding a debate on a political endorsement in the middle of a strike, for example, may undermine the union's power by diverting energy from the immediate crisis; or it may strengthen that power if the politician, once elected, plays a hand in the strike. During the early phases of organizing a union, for another example, the emphasis may be on practices that make the union as open as possible to new people—holding small, informal meetings by work group, for instance. As the union develops, more emphasis is needed on developing leaders. Larger, more structured meetings might be organized with several members giving reports and leading discussions.

Or consider a large workplace like a factory where most members are in one or two big job classifications. Should each of the smaller classifications—skilled trades, clerical, professional, janitors—have its own bargaining representative? If so, the ratio of representation for the small groups will be much higher than for the large classifications. Perhaps instead the rule should be one bargainer per a certain number of members. The answer will depend on the unit's history and situation: are the concerns of the smaller classifications sufficiently addressed under the second scheme? Have the higher-skilled classifications traditionally had more voice in the union than their numbers warrant? The key question is which procedure will increase member involvement and the power of the union. Either falls within the realm of democracy.

The point is not to get hung up on procedures and bylaws if the

Rank and File Organization Makes the Difference

In 1996, the Laborers union held its first-ever direct election for international president and secretary-treasurer. Only about 15 percent of the members voted (compared to around 30 percent turnout in the Teamsters). Some observers said the low turnout reflected the lack of a real choice in this historically corrupt union. Incumbent President Arthur Coia, reputed to be an associate of a New England crime family, was challenged by Bruno Caruso, himself believed to have ties with the Chicago mob. One activist said it looked to members like the organized crime version of "Family Feud." Coia won, by about two to one.

Those voting did choose by about 78 percent to change the constitution: starting in 2001, all international officers, not just the top two, are to be directly elected by the members. But without an organized reform network, future elections are likely to replay the 1996 contest.

The federal government also took action against the Hotel Employees and Restaurant Employees, an international with a similar long history of apparent corruption. Under an agreement with the Justice Department, HERE had an independent monitor for 30 months in 1995-98, but no new elections. Federal investigators quietly pushed several corrupt officials to resign, and a new, clean president took over. But there was no established reform group strong enough to take advantage of these minimal changes, and the monitorship did not alter union's top-down culture.

members and the leaders are in touch and the union is strong. That said—although procedures are neither the substance of democracy nor the route to achieving it—they are important tools. They can either reinforce democratic values or get in the way of members' power. We offer here some guidelines for evaluating union procedures and how they contribute to a democratic culture.

1. Members must have the right to organize for a viewpoint.

Organizations *within* the union are critical for its democracy. Caucuses, slates, or networks are ways for members to hold leadership accountable. Few union constitutions provide for or mention union caucuses. Yet it is the ability to easily form such organizations that is the most important pressure for democracy within the union.

The right to speak your mind is not worth much if you don't also have the right to organize for your point of view. Therefore the right to join and promote a caucus without retribution is a priority. A union does not have to have an opposition caucus in order to be democratic. But in a democratic union members can easily form caucuses, if only temporarily around some issue, such as a rank and file Pension Improvement Committee.

2. Members must have the right, ability, and self-confidence to act on their own behalf.

Members should have the right to initiate and write their own grievances, and to form a committee to go to the boss about it. If a violation is not even recognized until an officer happens to see it, and nothing is done unless an official takes formal action, the union is weak. An active membership demands more of its leaders and therefore pushes them to a higher level of performance.

3. Members must have ways to hold leaders accountable.

Ultimately the election process is the main accountability mechanism. Between elections, the pressure on officers to appear democratic is still great, if only because too many clearly undemocratic actions will be remembered at election time. So a large group of members speaking out at a meeting, or circulating petitions and distributing flyers, will often inspire officials to reassess their actions. These informal mechanisms require the right to organize mentioned above.

A healthy union will also have mechanisms of accountability that can deal formally with smaller issues and do not require waiting for the next election. The ability of the membership meeting to reverse or direct an action by the officers is an example of such a mechanism. The right of members to initiate a bylaws change is another.

4. The union needs to protect both majority rule and minority rights.

Majority rule, that key to democracy, only works when the minority can organize for its point of view. For one thing, members have power to decide only if they have options to choose from. It is the minority of today, seeking to become the majority of tomorrow, that provides the democratic option to all members.

Second, when the majority respects the rights of the minority, the minority has every reason to support the organization as a whole—supporting a strike they voted against, for instance. If, on the other hand, minorities feel excluded, they have little incentive to act in solidarity with the majority's choice. Minority rights are essential to maintain the unity that gives the union (and therefore the majority) its strength.

The rights of minorities can be a thorny question for reformers who have won office over an "old guard" that then becomes a well-organized minority. See Chapter 6 for more on dealing with political opponents when in office.

Finally, it's especially important to respect the concerns of racial and gender minorities. Management can easily see and exploit such divisions, and the danger to unity is great.

5. Procedures should help to level the playing field.

Democracy works best on a level playing field where everyone has equal resources and equal opportunity. But our society is no level playing field. Every union member brings different resources, experiences, and skills to the organization.

Therefore union procedures should be evaluated for whether they level the playing field or increase the tilt. For instance, a group of registered nurses may tend to dominate a union they share with non-professional nurse aides; should the aides have a minimum number of seats on the board? In elections, incumbents generally have the advantage over challengers; how can challengers get a leg up? We will sort out some of these issues in Chapter 5.

The sharpest divisions in the workforce are typically based on race and gender job stratification, along with age, sexual orientation, and physical disabilities. While some unions have distinguished themselves in the fight for equality, others have a sad history of racial and other discrimination—one of the commonest crimes against democracy. The results of this history are to tilt the playing field inside the union in favor of white people and men. To ignore this history and insist on race-blind or gender-blind rules means that the playing field stays tipped. Unionists need to back affirmative action in hiring and promotion to get past obstacles to fairness in our own organizations.

Each section of the membership may have a different agenda of strongly felt needs, which must then be combined into a union agenda. To make this happen, all sections of the union need to be brought into the leadership. We consider this issue in Chapter 3.

6. The rules must be clear and simple.

Think of the many members who have come to a union meeting because there's an issue they want to deal with, but then can't get through the complex rules on motions and "points of order." Will they ever come back?

Properly used, rules make it easier for members, especially new ones, to get involved. Rules can let everyone know how things are supposed to work. For example, having a simple rule on how to introduce a motion means that a member with a concern is encouraged to bring it up.

The best constitutions, bylaws, and rules are brief, clear, and uncomplicated. TDU is a lively democratic group whose members vie for leadership positions within it—and its constitution fits on a sheet of legal paper. Examine almost any undemocratic organization and it is likely to have very complicated formal rules, and in practice abide by them only when they're useful to the leadership.

A clear set of rules reveals how decision-making works in the union—what can the staff or board decide, and what can membership meetings determine? If the union meeting is the highest authority, it should be clear how to bring questions there that are appropriate to that authority.

7. Surprise and secrecy are enemies of democracy.

Without the opportunity to gather information, talk to others, and organize a response, the right to vote has little meaning. Yet in many unions the membership meeting announcements posted at work list the agenda as "Old Business" and "New Business." How does that help members know what issues are up for discussion? Or in the name of preventing rumors, leaders do not give members advance copies of the contract before the ratification meeting.

One of the most insidious aspects of labor-management cooperation programs is the requirement of "confidentiality." Although one of the touted benefits of such programs is access to corporate information, access is limited to "team members" on a project, who are not allowed to discuss the information with union sisters and brothers. Unions should refuse participation in any activity with management that requires advance agreement to confidentiality.

Sometimes officers justify the usual secrecy around bargaining in the name of "not showing your hand to management." But the bargainers are certainly revealing their demands to management; that's what bargaining is. The only ones not shown the demands are the members. Leaders who rely on secrecy keep little from the employer but do build a huge barrier between themselves and the rank and file.

More commonly the secrecy around bargaining is acquiescence to the company's request not to "bargain in the press." Many unions, though, have found that the more members know about management's stance—through frequent bulletins, reports, and rank and file observers—the easier it is to mobilize support for bargainers.

Tactical surprise may give the union an advantage vis-a-vis an employer; one tactic of the Detroit newspaper strike, for example, was surprise pickets and sit-ins against secret targets. But the advantage of surprise has to be weighed against the cost to democracy (as well as the difficulty of keeping a secret among large numbers of people). Do union leaders have such a record of accountability that members trust them for a few secret decisions? If not, a non-sneak attack may inspire more long-term membership involvement.

8. Look for the long-term results.

We shouldn't let a short-term gain disguise a longer-term loss, as when management proposes a long-term gain for the company (holding wages down) in exchange for a short-term gain for us (a bonus). The same sort of trap can occur with union procedures. Paying lost-time for union activities may boost membership participation initially, but over time, members may refuse to participate unless they're paid—a disaster for democracy. Or a discussion of goals may seem like a waste of time at the outset of a contract campaign, if most members already agree on priorities. But holding such a discussion might have a big effect on members' involvement over the course of the struggle.

The Culture of a Reform Movement

A caucus within a union and the union itself are two quite different animals. You wouldn't want your reform caucus to mimic the structure and procedures of a union. But a democratic culture is indeed needed in a reform caucus.

One common pitfall of new organizations, including new reform caucuses in unions, is to over-structure a small group—to immedi-

---

How Does TDU Set National Policy And Strategy?

Formally, TDU is governed by annual conventions open to all members. The conventions elect an International Steering Committee which meets five times a year to guide the organization between conventions. But that's only part of the story; these bodies are not guaranteed to represent the views of most TDU members.

In general they do, and that's by conscious effort: TDU lives or dies by its ability to voice the concerns of most of its members and supporters—to act democratically. The organization's leaders are able to do that through frequent, informal communication with and among activists in local TDU chapters. The most common kind of question a TDU national leader asks a local organizer is "What are people saying about _____?" The activists who can answer that are the best recruiters—in closest touch with other Teamsters—and the most influential in the national organization.

They are also the most successful in building a local reform caucus. Local activists distribute TDU information and bulletins, talk up the issues among members, hear what they think, and communicate responses and new concerns back to the national leaders. Based on this local organizing, they have ideas for national strategy.

ately formulate long bylaws and reporting procedures, elect six officers and four standing committees. Is all that really helpful? An elected steering committee and simple financial reports may be plenty of organizational structure. The caucus's culture is more important.

For one thing, modeling a democratic culture within the caucus helps people learn how that can work—how members taking initiative can generate creative strategies, how active inclusion of racial or gender minorities can strengthen the whole group, how encouraging new leadership can also encourage new activism.

Second, a caucus depends as much on member involvement as the union does—maybe more, since dues payments are totally voluntary. So to organize a caucus, its leaders have to be in close touch with members and potential members to be sure the caucus is taking on problems that people think are important and fixable. The same interchange between leaders and members that we discussed for unions has to happen within a caucus.

To stay relevant and avoid burn-out, a caucus needs to continually bring in new leaders. Bringing new leaders along can be harder than it sounds. It requires asking a lot of different people to volunteer in a lot of different ways. The difficulty is not just that sometimes volunteers don't get their assignments done, which can be upsetting for the committed caucus leader who asked them to help. So often it's just easier to do the work yourself; coordinating a newsletter committee is a lot more time-consuming than simply sitting down and typing it out. Caucus leaders, like union leaders, should be very careful about how much they put getting work done ahead of getting new people involved in doing it.

The main reason, of course, for building a democratic culture in your reform caucus (as in the union) is to make it more effective!

Notes

1. For one explanation, see Chapter 2 of *A Troublemaker's Handbook*, by Dan La Botz, a Labor Notes book.

2. For more information on such programs, see two Labor Notes books: *Inside the Circle: A Union Guide to QWL*, by Mike Parker; and *Working Smart: A Union Guide to Participation Programs and Reengineering*, by Mike Parker and Jane Slaughter.

3. *4th Bundle*, a publication of the NALC New Vision caucus, 1997.

4. See Irving Howe and B.J. Widdick. *The UAW and Walter Reuther;* New York, Random House, 1949; Jordan Sims, "Going for Broke," in Alice and Staughton Lynd, eds., *Rank and File: Personal Histories of Working Class Organizers,* New York, Monthly Review Press, 1988.

5. Robert Michels, *Political Parties: A Sociological Study of the Oligarchical Tendencies of Modern Democracy,* New York, The Free Press, 1962, pp. 342, 379.

6. Steven Greenhouse, "Union Coalition Grapples with Troubles," New York Times, February 9, 1998, p. A16.

7. For some exceptions see Nelson Lichtenstein, *The Most Dangerous Man in Detroit: Walter Reuther and the Fate of American Labor,* New York: Basic Books, 1995; Farrell Dobbs, *Teamster Rebellion,* New York, 1972; Art Preis, *Labor's Giant Step, Twenty Years of the CIO,* New York, Pioneer Publishers, 1964.

8. Walter Reuther, quoted in "Statements of Liberal Americans and Labor on the Activities of the Un-American Activities Committee," UAW-CIO Local 600 "Ford Facts," Vol. 16, No. 7, February 16, 1952, p. 6.

3. Inclusion and Equality: Keys to Democracy

If union democracy is the "rule of the people" within the union, then it needs to include all the people. We've talked about many kinds of obstacles to democracy and participation; now let's discuss the ones that many people find it difficult to talk about: racial and gender barriers. These are barriers that exclude people because of prejudice or because of institutions of discrimination.

Racism exists within unions just as it does within society. Most white union members don't like to think of themselves as prejudiced, yet it is difficult not to carry some unconscious baggage in a society so long marked by inequality and the need to rationalize that inequality. The competition for jobs feeds into fear, prejudice, and resentment. At the personal level it may be hard for whites or men to understand the pain inflicted by a casual remark with racial or sexist overtones. But even such incidents undermine union solidarity.

In fighting for union democracy we have no choice but to take on these fears and hidden prejudices. The alternative to racism or sexism has always been to demonstrate that the power of working people, of the union, lies in the mobilization of members on a demo-

[Note: This chapter owes much to the work and writing of Kim Moody, Labor Notes' director and a former activist in the Communications Workers.]

cratic, inclusive, and equal basis. In the context of struggle for a better life, people change.

Unions are among the most racially diverse institutions in America's racially divided society. They are more integrated than most schools or neighborhoods, more racially diverse than most churches. African Americans are 15 percent of union members, compared to 11 percent of the employed workforce. Latinos make up another nine percent, slightly less than their share of the employed workforce but the fastest-growing ethnic group in the unions. Asian Americans and Pacific Islanders are 3.6 percent of the workforce and 3.3 percent of union members. Exclude all these people of color and organized labor would lose a quarter of its membership.

That may sound absurd, but time was when many unions did exclude Blacks, Latinos, and Asians. Even more recently, unions that admitted people of color did so on an unequal basis, in separate or "Jim Crow" locals. Union practices that exclude people of color from skilled jobs are still common today. The problems of racism and sexism, prejudice and discrimination have not disappeared. They affect all of us in one way or another. They definitely affect

Who Belongs to Unions?

Percent of workforce in unions, 1997

All workers	14.1 percent
Blacks	17.9 percent
Whites	13.6 percent
Latinos	11.8 percent
Asian Americans	12.6 percent
Men	16.3 percent
Women	11.6 percent
Black men	20.2 percent
Black women	16.0 percent
White men	16.0 percent
White women	10.9 percent
Latino men	12.6 percent
Latina women	10.6 percent
Asian American men	12.8 percent
Asian American women	12.4 percent

union politics and union power. These barriers can deprive unions of the talents of millions of potentially active members and leaders if they are not tackled.

Women too face barriers to participation due to discrimination and the "double shift": work on the job followed by housework and childcare at home. Women now make up 40 percent of all union members, a fraction that is rising. This is somewhat less than women's 46 percent of the workforce, but a big increase since the 1970s, when women were only 25 percent or less of union members. While women make up large portions of "traditional" female jobs like teaching, health care, and retail, they are found throughout the workforce. Women workers now make up a substantial proportion of better-unionized industries: 46 percent in telecommunications, 40 percent in non-durable manufacturing, 33 percent in urban transit, and 27 percent in durable manufacturing. (Durable goods are the ones expected to last at least three years.)

In 1987, two-thirds of all union members were white males. Today, they are just half. Those who still think of unions as "pale, male, and stale" just haven't been paying attention. Or rather, they have been looking only at the top leadership, which is still overwhelmingly white and male—a problem today's reform movements must address.

It's not enough to recognize or even celebrate diversity in the ranks, however. These days even corporations have "diversity" or racial and gender sensitivity training programs. The idea of these programs is to make people get along at work, not to promote equality or inclusion. Much of today's corporate concern with diversity is simply hypocrisy or has been imposed by law or court actions. It was employers who set discriminatory hiring and promotion policies in far more cases than the unions. Nevertheless, the existence of these programs does underline the failure of many unions to deal well with racial and gender inequality on the job and in the union.

Unionism and Discrimination

Workplace discrimination on the basis of race or gender goes back generations and rests on ideas and prejudices that often go unexamined. At one time, for example, it seemed "natural" that there were no women coal miners or construction workers. Today there are, but women still face an uphill fight to establish their rights because old ideas cast women as too "tender" for such jobs, even though they have proved they can do them as well as men. Similarly, following the Civil War and Reconstruction, African Americans were driven out of many skilled jobs they had previously performed, as craft unions attempted to protect their white members from labor market competition. To justify this, craft union leaders and members resorted to arguments that Black craftsmen were not (and could not be) qualified. The old ideas of racial inferiority that had been used to justify slavery were given a new life to justify job discrimination.

Thanks to both the many struggles of Black and Latino workers over the years and to the more progressive racial policies of some unions, particularly in the 1940s, modern unions no longer exclude people on the basis of race or gender. Many unions, however, have preserved more subtle forms of job protection based on discrimination. For example, until a reform movement took over the Pennsylvania Federation of the Brotherhood of Maintenance of Way Employees in the 1980s, unskilled workers had no way to bid into training for skilled jobs. Here the heritage of the last century lived on. The rule was not technically based on race, since many of the unskilled workers were white, so it wasn't illegal. Yet almost all the African Americans fell in the unskilled category due to past discrimination. When a reform movement took over the union, new officers negotiated a system that opened skilled jobs by seniority both to unskilled Blacks and to the many unskilled whites previously barred as well. The result was a more democratic, united union.

This story is the exception. All too often, most unions ignore such "legal" or even illegal discrimination. For decades, African Americans, Latinos, Asians, and women have had to go to court and to the streets to challenge discriminatory practices. With some exceptions, like the United Packinghouse Workers (now part of the United Food and Commercial Workers), the unions did little. Typically, union leaders would blame such inaction on the prejudice of white and/or male members, even arguing that it would be undemocratic to go against the wishes of the majority or to violate local autonomy. This reasoning assumes a false idea of democracy. As we argue elsewhere, the job of leaders is not simply to reflect the current views of the membership, but to point to the most effective ways to advance the interests of all members and, indeed, of working people generally—in other words, to lead by persuasion and example.

What's behind the conservative approach? Part of the reason is that dealing with institutional racism—the results of historic discrimination—is extremely difficult. Even the best union leaders are overwhelmed with the tasks they face. The path of least resistance may seem to be ignoring backward ideas among the ranks or discrimination on the job, or to opt for tokenism that does not challenge any established relations.

This tendency is multiplied many times by the dynamics of bureaucracy and business unionism. Bureaucracies protect themselves first, last, and always. If entrenched leaders see political risks in fighting discrimination, they will avoid it just as they avoid other confrontations when possible. This behavior is backed by business union ideology, which emphasizes normal contract administration, stable bargaining relationships with employers, and a passive membership. Civil rights and social equality are matters best left to legislation, according to this view. Thus we often see the contradictory phenomenon of unions that support civil rights legislation but ignore discrimination by the employers or within the union itself. Discrimination is a source of disunity and weakness long tolerated or promoted by business unionism. Union reformers need to fight this aspect of business unionism just as they do any other.

Aside from the fact that hypocrisy is never a good foundation on which to base an organization, ignoring discrimination or leaving it to some other agency runs afoul of basic trade union principles. Equal pay for equal work; seniority as opposed to favoritism; equal access to grievance and other procedures; one member, one vote: all of these are the basis of equality and solidarity that allows a union to make gains.

After all, the notion of "taking labor out of competition" is the economic basis of unionism. The union sets a pattern on pay, benefits, conditions so employers can't whipsaw one set of workers against another and thus ratchet wages down. Where inequality is allowed to exist, workers are set up to compete amongst each other. Where competition exists, the only direction for wages and conditions is down. Legislation can help tame that competition, but ultimately it is the union that must enforce standards, whether it is civil rights or health and safety legislation or the union contract.

In the past, unions have sometimes "taken labor out of competition" by exclusion. This was the practice of many building trades unions at the very birth of business unionism over a hundred years ago. These unions were able to exclude certain workers and thus maintain a "monopoly" over the labor markets they had organized. The payoff for these skilled workers was substantial. Because of the racism that pervaded society, race became one obvious and easy basis for exclusion. This system of racial exclusion rested on three premises. The first and easiest was the agreement of the employers, who were generally no less racist than their workers. The second was the limited nature of the labor markets involved. In those days both the construction industry and the contractors, who were small firms, were local and within the reach of the union. The third was a social consensus among the white population, including most employers, that supported formal segregation even where it was not as extensive or underwritten by law as in the South.

Except possibly for the first premise, the conditions on which this racial labor monopoly rested have eroded. The rise of national and even international construction firms, the differentiation of construction products and markets (high-rise buildings, mammoth public projects, tract housing) combined with urban sprawl ended "monopoly" conditions for the building trades. The consensus that upheld segregation, North and South, legal or unwritten, began to unravel in the era of the civil rights movement. Under these conditions, craft unions could no longer maintain a labor market monopoly for their members. The craft unions, however, did not abandon their exclusionary policies, or did so only marginally. The result is clear. The union share of construction in the United States fell from 87 percent in the 1950s to less than 20 percent in 1997. The racial exclusion that "paid off" when the U.S. was still a patchwork of local construction markets and small contractors could not protect white workers in the era of multinational corporations, market differentiation, urban sprawl, and globalization.

African Americans in Skilled Occupations

Skilled Occupation	1983	1996
Construction (nonsupervisory)	7.1 percent	7.9 percent
Precision production	7.3 percent	9.0 percent
Telephone install/repair	7.8 percent	11.9 percent
Aircraft mechanic	4.0 percent	11.3 percent
Data equipment repair	6.1 percent	9.9 percent
Percent of U.S. population	11.9 percent	12.6 percent

Discrimination in skilled trades jobs is still the norm despite economic changes, mass movements, new laws, and countless court challenges. As the chart shows, African Americans have made some gains in skilled occupations, but progress is slow and inadequate. Nor is there much doubt that most union leaderships remain complicit in practices that shelter skilled jobs for whites. Unlike the racial monopoly of yesterday, however, these forms of discrimination no longer manage to take labor out of competition even where they exclude all but a few women or people of color. The railroad machinist or engineer, the construction worker, or the tool and die maker in an auto plant are no safer from the competitive pressures of today's wide open, de-unionized, worldwide economy because the majority of their co-workers are white. They certainly benefit from having these better jobs, which would tend to be relatively better paid no matter who held them, but their wages, benefits, and conditions are threatened in the same way as their less skilled fellow workers. The relative scarcity of their skills provides some shelter and income advantage, but the fact is that skilled blue-collar workers too are seeing their conditions erode. From 1980 through 1996 construction workers saw their real hourly earnings drop by 16.5 percent, compared to only five percent for manufacturing workers. The wage advantage of construction workers over those in manufacturing declined from 37 percent to 21 percent.

The strategy of exclusion cannot address these economic forces. All discrimination can do is to undermine the trust between white skilled workers and less skilled workers of color in the same industries.

If we are right in assuming that the main reason union activists want a more democratic union is that they want a more effective union, then questions of racial and gender equality become basic to union reform and democracy. There are a million human reasons people fight for equality, as so many have again and again, and a million moral reasons everyone should support them. For the union and its members, however, the underlying reason is that without inclusion and equality, the economic basis of unionism falls apart and solidarity inevitably crumbles. Our ability to fight *effectively* is undermined. When it comes to a strike, almost everyone understands this simple point. When it comes to internal union affairs or day-to-day workplace life, however, it is often lost sight of by a complacent white majority and borne silently in angry frustration by those who feel the reality of racism or sexism.

How Unions Affect Inequality

Winning a union contract reduces inequality between the races. In 1979, in the U.S. as a whole, Blacks performing the same work as whites earned 10.9 percent less, on average. In the mainly nonunion South, this gap was 14 percent. But in the then highly unionized

Racism: Win-Lose or Lose-Lose?

Racial wage gaps and unequal employment patterns continue to be the rule. Whites clearly get the better deal. This gives them an economic incentive to hang on to the old ways of discrimination. But does this really pay? In relative terms, yes. The gap in wages between white males and Black males widened from 24 percent in 1979 to 32 percent in 1997, as the real wages of African American men plunged some 9.5 percent. But the growing racial wage gap didn't buy the average white male wage earner a thing. His real hourly wage dropped by 3.4 percent.

The drop in everyone's real wages is partly due to employer aggression. In the era of concessions and union decline, the average annual wage increase in major collective bargaining agreements dropped from almost 10 percent in 1980 to 2.4 percent in 1995. Another reason is the society-wide loss of unionized industrial jobs and their replacement by lower-paid nonunion jobs of all kinds. In both these cases, business unionism must take part of the blame—for refusing to fight and for failing to organize the new nonunion sectors.

Another clue that racial wage gaps don't pay off for anyone is that the region of the greatest historical segregation and discrimination, the Old South, is also the country's lowest-wage region. The average hourly private sector wage in the U.S. in 1997 was $13.26. Of the ten deep South states only Virginia reached the national average. Georgia came close, but the rest were well over a dollar an hour lower.

The white advantage accrued from centuries of racism has never prevented low wages for many white workers nor employer attacks on white workers' living standards. On the contrary, it weakens the ability of unions to fight to raise everyone's living standards. As one speaker at a UAW New Directions conference a few years ago put it, "Racism is the greatest wage reduction program in history."

industrial Midwest, the racial wage gap was less than one percent. Industrial union contracts, alongside equal employment laws, had all but eliminated this particular form of social inequality! The decline of unions in that region since that time, along with concessions and the decay of pattern bargaining, brought the Black-white wage gap among workers in the Midwest doing the same work back up to 14 percent by 1989. Not coincidentally, everyone's real pay fell during the same period and on into the 1990s. From 1978 to 1998, real wages for the population as a whole fell 12 percent. The lesson should be clear enough: when unions do their job best, everyone benefits more. When they don't, everyone loses. Everyone except the employers.

Industrial unionism won equal pay for equal work, but it did not eliminate the wage gap between Blacks and whites or men and women that results from unequal employment opportunities. Due to past and present discrimination, Blacks and Latinos tend to hold different jobs from whites, women different jobs from men. Typically, the jobs held by people of color or women pay less than those held by whites in general or by white males in particular. In 1997, Blacks still made 21 percent less than whites and women made 23 percent less than men on average across the economy. While some unions fought in the 1940s and again in the 1960s to lower the barriers of discrimination in hiring, most have stuck to dealing with the problems of current members and left the fight against discrimination to the legislative arena if they tackled it at all.

Despite this failure, union members of all races and both genders make more than nonunion workers. The union wage advantage for all workers was about 24 percent in 1997. White males who belonged to unions earned 14 percent more than those who didn't. For Black males, however, the union wage difference was 29 percent, for Black women 40 percent, and for white women 35 percent. In other words, at least in the area of wages, union membership is even more advantageous for Blacks and women than for white men. So women and people of color have a special stake in making the unions more effective again, that is, a special stake in union democracy and reform.

Official Efforts to Deal with Racism and Sexism

Organizations based on ethnicity, race, and gender have a long history in the U.S. labor movement. From the National Colored Labor Union of the 1860s, through the Molly Maguires of the 1870s, the Working Women's Union and Ladies' Federal Labor Union of

Affirmative Action

To many whites whose job security is endangered by today's economic conditions, affirmative action seems threatening and unfair. "Why don't we just make employment opportunities equal now and forget about the past?" might be one of the more generous attitudes out there today. The problem is that the past won't go away so simply. Since colonial times, both during and after slavery, white males were assumed to have a natural right to the better jobs when there was even a question of competition from people of color or women. This mindset only began to be modified thirty years ago.

So ingrained into the fabric of our society is this old set-up that most whites thought of it is as natural until very recently. Many still do. Yet it took effort to convince people it was natural. New laws had to be passed, institutions constructed to enforce them, the mythology of racial inferiority invented and refined, and jobs classified by race and gender. The undoing of this complex structure and way of thinking will also require effort.

After thirty years of equal employment legislation, employment is still unequal. Affirmative action seeks to accelerate a process that would otherwise take decades or more. It is not a program of quotas or of advancing the unqualified, but of giving women and people of color the ability to reach employment levels more or less comparable to their proportion of the workforce or population.

Seniority is a key principle of unionism. For one thing, it limits employer favoritism. Sometimes, however, it can mask old patterns of discrimination. We gave the example of the separate seniority lists for moving into apprenticeships on the railroad, that were later merged by union reformers. In other cases, a single seniority list can be a roadblock, where a group was the "last hired, first fired." Here women or people of color were denied the chance to accumulate the seniority that could get them a shot at the better jobs or improve their job security.

the 1880s, the United Hebrew Trades of the early 1900s, the Negro American Labor Council of the 1950s and early 1960s, and many more, various groups have seen the need to pull together to further their interests. During World War II and in the 1960s, Blacks and Latinos organized inside the unions to force them to deal with discrimination and to gain a greater share in leadership. They were supported by the massive civil rights movements of the times. As Black

Affirmative action plans do not eliminate seniority. Rather they modify the list for a period of time in order to equalize opportunities, without giving the employer the ability to play favorites. In the past, some unions and companies were put under a court-ordered consent decree to ensure the hiring and promotion of women or minorities. The best course for union reformers is to get the union to negotiate any affirmative action modification of seniority. This would benefit workers of color or women, but also give the union more control over implementation.

In some cases the best affirmative action policy can be to strengthen seniority. For example, getting into skilled trades apprenticeships in the auto industry now depends on tests which favor formal education over experience, and give no value to seniority. If production workers (of whom significant numbers are minorities) got priority for apprenticeships, with weight given to seniority, the racial and gender composition of the skilled trades would be greatly improved.

It cannot be denied that in some cases affirmative action can have a negative impact on some members of the groups who have gained from past discrimination, generally whites and males. In actual fact, however, it is impossible to argue that the current decline in living and working conditions being experienced by whites or men as a group has been caused by affirmative action. The evidence for this idea produced by right-wingers and racists is always anecdotal—this white student didn't get admitted, that male worker lost out to a woman, etc. Unfortunately, tough economic times tend to inflame racist ideas and racial conflict. Scapegoat explanations ("the Blacks," immigrants, welfare mothers) flourish in this atmosphere of economic insecurity. *The cause of the declining prospects for good jobs and the lowered standard of living experienced by most working people these days is corporate profit lust, uncontrolled business competition, and right-wing economic and social policies,* not the gains of the disadvantaged. Along with countering false explanations, we need to provide the real ones.

and Latino workers poured into the labor-starved factories of the early 1940s, they demanded equal treatment in hiring and promotions. In 1941, the March on Washington Movement, headed by A. Philip Randolph of the Brotherhood of Sleeping Car Porters, underlined their demands by threatening a mass march of African Americans on the nation's capital just as the country moved toward war. The government issued a Fair Employment Practices Code that was supposed to prevent discrimination in the war plants. In response, some of the new industrial unions set up national and local union Fair Employment Practices Committees. In a like manner, the civil rights movement of the 1960s encouraged the formation of union civil rights committees at all levels. The women's movement of the 1960s and 1970s produced women's departments and committees in many unions. Equally important, these periods saw the inclusion of anti-discrimination clauses in many contracts.

The Fair Employment Practices Committees, civil rights and women's committees and departments provided a place for women and workers of color to express grievances and try to enforce laws and contract clauses prohibiting discrimination. One could probably find thousands of individual cases where they have made a difference. But if we are to judge by overall results, including the slipping employment prospects and real wages of so many Black, Latino, and women workers, we would have to conclude that their effectiveness has been limited. Writing in the mid-1960s, Ray Marshall, who would later become U.S. Secretary of Labor, characterized the UAW's Fair Employment Practices Department, for example, as "ceremonial and symbolic." Racism in the ranks and corporate intransigence explain some of this, but we are also forced to return once again to the fundamental inertia of business unionism. Indeed, in an attack on the shortcomings of the UAW's racial policies in the early 1960s, African American UAW leader Horace Sheffield contrasted the union's growing "business unionism" with the "crusading spirit" of contemporary civil rights activists and of "the CIO in the 1930s."

This inertia isn't just a matter of union "maturity" or the caution that comes with age. It is a political phenomenon of bureaucracy— bureaucracy abhors dissent or conflict. Raising issues of racism or sexism will naturally produce opposition and controversy. Furthermore, the business union bureaucracy often counts on support from the better-paid skilled workers, who tend to be white. Confronting racism will challenge these and other political alignments in union politics, forcing leaders to take sides. This kind of politics is anathema to bureaucrats and to business unionism in general. The only kind of racial harmony that comes out of this bureaucratic response is that which unites incumbent officials of all races and both genders in the "now is not the time" line they will hand the aggrieved.

A similar problem exists with many of the official and semi-official organizations of women and people of color within the labor movement. The A. Philip Randolph Institute, the Labor Council for Latin American Advancement, the Coalition of Labor Union Women, and the Asian Pacific American Labor Alliance all have an official connection to the AFL-CIO. As May Chen and Kent Wong point out, with the exception of APALA all these groups "were formed under the initiative and control of the AFL-CIO in response to an insurgent population of rank and file workers."[1]

Others, such as the Coalition of Black Trade Unionists or the Minority Caucus of the Communications Workers of America, were organized independently. Whatever their origins, over time most of these organizations have become dominated by those possessing or seeking a career in the labor hierarchy. Some local chapters of these groups remain active and effective. Some provide training in organizing and basic union skills. As far as fighting for equality, however, the tendency has been for them to become largely ceremonial in nature. Unlike Randolph's Negro American Labor Council in the 1950s and early 1960s, the Trade Union Leadership Council of the same period, or the more militant Black caucuses of the late 1960s, today's official and semi-official organizations of women and people of color seldom challenge the status quo.

One obvious reason is that most of these groups are themselves dominated by high-level officials with close ties to incumbent white or male officers. Women and people of color are no more immune to bureaucratic functioning and loyalty than the white males who preceded them. The siren call of high pay, a nice work environment, power breakfasts with big-name politicians, and all the rest has tamed many a militant. In this situation, official caucuses or organizations of women or people of color can become a way for the bureaucracy as a whole to keep control of union affairs.

Caucuses of Women and People of Color

In the 1960s and early 1970s, under the influence of the mass social movements of that time, rank and file-based Black caucuses formed in some United Auto Workers locals. Very militant against the companies, who continued to place Blacks in the worst jobs, these groups argued that union officials had ignored Black workers' concerns and that Black workers needed their own organizations within the unions to press their demands.

Today there are few such rank and file, not officially-approved groups. In part this is because there is little social movement in society to encourage such initiatives. Organizations such as the Black Rank and File Exchange, founded at the 1983 Labor Notes conference; Pride at Work, a national caucus of gay and lesbian union activists; and Latinos United in Labor are current examples of workers organizing against discrimination (Pride at Work began independently and later affiliated with the AFL-CIO).

Perhaps one reason there are few unofficial caucuses inside unions today is that women and people of color still run into criticism when they attempt to organize on their own behalf—even when the women's conference, for example, is officially sponsored by the international union. Organizations that promote one group within the union are accused of creating disunity. Isn't this separatism and exclusion? they're asked. Aren't you breaking down solidarity, especially if the meeting or group is not open to all?

In truth, such organizations ultimately aid solidarity. They are after equality, and equality is the basis of solidarity and union economic power. The decision to organize a caucus, committee, or movement along lines of race, gender, or sexual preference is up to those who have suffered discrimination—just as the right to organize a rank and file reform movement is up to the rank and file activists, not the officialdom. We want to take this a step further, however, and argue that organizations based on fighting racial or gender discrimination, where they are not just comfortable parts of the labor establishment, should be viewed as part of the broader union reform movement. For one thing, they will tend to promote a fight with management. For another, fights for equality, just like any other reform cause, tend to open up the politics of the union. They also prepare the basis for broader coalitions in the reform process.

Historically, the late 1960s and early 1970s, when Black and Latino caucuses were forming, was also an era of racially integrated union reform movements such as the United National Caucus in the UAW, Miners for Democracy, Teamsters United Rank and File, Steelworkers Fightback, and others that never became formal organizations. The relationship between the different types of rank and file-based organizations was often complex and sometimes tense. But the fact was that they all pushed in the direction of greater union democracy and power.

Inclusion in Reform Movements: Out of the Comfort Zone

Just as union structures should reflect the membership, so must reform caucuses. Most of the growing and successful reform movements we know of are diverse in terms of race and gender. These organizations have attempted to develop a leadership that reflects the diversity of the membership, and to do so from the start. For example, while TDU had its origins among the largely white and male trucking sectors of the union, it always included Blacks and women on its leadership body. Later, as it expanded into the largely Latino food processing industries of the West Coast, Latinos joined as members and leaders locally and nationally. Other reform organizations that have achieved electoral success at one or another level such as the New Directions caucus in Transport Workers Union Local 100 in New York City, the Caucus for a Democratic Union in the California State Employees/SEIU Local 1000, or UAW New Directions have always made a point of developing a diverse leadership.

One barrier to equal involvement of workers of color or women is that the whole arena of union politics, including dissident caucuses, can look like the inaccessible domain of white men. If the union hall seems to have the culture of a white male comfort zone, suspicion of union politics will run high among Blacks, Latinos, women, and other left-out groups. This suspicion is mixed with the cynicism most union members of all races have about union "politics" and politicians.

These aren't easy problems, but, as we argue throughout this book, a workplace-based approach may be the most effective: the reform group should act around issues such as sexual or racial

harassment, unfair contract clauses, or any barrier to equal conditions on the job, as well as workplace problems that affect members
across racial, gender, occupational, or departmental lines.

Campaigns around improving representation or around contract
clauses that affect everyone often bear positively on race and gender
questions as well. For example, say a large local is majority white
but some departments have Black or Latino or women majorities.
Winning a new bylaw to require elected stewards will improve representation for all while increasing the chances that the stewards
council—and the pool of experienced, potential new local leaders—
is more diverse.

To build an inclusive rank and file movement, it is crucial that
issues of importance to each group receive the attention of the entire
group. Newly elected reform leaders, after all, will come under
many of the same pressures that led the old guard to ignore racial or
gender injustices, particularly where the majority of union members
are white and/or male. The emphasis should be on what the group
does—winning a case of sexual harassment or discrimination in promotion, passing a by-laws change that eliminates a barrier to running
for office, or getting a paid holiday for Martin Luther King's birth-
day—rather than passing resolutions, which are the specialty of
business unionism.

Campaigns, Coalitions and Election Slates

Reform movements seldom grow simply by one organization
becoming bigger and bigger. Along the way new organizations are
formed for different purposes, say a contract campaign: coalitions
are struck, and a broader base is established. The reform movement
in Local 100 of the Transport Workers Union, the 35,000-member
union in New York City's Transit Authority, provides a good example. This movement began as a newsletter called *Hell on Wheels* put
out by a small group with a diverse membership. The group became
well known for its campaigns for better contracts, similar to those
waged by TDU. For the group to become a successful challenger in
executive board elections, however, it had to form coalitions with
other organizations or their leaders. Early in its life, the *Hell on
Wheels* group united with leaders of the Nubian Society, a Black fraternal order. A more recent alliance involved a leader of the Emerald
Society, an Irish fraternal order. Eventually an alliance was formed
around an election slate called New Directions, which eventually
became a unified organization (that narrowly lost the 1998 race for

top officers).

Elections offer a time to build broader coalitions and recruit a more diverse membership to the reform movement. The formation of a representative slate for elections speaks louder than words; it must reflect the union membership to the greatest extent possible. One of the most frequent barriers to accomplishing this is the often unspoken assumption that people only vote for "their own kind." Without denying the existence of sexism and racism, it's important to remember that at their best, union politics *are* different. As TDU leader Ken Paff put it, "The union context tends to bring out the best in people." The union, after all, is one of the few places in society where people of all races work together for common goals. So white male Teamsters will vote heavily for a slate that includes Blacks, Latinos, and women, as they did in international elections in 1991 and again in 1996. In 1998, the Teamster reformers put forth the most diverse slate ever run in that union. Tens of thousands of white Teamsters supported the Tom Leedham Rank and File Power Slate. At the GM assembly plant in Newark, Delaware in 1997, a majority Black and white male workforce elected an Asian woman and New Directions leader as shop chair, a position long held by white men in most auto plants. In Teamsters Local 2000, which represents Northwest Airlines flight attendants, the vast majority of them white, an African American woman and TDU member took the presidency and carried her entire TDU slate to victory. Why? Because these reformers were saying and doing something the rank and file majority knew they needed. Union politics had been taken out of the bureaucratic comfort zone and the old divisions were broken down. As so often happens, a struggle around one issue opened people's minds on more questions than one. The majority of members were able to recognize diversity in leadership as a strength, not a weakness, a source of unity, not division.

Anyone in the business of changing the status quo needs to remember that when the circumstances call for it, and leaders and movements arise to offer an alternative, people will change. People will suppress, overcome, or even abandon their old ideas, prejudices, and suspicions when a genuine alternative shows itself.

Notes

1. Gregory Mantsios, ed., *A New Labor Movement for the New Century*, New York, Monthly Review Press, 1998, p. 191.

4. Promoting Involvement in the Union

In Chapters 5, 6, and 7 we will take up how the union's formal structures and procedures affect its democratic culture. In this chapter we'll concentrate on the mostly informal procedures that often determine whether the members are really in control.

The bottom line is the culture of the union we described in Chapter 2. Do the members see themselves as controlling their own union and responsible for initiating ideas and activity, or do they see themselves as consumers of a service? Do the leaders trust the members, and see the members' ideas as resources? Do the members hold leaders accountable?

Start with the Contract

Union democracy has to start with the reason workers belong to unions—it's the only effective way to negotiate a contract and to deal with an employer on a day-to-day basis. The relationship of the members to these two activities fundamentally determines their relationship to the union. If members believe they can't influence what they get at contract time or how grievances are handled or what rights they have on the job, then there is little reason for them to care how elections are conducted or how many people show up at union meetings. Interest and involvement in the union is higher during contract negotiations than at any other time. How decisions about contracts are made goes a long way toward determining the culture of the union.

Some democracy/power issues in bargaining:

Formulating demands and setting priorities

In most unions members are invited to submit contract proposals. But all too often members believe correctly that what they say makes little difference and that leaders will do what they want anyway.

The process of formulating demands and setting priorities should include some give and take among the members. Individuals should be invited to submit ideas, maybe as part of a survey. But another part of the process is newsletters and leaflets that talk about the importance of some issues (produced by officials and by rank and file activists), as well as discussions in meetings and lunch rooms. It is as important that members hear each other's views on contract goals as it is that leaders hear and react to the members.

No contract campaign can demand everything at once. Focus on a few issues that—it's clear to everyone on both sides—must be addressed to achieve a settlement. A union that approaches bargaining with a shopping list, without two or three priorities at the top, shows that there is no membership campaign behind the bargainers, and that leaders themselves are confused about where they're headed. It may be tempting to include all suggested demands as a way to make more members feel connected to the campaign. But too many issues cloud the focus and can lead to an unnecessary sense of defeat.

Rank and filers on the bargaining team

While the bargaining committee must include experienced officers, electing rank and filers to join them on the team brings in the insights of those who will work under the new contract. A work rule is less likely to be given away when the bargaining team knows just how much harder such a concession will make them work on Monday. Bringing in rank and filers tightens the relationship between members and bargainers and gives other members the sense that they're represented by one of their own. Some locals have elected bargaining committees that number in the hundreds to facilitate the spread of firsthand information from the bargaining table back to the ranks—what the employer is saying and what's his demeanor. (A local that did this is HERE Local 26, which represents hotel workers in Boston. One negotiating committee had 165 members speaking 10 languages.) The Teamsters have included rank and filers on national negotiating committees.

Open bargaining

You can tell that business unionism rules when members accept the notion that bargaining should be done behind closed doors. Often the formula is to go off-site and impose a "blackout" on information. Notice that the blackout applies to the public and to union members, but not to the superiors of the management bargainers. Upper management is well informed and in control of their side. Closed bargaining only reduces members' involvement. The bargaining, like the contract, belongs to them. Members are entitled to regular reports of what is going on, regular consultation, and input into critical decisions, just like the employer top brass gets.

Cutting leaders off from members is a central, though unspoken, tenet of "mutual gains bargaining," pushed by management and some academics in recent years as a part of cooperation programs. The emphasis on mutuality tends to make union bargainers see what they have in common with their "management counterparts"—that is, the need to reach an agreement they can "sell" to the members. The extent to which this approach undermines union democracy cannot be exaggerated. For more discussion see Chapter 15 of Labor Notes' book *Working Smart.*

The contract campaign

The old saying that you can't win in the peace treaty what you can't win on the battlefield applies to contract bargaining. The contract is not the work of clever bargainers (although bad bargainers can lose a lot) but the result of members' organization and resolve. Members' willingness to act for what they believe in—up to and including a strike—provides the pressure that can get a good contract.

Many unions have developed detailed materials on running contract campaigns (although you should look out for the top-down approach we warned against in Chapter 1). See also Labor Notes' *A Troublemaker's Handbook* and the box on the Teamsters campaign at UPS. Here we will use TDU's contract campaigns as an example of how a reform caucus not in power can press for a better settlement. Over the years much of TDU's organizing has been around the national trucking and UPS contracts (the same principles will apply to local agreements). The description that follows is about TDU's contract campaigns before reformers were elected to international office in 1991; after that, TDU did much of the same work, but in combination with a leadership that was trying to involve the members.

Any contract campaign starts with deciding on priorities and what members are willing to fight for. TDU didn't have the means to survey 125,000 freight Teamsters, but local activists talked with many members, individually and in rank and file-sponsored meetings and over several years' time, so they had a good picture of what the key issues were as national bargaining approached.

To put these issues down on paper, TDU staff recruited a representative committee of activists from around the country. The TDU contract committee met by phone or sometimes in person and formulated goals for bargaining. Most or all on the committee were rank and filers; this was by necessity, but it also meant they had a keen idea of what working under the current agreement was like.

The contract committee didn't try to analyze every word in the current contract. They just needed to choose a handful of improvements that they'd heard from members were important. Then they had to decide what could be won on those issues. The goals were always specific: not "a better grievance procedure" but "innocent until proven guilty"; not "fair pensions," but "$3,000 for 30 years at any age." Activists sometimes collected petition signatures for a set of demands and sent the petitions to bargainers. Making the goals specific means that it's clear whether a goal was met; members may choose to accept less, but they can't be told that doing so is actually a victory.

TDU didn't have the resources for in-depth analysis of corporate financial health, although members did watch and publish basic information on profitability. They set goals by deciding what seemed fair and winnable, and also beyond what the companies would be willing to give with no pressure—which is what the Teamsters old guard generally brought back.

The range of pressure tactics available to TDU was limited by the fact that as a caucus TDU lacked many union resources, could not coordinate with bargainers (who were hostile), and was not as strong in some areas as others. A local or national union would have the chance during bargaining to organize increasingly militant displays of solidarity, possibly including disruptions of work. TDU's main strategy was to prepare members to vote down an agreement that didn't meet their goals, by getting local activists to talk up issues and distribute literature. The expectation was that company negotiators were looking for the least that members would accept, and the contract campaign could raise that floor.

Much of what made TDU contract campaigns successful was members' hunger for information—on the progress of bargaining, on the demands from each side, on what other members wanted in the new contract, and on the details of tentative agreements. TDU "contract bulletins" were the only information available to members, and they were eagerly sought even by those who had no other interest in TDU. Caucus leaders worked hard to dig out and provide information, but were always careful that what they published was correct. That way, even people who might not agree with TDU's philosophy could count on getting good information from the bulletins.

(Later, the international under reform leadership published a series of bulletins for each set of national negotiations. Most they distributed through local unions, but many old guard local leaders could not be trusted to get the bulletins to members. So after putting out a few bulletins through locals, the international would mail an issue directly to members' homes. This bulletin would include pictures of the previous ones, alerting members that if they hadn't seen them they should contact their local.)

After international bargainers announced a tentative agreement, the TDU campaign kicked into high gear. The first job was to get information—not an easy task. In the Teamsters at the time, the complete contract was given only to the "two-man committee," made up of two officers from each local that had members covered by the contract. In the time before fax machines, getting a copy of the tentative agreement quickly often meant a TDU organizer flying to another city to meet a sympathetic officer.

Then the document had to be sent to TDU leaders and analyzed. How closely did it meet TDU's goals? What concessions were included? TDU contract committees usually found the agreements wanting. Sometimes wages and benefits were just too low; sometimes the union had given the company concessions on working conditions, always bargainers had not used the full power of the membership. TDU's role was to help members demand more than the company was willing to give, by voting "no."

By the mid-1980s, after several years of rank and file contract campaigns, TDU had enough clout among Teamsters covered by the major national trucking contracts to get a majority "no" vote. The National Master Freight Agreement, the UPS national contract, and the national carhaulers agreement were all voted down even though leaders were united in selling them. In 1988 the NMFA was rejected by a whopping 64 percent, still short of the two-thirds then required in the Teamster constitution to prevent implementation.

TDU's contract campaigns show the worth of leaders learning about workplace conditions long before negotiations start—talking with members over the entire contract period instead of relying on a one-time survey. TDU's work also shows the importance of information; members' ability to get a full picture of the proposed contracts meant they could have the confidence to say "no." The embarrassment that international leaders felt over signing contracts that were voted down (how could they defend that, really?) pushed them to quietly give members the right to majority rule on contracts in 1988. TDU's campaigns show it's possible for the ranks to put heavy pressure on employers no matter who's in office.

Ratification: The Most Important Election of All

Contract ratification is a more important vote than any officers' election because it more directly determines how the union fulfills its purpose: power on the job. A local that denies members the right to ratify or that doesn't protect the legitimacy of ratification votes is guaranteed to have an undemocratic culture. The UFCW constitution, for example, allows local executive boards to sign contracts that have been voted down if a strike was not also approved by at least two-thirds.

In most unions members do have the right to ratify, but often they face ratification practices that frustrate their right to a real choice.

You need time and information.

The right to vote on contracts is most often undermined when members can't make an informed decision. They need accurate contract language, the opportunity for alternative leaders to analyze the proposal, time to discuss the likely implications, and time to perhaps

The Right to an Informed Vote

Here is a sample resolution for amending local bylaws to include the right to an informed vote. The amendment will be stronger if you can set firm time limits in parts b and c that are reasonable for each different bargaining unit covered.

◆ ◆ ◆

Whereas the right to vote on contracts is meaningful if it is an informed vote;

Whereas it is possible for different people to summarize a lengthy contract in different ways;

Whereas the contract contains many technical sections, and it is sometimes necessary to seek expert analysis on these sections;

Whereas the opportunity to hear alternative views and analyses is critical for informed and democratic decision-making;

Whereas common sense dictates that members approve contracts after the opportunity to read them and consult about them;

Whereas common sense and labor law both hold that the right to vote includes the right to pre-ratification information;

Whereas new electronic/computer forms are available for rapidly transmitting large amounts of information;

Therefore the bylaws shall be amended to add the following paragraph:

When a bargaining committee achieves a tentative agreement with an employer:

(a) Within 24 hours of the tentative agreement, copies of it, marked with additions and strikeouts to indicate changes from the previous agreement, will be made available for inspection during office hours at the local union office and will be provided in either hard copy or electronic form to any member who requests, and who has pre-paid a reasonable fee to cover duplication and shipment costs.

(b) The union will prepare and distribute an accurate summary of the provisions of the tentative agreement, including both gains and losses, a reasonable time before the ratification vote. Minority reports of bargaining committee members, if any, will be included.

(c) An adequate period will be provided before the ratification vote for consideration of the tentative agreement and for formulation and distribution of alternative views, if any.

campaign among co-workers for a "no" vote. In most unions all are short-circuited.

In many cases members never get to see the full contract, only a summary version, usually with the most positive spin and even dubbed "Highlights." Are there really never any "lowlights" that the

Democracy ≠ Voting

During the UPS strike in the summer of 1997, management spin-doctors complained that it was "undemocratic" for Teamster leaders not to send management's "final offer" to the members for a vote.

Teamsters leaders countered that it was up to the union, not the company, to decide when it was appropriate to put a proposal up for a vote. Besides, they added, the company's offer was so clearly unacceptable that it was not worth a vote.

It was widely understood among the membership that the only Teamsters who wanted a vote were the ones who wanted to accept the offer. Most preferred to stick with the strike. A few members interviewed by the press had a hard time explaining why following their leaders on this particular decision was consistent with democracy; as we discussed in Chapter 2, the role of leaders in a democratic organization is not always understood. Still, most members' reaction was to trust the leaders. Although UPS did get some to phone the union and complain, there was no widespread outcry for a vote.

The story might have gone another way. Union officials could have denounced UPS's pretense of being concerned about democracy, but nevertheless put the company's proposal to a vote. In essence, this would be like taking a strike vote in the middle of a strike, with members having a detailed view of what they'd get for going back to work. An overwhelming rejection would have been a big victory for the union and an undeniable refutation of UPS's contention that management cared more about the workers than union officials did.

Union democracy did not require that the vote be taken; this was a strategy decision, which had to take into account the difficulty and expense of a national vote. Perhaps a vote could have strengthened the union by proving how much the members supported the strike. Or perhaps the union showed more strength by resisting outright UPS's attempted intrusion into union business.

members should know about? Few unions allow, let alone encourage, minority reports from the bargaining committee, which would help members quickly focus on the pros and cons. The California State Employees Association, SEIU 1000, even brought charges against a bargaining committee member who campaigned against an agreement the top leaders supported. These leaders had promised the employer that all union officials would support the contract, and felt that fulfilling this promise was more important than members' right to hear alternative views.

Any serious critique of the contract requires reasonable time to study it, get expert assistance on technical questions, and communicate with others. Too short a time between bargaining and voting denies the right to organize a potential opposition.

In the past union officials used logistical arguments against making the full contract available to the members in ample time. The contract is too long, it's too expensive to get it out to everyone, and it would delay ratification. There was some truth to the argument. UAW-Big Three draft contracts, for example, can be over a thousand pages long, including benefits packages, riders, and supplements. On the other hand, the Teamsters International has found it worth the expense to mail copies of all tentative changes to national contracts, to each member covered, before ratification.

This is one area where technology aids democracy and overcomes most objections about cost or time delay. Within minutes of an agreement the draft documents can be posted on a web site. The entire contract can be downloaded in under two hours. Using the web, people can easily choose which portions they want to read and/or download. And the internet makes it easy to circulate analysis and discussion among those equipped with computers.

For instance, in 1996-97 a group of American Airlines pilots, members of the Allied Pilots Association, used a web site to distribute information among their widely spread, highly mobile workforce. This group, APA Pilots Defending the Profession, was concerned about American's moving work to regional subsidiaries that operate "small jets." They were able to organize a sound rejection of one concessionary contract; a second contract proposal—still flawed but with $200 million more money for the pilots—was later passed.

Web distribution of material, though quite helpful, must be in addition to written versions. Relying totally on the web would exclude large portions of many unions, especially those with members too low-paid to afford a computer. And as Mark Hunnibell, main technician for the Pilots Defending the Profession web site, said, "Technology is not enough by itself."[1] The web can never replace personal interaction for organizing.

Leaders' report on the tentative agreement is a real test of the democratic culture in the union and the degree of trust between leaders and members. Forget snow jobs. Bargainers need to come to the members with the truth about the contract, losses as well as gains, and particularly the areas where language is ambiguous and will require membership action to properly enforce. It's up to the members to balance these downsides against the costs of continuing without a contract and maybe going on strike. Of course a real leader will make a recommendation, not try to duck trouble. If it's not a great contract but officers think a strike is too risky, they should say so, and why. Telling members only that they should "vote their conscience" is a cop out.

Getting a fair contract vote

First are the physical conditions. Are the times and voting places accessible to members? Are ballots counted fairly? At a Honeywell plant in Minneapolis, the lights went out during a vote on whether to end a strike. When a return to work was passed by eight votes out of 2,040 cast, many members doubted the vote's validity.

Even more important are the political conditions of voting. Does voting on the contract matter? Many unions use practices that make the vote next to meaningless because they so heavily slant the vote in favor of ratification:

- "You will vote until you get it right." Leaders sometimes make it clear that if members turn the offer down they will get nothing better. They may go through the motions of bargaining and resubmit the same contract several times with cosmetic changes until a ratification vote succeeds. They realize they can't get improvements by themselves, and they're not willing to bring membership pressure to bear beyond the bargaining table.

- "If you turn it down you must go on strike." By making a contract ratification vote serve as a strike vote—either vote yes and work, or vote no and strike—officers may hope to frighten members into ratification. This tactic is especially effective where there has been no contract campaign or any involvement that would prepare members to strike and win. In truth, voting "no" and striking are two separate issues. A strike is often not the best strategic response to a failed contract bargaining. A better one may be to escalate the contract campaign on the inside while continuing to bargain.

- "Settle now because the signing bonus is a one-time offer." A number of companies and unions now use the signing bonus as a way to try to stampede members into quick ratification. This is a terrible practice for democratic unionism because it is designed to keep the membership from careful consideration of the long-term impact of the contract. Bonuses are worth much less than the same dollar wage increase. They have to be renegotiated each time, whereas a wage increase tends to raise the floor for the next round of bargaining. Bonuses also add no value to the multitude of benefits calculated from the basic wages (overtime, holiday pay, and in many cases pensions). A union leadership that has negotiated a signing bonus will often foster the illusion about one-time opportunity. In most cases, if the company really wants a settlement the money will be there.

- "It is impossible to defeat." Tight control of information combined with mobilization of the union staff and appointees to campaign for the contract make it difficult to generate an opposition. A high-pressure sales job gives the sense that ratification is not really debatable.

- "The fight is over—we may as well accept it and get on with our lives." This sentiment usually prevails when the vote does not take place until, say, a week after members have gone back to work after a strike and everything has returned to normal. On the one hand, few people want to maintain a strike needlessly when the issues appear to be settled, and this method has the advantage of giving members plenty of time to study and debate the contract. Yet it can take the wind out of any mobilization and make acceptance seem a done deal.

The answer lies in continuing the mobilization. The union may decide strategically that members should return to work while waiting for the ratification vote, but make clear to management that the members still have the say and are still mobilized for action if they turn the contract down. In a good contract campaign, the members are mobilized and active well before the expiration date, while they're still on the job. They can maintain a similar level of activity after a tentative agreement has been reached, with the focus now on getting out information and debating the proposal. The union can refuse to sanction overtime, for example, or any other effort that might help the company undermine the union if bargaining resumes.

How should a ratification vote be conducted—by a mail ballot or at a meeting? Wherever possible contract voting should take place in conjunction with a (presumably mass) meeting. If the group is too large for paper ballots to be collected right in the meeting, then voting machines can be used.

The reason for getting members together to vote is that decisions on contracts, with sometimes complex issues, depend not only on what's in the contract but also on what other members think about it. A member who arrives at the meeting unhappy with the terms but unsure whether more can be won will be emboldened to try if she sees others who want to put up a fight. Accepting contract terms is a group decision because it always depends on what the group is willing to struggle for. Conversely, those who want to push a contract through prefer to keep members dispersed and thinking purely in terms of individual gain or loss.

Use Grievances to Organize

The way a union handles the contract overlaps with democracy on the shop floor. If the contract was debated and decided by the members, they'll be better prepared to take day-to-day initiative in enforcing contract rights.

The difference between a truly democratic union and one that follows a servicing model is stark when it comes to grievance handling. In a strong democratic union there may not even be many grievances; members organize to convince supervisors to stop violating the contract without having to use the formal procedure. In the servicing model, the member is not encouraged to get involved at all but to turn the grievance over to the "expert." Even in unions that seek membership mobilization, the service model of grievance handling prevails: members may be mobilized to act for certain grievance issues, but they take no leadership role—no responsibility or initiative.

But a different approach is possible:

1. Get the grievant(s) directly involved. Let the member carry the grievance as far as possible. In many contracts it is possible for the member to initiate and write the first-level grievance. Train the members to write their own grievances and to do the research that makes the grievance winnable. The stewards then become advisers and trainers, not simply grievance filers.

As the grievance goes through the procedure, the member should participate in planning the case, talking to witnesses, talking to other members about what's going on. Where it is not possible for a member to be present at meetings with management, make sure the member is consulted about each decision and notified immediately of any changes or progress.

2. Involve other members in winning the grievance. Wherever possible, make the content public. While there may be privacy issues here, it should be possible to at least list the type of grievance and chart its progress. (Computer programs for grievance tracking are available; a personal computer could be set up someplace where stewards have access to it.) One of management's attacks on unions

is to try to divide the "5 percent who have grievances and need the union" from the 95 percent who presumably never have trouble and therefore do not need the union. Making grievances public helps drive home the point that a member's grievance is a battle for everyone, not only in the sense of general solidarity and "it could happen to you," but in the sense that grievance results define the meaning of workplace rules. It also brings the membership into discussions of how well grievances are being handled.

If the grievance clearly and directly affects others, make it a group grievance, with as many signers as possible. Get signers together to work on gathering information and support. Having more people involved will generate pressure on management beyond the formal grievance system. While some grievants prepare the case, others can be distributing information and buttons, urging co-workers to bring up the topic when a manager stops by their cubicles, or bugging managers themselves.

Some unions use a "wheel signature" for group grievances and petitions. On the paper, the signature lines are like spokes around a hub—no top and no bottom—and people sign anywhere they want. The idea is to make all signers equal, either to share credit or to prevent the employer from singling out the originators.

To make membership initiative a reality in handling grievances, union reps and stewards need the same leadership qualities we look for in top leaders: ability to share authority with others, to train others and share credit for union wins, and to delegate tasks and support others if they make mistakes.

Why Members Don't Participate

A major hurdle for building democracy is member apathy; the union can't be run by the members if they don't take part at all. Local officers are often frustrated with low attendance at union meetings and a lack of volunteers for committees—and then they get an earful of member complaints about how the union is run. "We're not keeping anybody out," these officers say. "We'd love to have more involvement, but all we can do is open the door."

Members do need to get off their duffs and take custody of their own fate. Officers who are trying to promote member involvement are up against decades of training in the passive, "let the experts do it" style that we learn in community life as well as in unions. The schools and the media promote corporate values and portray unions in a negative light. Passivity is reinforced by the very real forces that make management dominant, from globalization to pro-business politicians, and that make members feel powerless.

But the hard truth is that a good part of the reason for low participation is not member ignorance but rather a legitimate conclusion from real experiences in the workplace and the union. If the union seems to have no power to achieve the goals you want, then what's the point in participating? As AFL-CIO Education Director Bill Fletcher puts it: "Union democracy is a dead issue if union members believe that the union is irrelevant to their concerns."[2]

Even if the union does appear to have power and to deal with relevant issues, plenty of members still don't get involved, because they feel that their participation will make no difference to the outcome. There are two versions of this "not making a difference" mentality.

The first is the experience that the union is operated in such a way that members as a group don't seem to make a difference. When members find that a contract they have turned down is forced down their throats by a "vote until you get it right" policy, or that elections are determined by an army of appointees campaigning on company time, they may reasonably draw the conclusion that it is a waste of their time to participate. Even if officer elections seem honest, if that vote is the only choice members make over the course of three years—which leader will have the union in his or her hands—the main impression is that the members don't count. Intentionally or not, the union has made these members feel powerless, which gives them no reason to get involved.

The second version of the "not making a difference" mentality comes from the problem that one individual seems insignificant compared to the whole group. Leaders and activist members frequently complain that members who are not active are freeloaders: people who take the benefits of union membership without contributing to it. But "freeloading" is built into a world where we all have competing demands on our time. If an individual thinks in terms of her own immediate costs and benefits, she sees the situation this way:

> The union has 2,000 members. My two-hour participation at the picket line will have no noticeable effect on the union's success or failure in showing management we care about the contract. Reports on the

size of the picket line will not be accurate enough to even reflect whether or not I was there. So I can use the two hours for something where I do make a difference and/or that I enjoy (play with my daughter, do volunteer work for the church, read a book) versus something where my time and presence makes no difference.

Of course, every member could apply this reasoning. And if every member does, the picket line is a flop, the union is ineffective, and all members lose.

There is no easy answer to this individual/collective problem. But experience demonstrates that the guilt trip/lecturing approach doesn't work. Countermeasures will be based on realizing that it's not the members' fault if other demands on their time seem bigger, and on running the union in such a way that members' participation does make a difference.

When you get down to it, the reason most people get active in the union is to increase their power against the boss. When people see results from involvement, more will want to get involved. But winning victories is not easy these days, so the second reason people might have for being an activist—that it's enjoyable, fulfilling, stimulating, fun—needs to be consciously built into union activities as well. At the very least, the things that make it hard to participate need to be eliminated. Luckily, being effective and enjoying yourself tend to go together. Union work is enjoyable when the member feels that he's learning something, contributing something, making a difference—and that all of us together are doing those things. There's a feeling of community. And when people *are* contributing their talents, they're likely having a measurable effect on management too.

Why Members Do Participate

Here are some ways to make involvement more satisfying in and of itself, even when the union is not winning every battle:

• Accept and encourage initiative. For many people, putting themselves forward in any form is hard to do, as the example in the "Why Volunteer?" box demonstrates. Initiative, whether volunteering time, suggesting ideas, or planning and carrying out a project, should be highly respected by acknowledging it and taking it seriously. Volunteers can be thanked in the newsletter, asked to report their activities at a meeting, or phoned to ask how their project is going.

• Make sure individual contributions are recognized. Do this in the union newspaper, in public talks and private conversations. Create an atmosphere where people freely give credit to others for ideas and actions. Credit the small contributions too, to let members know they don't have to devote their lives in order to get involved.

• Make it easy for members to attend events by altering the time and place, when appropriate, arranging for childcare, and organizing car pools. Besides helping people attend, actions like these show that leaders really want members to come.

• Make sure that language that belittles any group of members is out of bounds in the union or workplace setting. Union leaders can set an example here. If one of his members starts to tell an ethnic joke, for example, BMWE organizer Paul Swanson suggests he change the group that's being ridiculed to "management." Such policies don't eliminate sexism or racism or prejudice, but they can make coming to work somewhat easier for those in the affected group.

Pay attention to the traditions of different sections of the membership. Don't hold meetings on important holidays. Recognize that many Americans do not celebrate Christmas: hold winter holiday parties with contributions from all cultures represented in the workplace.

• Include families in activities (more than just the annual picnic

Unions Fight Racism in the Community

The union shows it belongs to all the members when white workers step out and deal with racist problems without waiting for people of color to complain. The union can gain this reputation by taking action on community race issues.

For instance, in the mid-1970s, rank and filers in a mostly white tractor plant near Chicago, members of UAW Local 6, stood guard at a Black member's home after it was firebombed by racists. Members took turns watching the house from dusk to dawn for six months. At the same plant, the membership voted that the executive board should attend the trial of another African American member, who was brutally beaten by police after a traffic accident and then charged. In the 1990s, members of the Painters and Allied Trades in some areas have volunteered to repair homes that vandals have painted with racist slogans.

or winter holiday party). Hold kid-appropriate classes on unionism, perhaps during the union meeting, and have the kids put on a skit for the members.

• Remember members when they are sick and recognize key life events such as graduations or awards (not just deaths in the family). Honor members who are active in the community and encourage them to bring that activism into the union and vice versa.

You Have To Ask

Democracy is just a continuation of good organizing. If you want people to get involved, you have to ask them. A general call for volunteers in a newsletter, no matter how well defined the task, will not usually get people involved unless someone has talked to them

---

How Do We Know We're Organizing?

Building a participatory democracy means organizing people: helping them plan and carry out their own program to reach their own goals. The main sign of success is that members win some battles for their rights on the job. Here are some other signs to look for along the way to victory.

1. More members are involved in a passive way (reading a leaflet, checking out a union web site).

2. Other members are becoming more actively involved (wearing a button, signing a petition or group grievance, posting a leaflet at their workplace).

3. Still other members are taking on organizing tasks (selling raffle tickets, circulating petitions).

4. More and more members are becoming leaders (taking responsibility for organizing and coordinating activities).

5. Leaders and members are taking initiative; organizers' plans get adjusted by the rank and file.

6. Leaders sense that they're a team.

7. Leaders and members understand the union's strategic goals, and the union is making progress toward them.

8. People are enjoying themselves. "If you're not having fun, you're not organizing," says long-time organizer Suzanne Wall of the Oregon State Employees Union, SEIU Local 503.

personally. A member is much more likely to say "yes, I'll be there," if she knows her presence does count to someone she respects. This means that leader—board member, steward, workplace activist— needs to ask her personally to attend the rally, chat with her there, and tell her afterward it was good to see her, and what did she think? The leader who asks will hear what members did think about the rally, again making the participation a bit more meaningful.

Match the task you need help with to the person. A common unspoken dynamic goes something like this: Activist: "You see how much I do with the union; why don't you become an activist too?" Member: "Yes, I see how much you do. I am not prepared to be like you and devote so much of my life to the union." Leaders and

Why Volunteer?

Here is a standard exercise used at schools for new organizers:

The leader places three chairs in a row at the front of the room, facing the audience. The leader then asks for three volunteers to come up. Normally, after an embarrassing silence, three people will finally come up.

Now the leader asks those who didn't volunteer why they didn't. Typical answers:

"I didn't know what would be expected."
"I didn't know if I could do what you wanted."
"I didn't want to make a fool of myself."
"There was probably someone better."
"I prefer watching and taking notes."

The leader then asks the volunteers why they volunteered.

"Somebody had to do it."
"I wanted to help out."
"I like recognition."

Then the group discusses what would have made it easier for the people who held back to volunteer.

Note that in this exercise one piece is missing: the key question of relevance. Will volunteering to do the job make a difference to something people care about? But the lesson that members need clarity about the task they're being asked to do, and encouragement to take it on, is very clear.

activists need to keep in mind a list of distinct tasks that includes small jobs to be delegated as well as bigger responsibilities. Draw on widely different talents so that each prospective activist can pick the task that fits. Ask a person to do telephone banking. If that doesn't work, ask him to gather information on a topic needed for bargaining. People are most likely to say yes when the tasks are specific, clearly do-able, and rewarding. And don't forget the feedback loop: if you're getting a lot of no's, does the job you're asking people to do seem meaningful?

One outcome of the competing demands on people's time is that involvement is not a yes-no issue but a matter of degrees. People get involved in many different ways and often change their level of involvement depending on what else is going on in their lives. A successful organizer pays attention to and welcomes involvement at every level. Structures that depend only on members who are high-

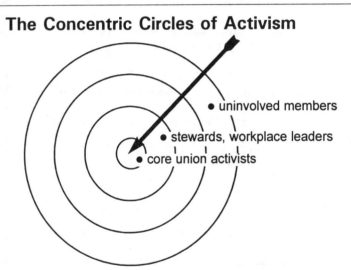

The Concentric Circles of Activism

- uninvolved members
- stewards, workplace leaders
- core union activists

The concentric circles illustrate members' different levels of participation. Each union activity—membership meetings, newsletter writing, newsletter reading—is aimed at those within a certain circle, not that others wouldn't be welcome. "Centrifugal force"—competing demands for time—will tend to draw people toward the outer circles. Leaders' job is to realize that each member's location on this diagram changes over time, and to keep drawing people into successive inner circles.

ly active all the time will make the union the property of an in-crowd. The task is to recognize the different levels of involvement and welcome members at all levels into increased activities.

TDU leader Joe Fahey says that activist members often play out the following scenario—and miss an opportunity:

> Fred: What happened at the union meeting yesterday?
>
> Activist: You should have been there to see; we need more people to come to meetings.

This response tells Fred that if he doesn't attend union meetings, he is out of the union loop, and there's no other way to find out what's going on. Fred is faced with the choice of deciding on his own whether he wants to increase his level of activity to attend meetings, or just leave the loop to those who "have more time" or "are activist types." Given the response he's gotten from Activist, chances are he will choose the latter and drift further away from the union. But suppose instead that Activist says: "We had a really interesting discussion about which jobs are threatened by the new machines. And we're getting people together to circulate a group grievance on XYZ—would you be willing to take one around?"

Some unions have a rule—no running for office without atten-dance at a certain percentage of union meetings—that penalizes members for their past inactivity, rather than inviting them to move from inactivity to activity. The existence of cliques does the same thing: if you're not active already, it's tough to butt your way in. Democracy means finding the barriers to involvement at every level, and abolishing them.

Relevance and the Game of Bridge

Bill Fletcher uses this exercise to start a discussion about member participation:

He announces that he is looking for people to join his bridge club, to play cards. He always gets few or no takers, so he then proceeds to lecture the students on their apathy and unwillingness to learn. This triggers a discussion on the nature of apathy and responses to it.[3] Isn't apathy a natural reaction to things that don't seem relevant? Would being lectured this way inspire anyone to come to a bridge party—or to a union meeting?

Union Education

Democratic unionism is not so complicated that only the anointed can practice it. At the same time, it's not a big part of modern culture, so there's much to learn from other activists. Unions must provide their own training programs to counter the pro-management passivity taught in most public education and the media; other organizations—political and community groups—can provide valuable experience, too.

Union training programs often provide the only opportunity for members and leaders to explore issues in depth from a union point of view. This becomes increasingly important as management uses its own training programs to subtly (or often grossly) undermine the basic principles of solidarity and democracy. How many people come away from team concept training programs with the idea that voting, majority rule, and arguing passionately for your position are bad things? (Consensus and "conflict resolution" are the only legitimate methods.) How many come away believing that all questions must be approached from the point of view of competitiveness and profitability (the company agenda) rather than rights, decent jobs, and solidarity (which should be the union agenda)?

This places a heavy burden on union training programs to cover everything from basic skills—public speaking and grievance handling—to union-friendly world views. Local unions don't have to do it all alone, although when it comes to training in membership democracy most unions are too timid about internal debate and opposition to do adequate training in democratic procedures (they teach Robert's Rules of Order instead). There are some exceptions; the United Electrical Workers (UE) provides its leaders with training materials that include some "why" and "how" on democratic procedures. Some college and university labor studies programs are excellent on this score. Labor Notes conferences and schools offer unusual opportunities for members to come in contact with activists from other unions who are struggling with questions of democracy.

On the level of a union world view, most unions have or are developing new videos and workbooks to help reestablish the idea of a union agenda. These are a mixed bag: many training materials are based on a service model of unionism and/or the ideal of partnership with the union's adversaries. But if you watch out for these unspoken assumptions, you may uncover valuable resources.

Another approach to education is to make sure members have contact with the best of the labor movement outside their own workplace. Some unions take seriously labor support activities, getting members to picket lines or caravaning to other locals' strikes. UAW Local 879 adopted a sister local in Mexico; many local, regional, and larger union bodies have sponsored visits by Mexican, U.S., and Canadian unionists to the other countries. Some locals help train their members by sending them to cross-union activities and conferences sponsored by the AFL-CIO, Jobs with Justice, or Labor Notes.

Another challenge to management ideology in the workplace comes from grassroots activist groups. Community groups working on issues from the environment to school funding help fill out an anti-corporate view of the world. Bringing in speakers from such groups and highlighting the work of members who belong to them helps expose members to a wider range of experiences fighting corporate power.

Membership Meetings

Membership meetings are not simply places for members to get information and cast votes, which could also be accomplished through newsletters and mail referendums. Meetings should give members a sense of power by bringing them together. They can see and feel that they are not alone, that others have similar problems, and that others have found solutions. Meetings should give members the opportunity to observe leaders and potential leaders in action. They can learn from each other, combine ideas, and build something bigger. If this doesn't sound like a union meeting you've ever been to, it's because most locals are unwittingly stuck in traditions that almost guarantee that a first-time attender will not come back, and only the most faithful will persevere.

Although many officers fret about low attendance levels, it is not necessary for democracy that all or most members attend membership meetings. Except at contract time and for other special events, most locals will see only a relatively small, dedicated minority at monthly meetings. Meetings, especially on a regular basis, are not for everyone.

But union meetings can be the chief organizing vehicle for that portion of the membership that takes union work most seriously— the activists. Coming to the monthly meeting is often one of the first things that a member tries when he's seeking to be more involved. It's important not to turn them off!

That means that the success of a meeting is not measured simply by the number attending but by how that meeting contributes to the control, involvement, activism, and self-confidence of all the members, *both those present and those not.* What "comes out of" the meeting—the plans made, assignments taken, feedback received—are more important than the meeting itself.

Making Meetings Interesting and Useful

To improve meetings and boost attendance, start by doing away with the standard meeting announcement that sets out the same uninformative agenda month after month:

President's Report
Committee Reports
Old Business
New Business
Adjourn (wake up)

Tell members instead what will actually come up at the meeting. Make sure they know how to propose agenda points covering their concerns. Distribute proposed motions in advance. Put important and controversial items on the agenda. Discuss issues that will directly affect work situations. Have votes on policy questions where the vote really makes a difference. Get rid of the boring reports. Print them out and distribute them in advance. Do them in multiple languages or on cassette tapes if appropriate, so members can come to meetings prepared.

Once we get over thinking that every member should attend regularly, then we can specialize some meetings. Plan each meeting to focus on a different section of the membership. Invite a few of those members to make a presentation on specific problems they're facing. Advertise that the September meeting, for example, will take up the question of repetitive strain injuries in the wrapping department, and recruit shop floor leaders and RSI victims to give presentations. October will focus on the problem of a particular supervisor in inspection. Treated this way, soon members will be clamoring to get their points on the agenda. Another possibility is to move the location of the meetings around to make them more convenient to different segments of the membership.

Use some imagination. Bring in outside speakers for brief talks and discussion. Use video clips. Give people—especially volunteers—recognition for what they have accomplished for the union. Break down into small groups on occasion to get more people participating. Have members do skits or role-playing to deal with challenges facing the union. For example, management offers controversial perks to some members.

Always have a point on the agenda called "members' concerns," where anyone can raise a problem or question without necessarily making a motion. In this portion the officers listen, make notes, and after the meeting see that some action or investigation begins. Not only do they report back to the person who has brought the concern, they also report back to the next union meeting.

Make sure several people are assigned to help any new members or first-timers understand the meeting procedures and help them accomplish what they came to the meeting for. Sit with them and explain what is going on. If a person uses procedure incorrectly, figure out his intent and help him through it. The chairperson should go out of her way to make the newcomers comfortable, give them recognition when possible, and draw them further into participation.

Invite spouses to the meetings as full participants (except for voting). Have good quality childcare so that the kids look forward to the meeting as well as the adults.

One technique we do not recommend is door prizes or lottery tickets to boost meeting attendance. It cheapens the purpose of the meeting and stresses seeing things in terms of "what's in it for me individually" rather than coming together to help all of us. On the other hand, Teamsters Local 174 in Seattle used a financial incentive to break the ice with new part-time UPS workers. Those who came to an introductory meeting were refunded their initiation fee. Union leaders thought the one-time appeal to self-interest was worth it, to make sure some of these young, high-turnover workers learned firsthand about the local's philosophy and how to get to the union hall.

At the end of the meeting it is sometimes useful to have a brief point on evaluation—what could be improved? Keep the meetings short so they don't dribble to a close as people drift out; leave time for informal discussion and socializing afterward.

Remember that the meeting is only one piece of the union's life; most members relate to the union outside of meetings. That's why every meeting should be an action meeting that leads to some other activity. Members and leaders should take assignments at the meeting, and these should be summed up at the end: "The president will check into x and report back to y body. John has volunteered to help the education committee put out a leaflet on xyz problem by x date. Everyone here in the abc department will take the group grievances and get them signed." Assignments should lead the work of the union back into the workplace where more members can be involved, not just to the next union meeting or committee meeting.

All of this discussion assumes that the leaders of the union want meetings that contribute to democratic control. If not—if you are a rank and filer facing an undemocratic administration—you need to know how to use the monthly meeting to further reform goals. See "Being Effective at Union Meetings," Appendix 1.

Ignore Robert's Rules

Most union bylaws say that meetings will be run according to Robert's Rules of Order Revised. The power of tradition is strong: this procedure is almost never questioned even though so many people find it intimidating and so few understand it. Ideally, unions that want to be democratic should start by discarding Robert's Rules, for three reasons:

For one, Robert's was designed for other situations in other times. Robert's conception of meetings is based on the British parliament in the 18th century—a period before microphones and amplifiers, when it was necessary to be an orator with a powerful voice to effectively participate in any meeting of over 100 people. It was before the invention of photocopying for easy duplication of printed motions and agendas. It was before mass telephone, fax, and e-mail for fast information distribution and retrieval, when members of organizations had to depend solely on the meeting for their information about its activities. These tools have radically altered communication possibilities and therefore the function of face-to-face meetings.

Second, Robert's is designed for legislative bodies, not for meetings that involve people in discussion to exchange information and ideas. For example, under Robert's every discussion must start with a motion, rather than starting with a problem and then through discussion and cooperation coming up with a plan of action.

Third, Robert's is not democratic. It was designed for bodies, like legislatures, made up of professional meeting-goers. It is certainly not designed to encourage participation from people who have come to their first union meeting. The current edition is 706 pages plus tables. Robert's is so complicated that it violates the most important democratic reason for having rules: to level the playing field by ensuring that everyone can know how to participate. Robert's is used frequently in the opposite way: to intimidate members, make them feel foolish, and rule them out of order.

In addition, Robert's is designed with a bias toward the *status quo.* The requirements for a two-thirds majority to pass certain motions, like changing the agenda or moving to a vote, don't just add to the complications. They also make it relatively easy for a minority to block or delay decisions and action.

So ingrained is the traditional genuflection to Robert's Rules that any attempt to change to different rules will usually meet resistance. There is no commonly known alternative so it is not usually worth the time and energy to try to dump Robert's. If you want to try anyway, you could start with the "Simplified Rules of Order" in Appendix 4.

But in general the best policy is to do openly what almost everybody does in practice, that is, simply ignore Robert's Rules, do what tradition calls for in your union, and mix it with common sense and fairness. Most people dislike procedural wrangles and are very supportive of proposals made to handle things in a fair, common sense kind of way. See Appendix 2 on how to lead an effective meeting for examples of this approach.

More on Meetings

See the Appendixes for more help on membership meetings:

1. Being Effective at Union Meetings (when the chair is undemocratic)

2. Leading Effective Union Meetings (when you are the elected leadership)

3. Hints on Robert's Rules (including a table of Robert's Rules)

4. Simplified Rules of Order (a set of proposed better meeting rules)

Reform Caucuses:
Show How Rank and File Power Works

Nearly all the democracy-building and membership involvement described in this chapter can be carried out by a rank and file
caucus, to a certain extent, if the union leadership is unwilling. In
fact, that's the main activity of the most successful reform caucuses.
So where we talk about getting members involved in grievances, it
may be a caucus leader who helps the grievant gather evidence and
pressure the rep to do a good job. Reformers often organize group
grievances; having lots of members signed on helps pressure officials as well as the company. Where we talk about getting members
information on bargaining, it's often up to reform activists to
demand, research, and then distribute information about contract
proposals and settlements.

As part of showing the need for democracy, reform caucuses
often find themselves using their own democratic practice to accomplish things the union is neglecting. This is because when you're
operating without staff support or resources, you're necessarily
going to depend on rank and file involvement to get things done. So
reform caucus members—say they're concentrating on an important
grievance that officials are ignoring—are forced to practice the same
kind of membership mobilization that they've been bugging the
union leadership to promote. They must deal with all the same issues
about participation, inclusion, and relevance. Members thus teach
themselves a new style of unionism. As TDU organizer Ken Paff
says about that movement's history, "We changed ourselves as much
as we changed the union."

Notes

1. Mark Hunnibell, "Defending the Profession: Pilot Union Activism at American
   Airlines," a paper presented at LaborTECH 97, July 12, 1997.
2. Bill Fletcher, "Whose Democracy? Organized Labor and Member Control," in
   Gregory Mantsios, ed., *A New Labor Movement for the New Century*, New
   York: Monthly Review Press, 1998, p. 20.
3. Fletcher, p. 22.

5. Elections

Voting is a core procedure for union democracy. First, some votes—on contract ratification, for example—allow the membership to make a key decision directly. Second, elections have an impact through their potential rather than their actual use. The fact that an election will take place is a kind of backstop. To the extent leaders believe that members can vote them out of office, they will try to listen to and deliver for the members.

Third, an election campaign can draw many members—both active ones (who formulate issues and campaign) and passive ones (who are exposed to the campaign and then vote)—into greater activity. The election season creates opportunities for more involvement and knowledge so that all kinds of choices (voting included) are more informed and meaningful.

At the same time, elections by themselves don't ensure democracy, and there are limitations on their usefulness. Elections are a snapshot of leadership-membership relations and priorities at the time of the vote. Since the union needs to respond to rapidly changing circumstances, interchange between leaders and members and development of members into new leaders has to go on between elections as well.

Elections also tend to put a premium on certain kinds of activities and personalities: the good talkers, the simple solutions. And elections take resources. The purpose of unions is not to have elections but to give members power in dealing with the boss. Elections are a crucial tool for giving the members power, but their use must be balanced against the time, money, and energy they require.

In this chapter we deal only with officer elections. See Chapter 4 for discussion of contract ratification votes.

What Are We Choosing?

Elections typically take the form of choosing individuals for individual offices. We elect a local president, vice-president, and executive board members. As voters we often see our task as choosing the most qualified person for the job. Sometimes we're admonished to vote for the platform, not the personality. Either of these is too simple a way to view elections. We can't just pick the most qualified candidate because qualifications matter little if the candidate doesn't carry out the right policies once in office. On the other hand, qualifications do matter: the best platform is useless if officers, once elected, can't get the platform carried through.

Elections are a chance to weigh potential leaders' personal attributes together with their viewpoints. At the same time, voters are often presented with a team, not just a group of individuals: who makes up the slate, how do they work together, who are the people they tend to work with most closely (the most militant stewards, or the skilled trades clique, for example)?

In a local where different forces are actively contending about the future of the union, a vote for officers is a vote about the policy and priorities of the local. The debate may be over militancy vs. partnership with employers. It could be over a choice between the servicing model and redefining the union based on rank and file activism. Most likely, the choice is not so clear-cut; it gets mixed up with personalities and the candidates' past actions. These are part of elections too. Which candidate has the character needed when the going gets tough, or in the face of temptation? Which ones will have the flexibility to respond when new issues come up? We hold old leaders accountable for their records.

But elections are not a one-way process where potential leaders present frozen positions and records and members simply choose among them. Leaders, including opinion leaders not in office, also shape members' sense of what's possible. Campaign rhetoric about militancy, for example, will tend to make members consider striking to be a real possibility next contract round. On the other hand, expectations are often kept low—vote for incumbent president Smith for more of the same, or for challenger candidate Jones for more of the same, only better. This is one reason for low turnout.

Individuals vs. Teams: Slate Voting

Slates may not be important in electing a steward. There we are mainly concerned with the individual's performance: does she write grievances well, stand up to the boss, organize the members? Because of the nature of the job we can evaluate the candidates first-hand.

But this kind of individual evaluation makes less sense the further away the candidate is from your direct experience. How do you decide between two candidates you've never met for treasurer of the local or the international? What counts is not the kind of job officers do individually but how well they do as a group. Slates help voters make decisions based on proposals for the union's direction, not who's made the most friends. Slates mean those on the leadership team take collective responsibility for the slate's platform and for the performance of any individual member of the slate. Slates also help balance representation in the leadership; as candidates put their lists together, they'll naturally want to include people from various parts of the union—racial and ethnic groups, job classifications, work locations—to help gain votes from all these parts.

Of course, members should also have the right to ignore the slates—to pick and choose among the candidates regardless of slate designation. But ballots that list slates, even allowing a single check mark to serve as a vote for a full slate, help clarify what the election is about.

Uncontested Elections

A leader of the International Alliance of Theatrical and Stage Employees declared in its "IA Bulletin" after their 1998 convention that "...this International has gone without an election and demonstrates to the world that this Union once and for all is united." One member saw the lack of an election differently; he commented on the internet, "The message from a convention without votes, without debate, without contending factions, without dissenting views, without opposing candidates, is a message from a top-down organization with a powerless, uninvolved membership."

By itself, this uncontested election doesn't prove one view or the other. Democracy requires not a certain number of elections, but a lack of barriers for members to put themselves forward as leaders. The fact that any given election is not contested may simply be a sign that the democratic process has been at work throughout the year—that new members are moving into leadership roles, elected or not, and that leaders are responsive to members.

Or an uncontested election may be a sign that members believe that leaders can't be replaced through voting, which becomes a self-fulfilling prophecy.

Election Procedures

Procedures for running elections should not only ensure an honest election and a fair campaign, they should also help the campaigners to focus on the direction of the union rather than personalities, pose real choices, and draw members into activity.

An honest election means it should be easy to vote, without intimidation or retribution, with polling places conveniently located and open for reasonable periods.

A Fair Campaign

Fairness requires that members not have to jump high hurdles to be eligible to run, such as a requirement for dozens of nominators. A bylaw that candidates must have attended most union meetings rules out nearly all members—and has been ruled illegal by the Department of Labor. Beyond that, the ideal of a fair contest implies something like a level playing field, when in most cases there is no way to make conditions truly equal. Factors that can put mountains on the playing field are incumbency, finances, and employer involvement. All these often work together against rank and file reform campaigns.

"How to Get an Honest Union Election"

"How to Get an Honest Union Election" is a 64-page booklet by longtime democracy activist Herman Benson, available from the Association for Union Democracy. It gives useful tips on the dangers of stolen elections, some safeguards, notes on the law, and a sample set of election rules. Paperback, $5.

Contact AUD, 500 State Street, Brooklyn NY 11217.

The power of incumbency

In the worst cases, selected candidates are given the advantage of incumbency before they're ever elected. In the International Brotherhood of Electrical Workers, for example, and in some other unions as well, a retiring international officer typically picks his successor in effect by leaving before the end of his term. On retiring he effectively chooses his replacement, who can then run as the incumbent.

Caucuses in some locals follow the same practice. This does "smooth the transition," as its defenders claim, if by "smoothing" we mean creating the sense that the results are already fixed and discouraging opposition. This practice is simply contempt for the election process and democracy.

Incumbents' advantages include:

• Access to members for campaigning

First, incumbents have the lists of members and where they work. Incumbents may not legally use the membership list for campaigning unless it's available to all candidates, but it's usually difficult to prove whether and how an incumbent used her access to the list to aid her campaign. In private sector unions all candidates have the right to have the union mail their campaign literature, at the candidate's expense, to all members or to subsets of members.

Federal law for private sector unions also gives any member the right to view all current labor contracts at the local's office. Teamster reformers have used this right to gain a list of work sites for their locals. Again, this is information easily available to incumbents in the course of their union work.

The most valuable lists can be developed only through face-to-face campaigning. These are the lists that "map" the local—listing not only names but who is in contact with whom and who the natural leaders are. Any challenger needs to make such a "map" for a serious campaign.

Incumbents also have an enormous advantage in campaigning at the work site. Employers can exclude union candidates from their property as long as they do it "equally." Incumbents or their appointees can assert that they're there on union business; the law allows them to campaign while on the clock if it's "incidental" to performing union business, and they certainly will.

• Control over events

By picking which grievances or which contract issues to pursue, incumbents can often determine the most visible issues. If they organize a group grievance on a health and safety issue shortly before the election, then challengers are more likely to be asked, "What would you do differently on health and safety?"

Incumbents may also be able to set the date of an election to their advantage—say, before or after a contract negotiation.

• Regular exposure to members

Incumbents achieve name recognition simply through meetings, union publications, and handling union business. This advantage can be partly compensated for by allowing challengers to publish campaign material in union newsletters and to give a campaign talk at a union meeting, and by the use of slate designations on ballots.

• Staff and appointees as campaigners

Incumbents can use appointments to both full-time and committee positions to staff a campaign organization. (Again, appointees'

Suggested Bylaws for Democratic Elections

Here are some ideas for bylaws to help ensure candidates' right and ability to campaign among the members:

• The recording secretary will provide all nominated candidates a list of all work sites represented by this local.

• Candidates may post election materials on union bulletin boards.

• The local will include statements of all candidates and/or slates in union newspapers.

• Ballots will include candidates' slate affiliation if designated.

• Before the election the local will sponsor a candidates' forum with a moderator agreeable to all candidates.

• The union will make all reasonable attempts to see that all candidates have access to non-work areas of work sites for campaigning.

campaigning must be off the clock or incidental to their union work to be legal.)

• Handing out favors

Incumbents can reward supporters with immediate benefits: appointments to offices, lost-time authorization to attend conferences, special handling of problems and grievances

Given these natural advantages of incumbency, fair election procedures should include some steps to balance the advantages out, as described in the box, without weakening the regular functioning of the union or the elected officers.

Of course, incumbency has potential disadvantages, too: incumbents are responsible for results. Where incumbents can talk convincingly about union successes, on organizing and building members' power for instance, having a record is a big plus. But when things are not going well (decline of the industry, technological change), members may take it out on their leaders even if the problems are due to external conditions. The members reasonably respond to the slogan "it's time for a change" and hope that a different leadership can get results. (It's not uncommon for reformers who win office and actually do a decent job to be defeated in the next election.)

In fact, incumbency is an advantage primarily because it offers the opportunity to take advantage of other factors that tilt the playing field: employer involvement and unequal financing.

Financing

Union elections, unlike elections for public office, are mostly won through person-to-person contact—conversations among co-workers. Still, in a local large enough to have full-time officers, election campaigns take money, and the incumbents usually have more. Besides the personal cost of taking time off work to contact members, the big expenses for an election campaign are usually printing and possibly mailing literature, and hosting any events like a barbecue or spaghetti dinner.

Full-time union officers generally have more money to spend on election campaigns than rank and file challengers because they're usually substantially higher paid than the members. In many cases they also have more high-paid friends and allies: fellow officers of the local, staff reps, officers of nearby locals, and often officers and staff of the international (especially in unions like the Teamsters, UFCW, or UAW where there's a union-wide reform organization and a set of officers trying to stop it). In large locals there may be a dozen or so appointees, usually business reps, who owe their jobs to the incumbent officers and can be expected to help their reelection bid.

To level the playing field, and make finances less a factor, unions should print uncensored statements from candidates in a pre-election newsletter that goes to all members. SEIU Local 509, whose members are Massachusetts state workers, gives candidates a limit on how many words they may write for the pre-election edition of the newsletter. (If they go over, the newsletter simply cuts them off, in mid-sentence if need be.) The Teamsters' international magazine provides a designated amount of space for each candidate; candidates may run any text, graphics, or photos they choose and slates may pool their space. However it's done, the point is to make a base level of campaign literature and distribution available to all candidates at no cost.

Election rules could also limit the size of donations to an amount that's affordable to most members. This may be hard to enforce, but will tend to limit the effects of widely different personal incomes, which is the goal.

Some unions, notably the Steelworkers and Service Employees, have rules on campaign fundraising whose main effect is to widen any difference between higher paid and lower paid candidates; in today's world this difference mostly occurs between incumbents and rank and filers. These unions say they don't want outside influence on elections, and therefore prohibit donations from anyone but current members.

Employers are already prohibited by law from donating, so they're not affected by this kind of rule. The effect is on donations from nonmembers who aren't in management.

A no-outside-donations rule doesn't protect an election's integrity, but does hinder democracy by placing a disproportionate burden on insurgent candidates; they're the ones most likely to need donations from nonmembers to try to close the funding gap—a few dollars from their sister-in-law, raffle tickets sold at the corner bar, or donations from reformers in another union. Incumbents who are able—as so many are—to put hundreds or thousands of dollars at a time into their war chest do not need to cast so wide a net. For instance, in larger locals incumbents might spend $10,000 on a reelection campaign. With several business reps and officers putting in $1,000 each, that's all the fundraising the incumbents need do. Meanwhile, rank and filers will have to pull together hundreds of much smaller contributions to build a budget even half that size. It's doable, but more difficult, and will tend to involve some supporters beyond the membership.

Since they help level the playing field, outside contributions to election campaigns should be allowed—except, of course, from employers or vendors. The difficulties faced by rank and file candidates today mean that candidates should also be allowed to accept donated legal help to enforce campaign rights.

Certainly laws against employer contributions should be strictly enforced. That's easier said than done; truly crooked campaigners will find ways to subvert any rules. A cumbersome attempt at prevention, like requiring that names and addresses of each contributor be reported, no matter how small the amount (as required of Teamsters international candidates for the 1998 rerun election), falls more heavily on rank and file challengers. A requirement for listing small contributions puts dissidents at risk of retribution, gives an advantage to those with access to accounting and other bureaucratic resources, makes all sides more prone to technical violations, and still doesn't guarantee honest data. While watching out for employer contributions is necessary, the best defense is education before and during the campaign period, to maximize the number of members who can recognize illegal interference and understand how it hurts the union. If too many mailings of too-glossy literature raises eyebrows and costs votes, and if an explicit employer endorsement would torpedo a campaign, the union gets some protections against employer influence without having to impede legitimate fundraising.

Employer involvement

Most of the power often ascribed to incumbency is actually incumbents' ability to make deals with employers. Many of the opportunities to provide favors to members are really deals brokered with management. A union officer, if he chooses to, can usually get a member special consideration on a grievance, or extra time off. This can be done by focusing the power of the union, or it can be done by an exchange of favors with a manager. The latter is frequently easier, although the leader now owes the manager.

Employers get involved in union elections in a variety of other ways. They may be suddenly willing to settle large grievances or offer a perk right before election time (as in HERE Local 6 in New York, when officers announced a new prescription benefit just before an unusual contested election). Or they may threaten to close the plant or lay off a shift if the wrong candidate wins, as General Motors and Ford did at two plants in Michigan (in both cases, the candidates' opponents in the union were the main purveyors of management's threats). Employers have been known to make it easy for certain members—supporters of the incumbents—to get time off to vote, shutting down certain assembly lines at one auto factory, for instance, and even providing transportation to and from the local union hall in some Teamster locals.

The worst employer involvement is harassment and firing of candidates and other campaigners; the problem is both widespread and difficult to prove. In the first-ever direct election of Teamsters top officers, dozens of protests were lodged by rank and file members who were disciplined or fired apparently for their campaign activity—nearly all of them supporters of reformer Ron Carey.

Employer involvement in elections is illegal. But it happens in a context: management's ongoing influence in the union through those who are either literally corrupt or just too cozy with the boss. So stopping such involvement is as much a matter of changing the culture of the union as it is a matter of enforcing the law.

Mechanics of Voting and Voter Turnout

Turnout by itself tells us nothing about the democratic quality of an election. Totalitarian one-party states can produce turnouts in the high 90 percent range (there's a penalty for not voting). Mob-dominated urban machines achieved high turnouts. A hotly contested election may produce a big vote, but if the choices are meaningless, the turnout is meaningless. There is nothing democratic about a greater number of voters choosing between Tweedledum and Tweedledee. What we want is the greatest number of people making as well-informed, meaningful a choice as possible.

Resources

How many polling places are needed? Should we use voting machines or paper ballots? How long should the polls be open? How many members of the election committee should be paid lost time to monitor the election? If the union had unlimited resources the answers might be easy.

But union resources are precious, so there are no ready answers to these questions. Where elections are hotly contested and/or there is any suspicion of dishonest behavior, then the union needs to spend more on voting machines and monitoring; it's not just the fact but also the appearance of election fairness that must be preserved. But at other times these expenses are a waste of money that could be used for activities that increase solidarity through the long period between elections.

Voting location and mail ballots

Should elections take place at the workplace, perhaps in the cafeteria; in the company parking lot using tents or trailers; at the local hall; or through the mail? Where possible, and where the union hall is a comfortable place for most members, elections should take place there; that's where it's easiest to build an atmosphere that voting is about what's best for all of us. But when the union hall is an intimidating place for many members, then mail balloting is better.

Turnout is usually highest at the work site because of convenience; that's a plus. But the disadvantages of voting at the workplace far outweigh the advantages. Elections held at work make management's presence and influence stronger. An incumbent can use her influence to get a supervisor to "release" the whole department to go vote. The atmosphere is company and company power. The company may well intervene in any disputes (like campaigning too near the polls) that arise at polling sites.

Although parking lots are technically company property, management is less likely to intervene there and more likely to allow the union to establish whatever kind of atmosphere it wants. A downside is that parking lot voting stations tend to encourage tailgate parties and thus a cliquish atmosphere.

Voting at the union hall has several advantages. Most important, the union atmosphere can be most easily established there. The act of voting itself helps familiarize people with getting to and using the hall. The disadvantage is that turnout will definitely be lower than at the workplace. Also, geography is rarely neutral, particularly in racially segregated areas. The location of the hall could influence the racial makeup of the voters.

The union hall itself may not be a neutral place. The hall is more or less the territory of the incumbents, a fact that can influence which members feel comfortable going there; in some unions, if you're not known to be a supporter of the incumbents, showing up to vote can feel like (or actually be) getting marked for retribution. For this reason, and in an uphill battle against voter apathy in the union, Teamster reformers usually work for local elections by mail ballot. TDU considered it a step forward when in 1992 the international recommended mail ballot elections in its revised model bylaws for locals. TDU members have sometimes applied to the international to require mail balloting where a history of intimidation is evident.

True, mail ballots can be more difficult to monitor than a small number of walk-in polling places. (Since most members, unfortunately, will not vote or even notice whether they received a ballot in the mail, there are many ways for blank ballots to fall into dishonest hands.) TDUers found that removing the process from under incumbents' stare to a member's own kitchen table reduced the fear of retribution and increased turnout. (Most Teamster locals cover dozens of workplaces, often over a large area, so the hall is not necessarily near any particular workplace.)

As we mentioned in Chapter 4, the reasons for holding votes in the union hall are stronger for contract ratification than for officers elections. In both cases, you want to remind members that they're all in this together, rather than individuals making personal decisions. But since officers' jobs aren't on the line with a contract vote, members have less reason to fear reprisals for voting "wrong."

Reform Through Elections: Organizing Comes First

A caucus striving to rebuild the union will probably decide to run for office at some point. They'll have the best chance of success—in the election and in rebuilding the union—if the election is part of ongoing organizing, not the caucus's only activity. If campaigning is part of building a *movement* for reform, then that movement can go on after the election, no matter who wins. Happily, involving a lot of people who see the effort as their own helps win the election, too.

Thus organizing is the key to any election. Ken Paff, TDU's

national organizer, says that when he talks to rank and file reformers about their local election campaigns, he typically asks first, "How many people are helping you? How many are passing out literature or talking up the campaign or getting other people to wear your campaign button or sticker?" Questions about monitoring the vote count come second.

While both challengers and incumbents will be concerned about the integrity of the election process, the first job of every campaign is to inspire members to vote for them in large numbers. The best monitoring cannot detect all possible election fraud without a huge investment of time and resources; a substantial vote in your favor is the best insurance. Herman Benson, former executive director of the Association for Union Democracy, always warned, "You may need 60 percent to get elected."

Exposing election fraud and demanding a rerun is a poor second to winning outright the first time. Even valid protests of violations may sound petty to many members, which can cost the protester votes in a rerun. Deciding when to protest an election that included violations is as much an organizing question as a legal one: are members mad about it? Do they feel that their right to vote was infringed? Even when the rerun produces an election victory, the victors have often lost much of their mobilization to a drawn-out legal process.

If your real purpose is not to win an election but to change the union, then your group can make important gains win or lose. If a large minority of members votes for a more militant challenger, a winning incumbent will take pains to sound—and hopefully act—more militant after the vote. No matter who wins, teamwork built through campaigning will help prepare new leaders for after the election.

6. Taking Power in the Local: the Campaign Continues

Taking office is a perilous time for local reform caucuses, and many don't make the cut. Reformers face a whole new set of problems once in office and a gaggle of forces to push them or pull them off course. At the same time, the window of opportunity to make changes is short. If change is not evident almost immediately, it is easy for the members to become cynical. They campaigned actively, elected new officers committed to reform, but everything seems to stay the same. Thus begins a vicious circle: member cynicism leads to passivity and withdrawal, which leads to greater dependence on officials, which leads to officials identifying themselves as "the union" that provides services to the member-customers.

On the other hand, the expectation of change and the new level of attention members are focusing on the union allow new officers to take actions immediately after an election that would be much harder to accomplish after everyone has settled into routine. The honeymoon period will not repeat itself. The success of reform depends on carrying the momentum and spirit of a successful election campaign into the operation of the local on a day-to-day basis.

[Note: This chapter owes much to the work and writing of Dan Campbell, a co-chair of Teamsters for a Democratic Union, who has been a UPS package car driver, Teamster organizer, local business agent, and executive assistant to the local president.]

It depends on the members.

The following suggestions are directed to reform leaders who have just taken office, particularly to the one designated by the constitution as the top leader. Here we will refer to this person as the president, although in some locals the title may be principal officer, business manager, secretary-treasurer, or chairperson. With some adjustments the suggestions are also relevant to current officeholders. But they will be much more useful if reformers think these issues through long before the election. Don't wait until the votes are counted to read this chapter.

The advice that follows mostly assumes a worst-case scenario: that your predecessors (we designate them "the old guard") were truly uninterested in serving the members, remain hostile to your administration, and are plotting their own return to power. If your local has a less contentious atmosphere and the ex-incumbents are willing to work with you, so much the better. We've also tailored our suggestions for large to medium-sized locals with full-time officers and staff, including those who represent the members on grievances (who may be called business agents or committeepersons),

Although we've written in the form of advice to the top officers,

Even Before You Campaign

Ideally you'll be thinking about how you'd handle a leadership post before you even start an election campaign. For the campaign itself, you'll be searching out members with skills for campaign organizing and leadership; you should think about the same questions for local union work. Which members show knowledge in special areas—literature production, grievance handling, health and safety, running meetings, computers?

How you conduct your campaign helps set the tone for the local once you take office.

During the campaign, therefore, don't make promises that you can't keep or that, if kept, would undermine your functioning. For example, don't promise an unlimited "open door policy." You can't be in the office and visiting work sites at the same time, and you wouldn't want to devote all your time to only those members who come to the office. Promise instead an open door during certain hours and stick to them.

success depends on the efforts of a solid reform caucus, not just a few people. That means the entire reform movement, at different levels, must understand and undertake the tasks at this critical stage of union democracy.

Now What?

Congratulations, your local reform group has won an election. Now what?

The goal was to make the union more powerful. You ran on a platform of member involvement and more aggressive representation. You promised more education. You denounced the cozy relationship your predecessors had with management. Perhaps you ridiculed them for never returning phone calls and because members never saw them except at election time.

Now you face a stack of problems: all the normal bargaining and grievance handling of the local demand action. In fact, it may be worse than normal, since your predecessors may have left you all the messes to clean up, and as little information as possible. You have dozens of committee and staff positions to reappoint, replace, or abolish, and many legal procedures and responsibilities to learn and do.

And then you face the question of how to start moving toward the goals that motivated your reform group in the first place.

When you try to make changes the union structures feel like they are built of concrete. Nothing seems to give. Other times they feel like Jello. They give easily but just bounce back the way they were as soon as your attention is diverted and you relieve the pressure.

Your defeated opponents may have already started a campaign to undermine you. And they have the contacts with management and with sections of the union you hardly know, as well as knowledge of the contracts and "the way it's always been done."

Your own supporters are inexperienced and need training. Some may be pressing you to do it all with one stroke of the pen. Others may be demanding an appointment or a pet project. Now that you're in office, crises are thrust on you both by management and by individual members that you can neither duck nor defer.

It all seems overwhelming. And this is where the first mistakes are so often made: the temptation is to reduce the number of tasks by leaving things the way they are. Keep the experienced business agents and staff on, and hope they will follow the program of the election winners. Don't change the procedures; just try to take charge of the old machine and make it your own.

It won't work. You need to build a smooth-running operation that belongs to the members and that gets the *right* things done. The old guard's machine was part of the problem and still is.

The assumptions leaders hold become embedded in the structure they create. If the leaders do not trust the members, then their organization will be set up to protect themselves from those members; one method is withholding information about how the local operates. If the former leaders thought of unionism as a business, and members as passive and uninvolved, then their structure will not serve your goal of involving members. You need to thoroughly revamp the organization.

If you try to take over the old machine, at best there will be tension and nothing will happen. The local will seem even less effective and the members will be demoralized. More likely, the machine will slowly but surely take you captive, and the members will see you becoming like the people you beat. You'll start to believe that the only way to get anything done will be to stop rocking the boat. A lot of bad union leaders started out as reformers with good intentions.

Member Involvement from the Get-Go

First and foremost the members want results. Many will still expect you to "service" them in the same old ways—only more and better. They may like nice people and be willing to give them a chance, but what they need is coordinated action and the focused use of power. This means carrying out the members' program to change the status quo against both great inertia and formidable opposition. Democracy requires a powerful force.

That means figuring out how you are going to build off the mobilization created for the election. The election probably involved more members in union activities than at any other time except contract votes. While you cannot expect all members to maintain this same high level of activity, many will be ready to be more involved than before and some will continue to be very active. The task is how to turn this energy and creativity into an ongoing union campaign. In dealing with all the problems you face in running a local, *this task of involving/mobilizing the members must frame everything.* Without it you gradually slip back into a more competent version of business unionism.

Here's one example of a small first step: when a reform movement won office in Teamsters Local 728 in Atlanta in May 1990, one of the first things the new leaders did was to ask the members to come help clean up and reorganize the union office. The clean-up was a weekend project that reinforced the feeling that the union hall now belonged to the members, while encouraging members to chip in and help the new administration. Members said they had a great time carting trash and mopping floors!

Another vital and visible first step is to start or re-work the union newsletter. A new piece of literature, delivered to every member, calls attention to new goals and new ways of meeting them. A revitalized newsletter requires coordination by someone who well understands the new administration's priorities and who has a sense of the conditions at the workplace. From the beginning, the newsletter should involve many members in its production—in planning and writing articles—as well as in its distribution.

It is overwhelming to try to build a new organization all by yourself. Luckily, one of the benefits of being part of a democratic reform · movement is that you don't have to do it by yourself. You won by mobilizing the energy and initiative of members, and this becomes your most important resource for running the local. In addition, you can draw on the experience and active support of reform officers in other locals and other unions. Be familiar with any resources available from your international.

Pull Together the Leadership Team

Chances are a leadership group was formed in the course of the successful campaign, but you may need some additional skills or experience. You may want to bring in someone from another local who has been through this sort of transition, to help you out in either an official or unofficial capacity. Here is a sketch of a leadership team for a medium to large local with a multi-person staff.

Getting beyond a one-person show

The top executive function should really be two to four people working together and led by the president. These people should support the goals of the reform movement, regularly share information, and have confidence in each other's decisions so that they can function separately but still in a united fashion. They can fill each other's shoes when necessary. Depending on the local, these may be the top officers, but may also include appointed executive assistants or other officers. These must be people who can function as part of a team rather than engaging in self-promotion; take group direction and criticism; give honest feedback and criticism to the president; listen well to the members and report accurately. They should have strengths and expertise in areas that complement those of the president.

Members of this executive group should be able to make decisions delegated by the president. For example, the president may delegate most actual decisions about lost-time approval to an assistant, without changing what the bylaws say about that authority. The buck still stops with the president, who has to take responsibility for the actions of the appointee. But everyone understands that the assistant has real authority because he is backed by the president.

Executive board

In many locals the board is little more than a rubber-stamp. It can be turned into a real leadership body by bringing as many questions as possible to the board in the initial stages of sounding them out. Board members should have areas of responsibility beyond the board meetings: perhaps representing certain sets of members, chairing committees, or coordinating volunteer organizers.

If the board includes members of your opposition, the process is more difficult, requiring caucusing and appraisals of how the opposition will vote on each item. Still, your allies on the board are key to the leadership team.

A broad leadership network

This is the officers, business agents, stewards, and rank and file activists who support the reform program and work together in the union structures to translate it into action—the broadly-defined leadership for the local. This group would likely form the core leadership of a rejuvenated stewards council, for example. Many but not all will belong to your reform caucus (see below), which in turn will be a source of new leaders. It's important not to limit the network just to those who campaigned for you or belonged to the reform group all along; rather it needs to co-opt former neutrals and those newly energized by the reforms you're undertaking. By going beyond the officials to include rank and filers, the network will be able to get reliable feedback from the members and mobilize one-on-one.

Reform caucus

The temptation is to allow the rank and file-based reform caucus that was the backbone of your campaign to dissolve, now that you have won. Now that you are in charge of the union, what do you need it for? You are going to make the union itself open to the rank and file.

Actually, you need an independent reform caucus now more than ever. The battle to change the union locally and perhaps nationally has moved ahead a step, but there is still much to be done. The hard task will still be dismantling the institutions and attitudes of business unionism that are embedded in the union.

The reform caucus, or course, should function independently of the union, not using union resources in any way not allowed to all caucuses. See the section titled "Reformers: Do You Need an Independent Reform Caucus After Winning Office?" for more on this subject.

Mobilizing coordinator

Delegate a key officer or staff member to be the Mobilizing Coordinator—someone who thinks of new ways to get members plugged in, stays on top of all the volunteer activities and which ones need a hand, and reminds leaders of their responsibility to recruit new activists. Remember that getting members involved is every leader's job; the coordinator is there to keep an eye on how it's going, not to be the sole member of the Mobilizing Department.

Advisors

Never assume that anything is a purely technical question that can be left to someone simply because he or she is an expert. All advisors come with their own outlook and agenda. Just keep Ron Carey's experience with his campaign consultants in mind: they backed his candidacy but were schooled in the ways of big party politics, so that making a buck off illegal contributions was part of the game. Be sure that your advisors understand and share the reform perspective.

Avoid consultants whose experience is working with businesses or traditional business unions; they will bring the wrong lessons. Administering a local based on democracy and membership involvement is not the same as administering a business or a union based on top-down control. For the same reasons, be careful with business self-help books. These may include some helpful advice, but remember, they are based on other assumptions and goals.

An advisor is only as good as her/his understanding of what your situation is. If you wait until a crisis or an immediate decision is required, then you have already lost important opportunities for choice and the advisor will be ill prepared. Pick your advisors early, give them the necessary background material, and keep them up to date and accountable.

Here are some types of advisors or consultants you may want. Please note that these are not necessarily hired consultants or paid staffers. The first place to look is in your own membership. It's likely you'll find a computer or desktop publishing specialist and often other surprising talents—maybe a cartoonist or someone who knows bookkeeping. Be sure to get them training as needed.

- Successful reform officers in other locals
- A contact person in the reform movement in your union/industry, if any
- A communications specialist
- A person who knows her/his way around the international
- A lawyer
- Contract specialists for key contracts
- A facilitator for your strategic planning meetings (see below)
- A union office administrator
- Someone experienced with running meetings and parliamentary procedure
- An accountant
- A computer/internet specialist
- A desktop publishing person

Your local may already have a lawyer on contract. Don't wait until you can change that arrangement. One way or another, find a lawyer who has some experience with rank and file unionism and whom you can trust. Lawyers are for legal advice. Unless they have otherwise established themselves, beware of their political and organizational advice.

Delegate

The critical word here is *teamwork.* The leadership skills you need to learn quickly are delegation and encouraging feedback.

Unless you are in a very small local, don't try to be everyone's steward. When you talk to members on the phone or visit them, listen, take notes, ask questions, and hear them out. But tell the member you will see that the concern will be looked into, and assign the task to the appropriate person. Make sure she gets back with the member. Don't get sucked into personal involvement with every investigation.

If you fail to delegate, you will soon lose your health, spouse, staff, and next election—probably in that order. Members know you aren't superhuman, so don't try to act that way. Respect and trust your fellow leaders. It's your responsibility to see that things get done, but it is not your job to do them personally.

Hold a Planning Meeting

Ideally you will have begun planning for your reform administration well before you're elected. But, assuming that most of your energy has gone into the election and that there is still much to do, take advantage of the lame-duck period to call a broad planning meeting. Now is not the time for a rest, even if you deserve one from an exhausting campaign.

Planning here serves two purposes. First, failing to plan means planning to fail. Second, the planning process itself is a good way to put your broad leadership and the reform forces on the same page. One of the important differences between top-down business organization and democratic unionism is that top-down depends on people doing what they are told. While there is still hierarchy in a democratic union structure, we try to depend on people taking initiative and making many decisions on their own because they have the same goals. The way unity of goals is achieved is through joint discussion, planning, feedback, and evaluation.

Have your strategic planning meeting somewhere you can be uninterrupted. If you can make it two or three days, the time is well spent. If you have not done strategic planning before, get some assistance; you might find help at a college labor studies department. Again, this is not simply a technical job. Make sure the advisor you get has experience with rank and file unionism. For more discussion of strategic planning see Labor Notes' *A Troublemaker's Handbook*.

At this meeting:

1. Identify your situation, both external and internal.

External: What are you facing from the employers? Remember, this is primarily why the members elected you.

Internal: Does the stewards system work? Which committees really function? Do you need new technology to track grievances? New staff? Who are your supporters in the local? Who is on the fence? Who can be won over? Is there an old guard already mobilizing to bring you down?

2. Set long-term goals and your strategy for reaching them. These will determine your plans for building support, making appointments, choosing priorities, and even how you run your meetings.

3. Determine priorities. Example: Rebuild the steward system, begin contract campaigns, set organizing targets, in that order. Remember that you must start some visible campaigns and changes immediately; also remember that priorities may change as you take office and start hearing more from members about what they want done.

4. Make crucial immediate decisions.

Brainstorm lists of tasks (look at the sample lists at the end of this chapter). Divide them into ones you can start now and ones that must wait until you take office. Turn them into assignment sheets. Here is a great opportunity to establish the model of delegating responsibility. The list would be overwhelming for one person. But if you developed a leadership team leading up to and in the course of your election campaign, you can divide them up and attack them successfully.

As you can see, our lists of sample tasks are long and the items range from big policy-type issues such as priority campaigns to detailed administrative questions. When you brainstorm, your lists will come out in no particular order. It is worth spending a little time to group similar tasks. But the main thing is to identify the priorities and get those, if not all the tasks, assigned, with people clear on what they are supposed to accomplish by when and to whom they must report back.

It's a good idea to have this kind of meeting on a regular basis. The longer ones usually work best if they are facilitated by someone outside the local but who works with the local so he understands the issues. Reform leaders in some locals have yearly meetings like this and shorter quarterly meetings to keep up to date. Plan these ahead and put them on your calendar in ink.

If at all possible, newly elected officers should find a way to get released from work to address these tasks. In a democratic union the old leadership would cooperate by insisting that the employers release you. But your predecessors may prefer to make your job difficult. If necessary, use vacation time or some other method. This is a critical period and the time invested now will pay off later.

Rebuild the Union
Around the Membership

This is your highest priority. There is no single way to do it. In some cases it will require new bodies or programs, and in other cases a radically different approach to the old ones. Looking for and encouraging new activists and leaders should be a daily concern of all officers and reps. Don't wait. Ask members to get involved even before you take office.

Start a newsletter immediately.

This will be one of your main devices for communicating with the membership. Get assistance from someone with experience, outside the local if necessary, so you can train your people to do it well.

Fix the steward system.

The stewards are the critical link between the members at the work site and the union as an organization. If your bylaws call for appointed stewards, make sure that you have good stewards in place. Then start working on alternate stewards. Then plan to move to an elected steward system. As a temporary measure you can always agree to appoint the stewards that members select in an unofficial election. Encourage the good stewards and find replacements for the bad ones.

Set up an intensive training program for stewards. Even experienced stewards will need this, since you are projecting different procedures for the union and a different role for stewards as the organizers of members' involvement. As you recruit good stewards, build a Stewards Council.

One of your top leaders should sit down with each steward so that you discover their strengths and weaknesses and develop a

Stewards Survey

This survey will help new union officers get to know stewards' strengths, weaknesses, and interests. It is ideally done one-on-one between a top local leader and the steward.

◆   ◆   ◆

Name

Phone numbers
        Home
        Can you be reached by phone at work?
                What number?

Family members

Steward experience

Experience in other unions
        Ever held union office?

Have you ever worked on a newsletter?
        Writing or editing?
        Production?

Do you have a computer?
        Programs you know:

What special skills do you have that can be used to build the union?
        Examples: song writing, drawing/graphic design, acting,
                sports organizing, silk-screening T-shirts

What community and/or religious organizations are you a member of?
        Would you be willing to serve as union liaison to this
                organization?

training plan for each. Devise a plan for doing this with each new replacement in the future.

Give the stewards useful tools. See that each one gets a copy of *The Legal Rights of Union Stewards* by Robert Schwartz. Get a bulk subscription to *Labor Notes* to help give stewards a sense of being part of a broader reform movement as well as useful nuts and bolts tips on organizing.

Make the union committees functional.

Committees might include a newsletter committee, organizing

Could you make a "map" of the members in your district?
(Explain "mapping the workplace.")

What parts of the contract do you feel you know best?

On what parts of the contract do you want some assistance or training?

What do you like best about being a steward?

What do you like least?

Are there any union committees in which you would like to be active?
(list which committees are available)

Are there new committees you think we should form and that you would like to be part of?

Are there skills you would like more training in?

Speaking
Writing grievances
Writing articles
Note taking
Computer

Here are some of the training programs available to the local union. Note that most require you to use your own time. In some the local union can help defray part of the cost, but our resources are limited. Which look most interesting or useful to you?
(list programs)

committee, civil rights committee, community relations committee, and others. Committees should reflect the union's priorities: if legislation on bargaining rights is key, for example, you'll need an active committee to coordinate pressure on legislators. Post descriptions of the committees and invite volunteers (don't promise that all volunteers will be on the committee!). Discuss the committees' work at one or more union meetings. Appoint people you can count on to chair the committees. Recruit potential leaders you and the reps have identified. Carefully build the committees so that they can succeed; this may mean excluding some "old guard" members. Give the committees the resources, independence, and flexibility they need and let them go. If they don't go, find out why and appoint new people.

Tools for Stewards

Labor Notes, an independent monthly newsletter by and for the activists who are putting the movement back in the labor movement. A monthly bulk order costs 35 cents per copy (minimum five copies), plus shipping. To order, see back cover.

Labor Party Press, bimonthly publication of the Labor Party, is full of well-researched articles with facts activists can use. PO Box 53177, Washington, DC 20009; phone 202/319-1932.

The Legal Rights of Union Stewards, by Robert M. Schwartz. 1994 (second edition). Paperback, 180 pages, $9.95. Available from Work Rights Press, 800/576-4552.

Labor Notes books (see back cover):

Stopping Sexual Harassment, by Camille Colatosti and Elissa Karg. A handbook on contractual, legal, and—most important—organizing solutions, including some for members of an unhelpful union.

A Troublemaker's Handbook: How to Fight Back Where You Work—and Win! by Dan La Botz. Gives examples of styles and tactics for workplace organizing, many told by the activists involved.

Working Smart: A Union Guide to Participation Programs and Reengineering, by Mike Parker and Jane Slaughter. An in-depth look at what's behind all the feel-good rhetoric, and what unionists can do (and many have done) to keep organized.

Get member mobilization campaigns going.

A contract campaign? A major grievance issue? A battle against a cooperation program? A political or lobbying initiative? Any of these may be good places to start. To decide, you might begin with a membership survey to supplement what you already know through your campaign work. A survey is a great signal to the rank and file that something different is going on. NOTICE! If you ask members what they want, you will have to plan to take seriously what they propose. The worst thing you can do is ask people what they want with no plan to follow through.

The membership surveys and your strategic planning meetings should have identified priority campaigns for the union. Get them moving and get the members involved at all phases of decision making and control. See the box for an example of a campaign that tapped members' creativity.

Begin external organizing.

Organizing new members depends on getting current members involved in the campaign. But you are advised to get help from experienced organizers. Setting up an organizing drive is a difficult task; good training for volunteers and/or staff helps a lot. Organizing also requires a substantial budget; you want to make sure the resources are used effectively. You might target suppliers to your employer, non-union units within your workplace, or, if you are in a "right-to-work" state, the nonmembers within your bargaining unit.

Take the union to the members.

Since most members will not attend the general membership meeting, take the union to the members. Think about meetings by shift, department, or job classification, at times and locations that members can attend. Serve food. Have meetings in the parking lot or break rooms, if possible. Put the members themselves in charge of arrangements. If the union covers a wide geographical area, consider moving union meetings to different locations.

Make work site visits your top priority.

You know the common complaint: "We never see anyone from the union office unless there's an election." It's very easy to get chained to your desk, buried with the details of administrative projects like the new computer or voice message system. It's easy to get swamped following through on grievance appeals.

A Member Mobilization Campaign to Fight Team Concept

The remarkable rank and file unity and involvement that won the 1997 Teamsters' strike against UPS was foreshadowed by an earlier union campaign. The international union initiated a campaign against a management program called "team concept," and the organizing was also pushed from below by TDU. In some locals old guard leaders had endorsed team concept and allowed UPS to do whatever it wanted in this area.

The international's Education Department developed a series of materials, including a 15-minute video, on the UPS team programs, and held regional workshops for business agents, stewards, and rank and filers on members' rights in the programs and tactics for dealing with them. "Our campaign focused on trust," said John Braxton, a TDU leader and Education Department staffer. "Management kept saying that we would work better with 'trust.' And we kept pointing out that 'actions speak louder than words' (the video's title)." The union pushed the issues, and management's record on these, instead of debating team concept abstractly. The battle took different shapes in different locals. Here are examples of how rank and filers or local leaders took the ball and ran with it:

• At the Madison Heights, Michigan UPS center, management made the team meetings compulsory. Activists used the meetings to shift to their own agenda. "When the company would try to get us to talk about costs, we talked about the cost of living and wages for part-timers. When they would talk about productivity, we would discuss health and safety," explains Dave Staiger, a TDU activist.

The company appointed team leaders for package sorting lines. Under union pressure the job was changed to a seniority bid. A few people saw this job as a steppingstone to management, but others took it because they wanted it to be held by a pro-union person.

"Management hoped these team leaders would be the scab leaders for the upcoming contract," Staiger says. "But during the pre-strike contract campaign we asked many team leaders to be the contract campaign coordinators—which made sense since they were often the natural leaders of the work groups." These team leaders actively promoted the contract campaign and were solid during the strike. Afterwards, the company abolished the team leader positions.

• At a UPS center outside Modesto, California, a union member got up and declared himself team-leader-for-life and all the other team members bowed down before him. In six weeks management threw in the towel and declared the program over.

• At the Redmond, Washington center, UPS kept bringing up ideas in their "clean sheet" meetings that were clearly bargaining issues: incentive pay, worker involvement in screening new-hires, Teamsters auditing fellow Teamsters for mistakes. "The company blitzed us with meetings—weekly and sometimes twice weekly," said steward John Misich. Misich filed a grievance when the company refused to pay him as a steward to attend every team meeting it called, since contractual issues were always discussed. Members circulated a petition to back the grievance, saying they wanted union representation at these meetings.

One member worked very hard to design a new delivery route, believing that this would remove some of the work overload. But when the company used the route without posting it for bidding, it was clear that management cared only for its own flexibility and not about reducing workloads. It took a union grievance to force the route to go to bid.

After six months, attendance at the voluntary meetings dropped to a trickle, and that mainly for the easy overtime pay.

• In San Antonio, steward Nancy Crittenden says that the meetings started out quite pleasantly: an hour of overtime and free breakfast. But "we tried to get the company to use first-line tires on the trucks for safety, and the company used the meetings to show us propaganda films about retreads." Her local supplemented the international's educational materials with its own *Brown Dog News*. The union materials and company actions "got us all to understand that we had to act together, and people stopped going," says Crittenden.

• In Cleveland, clerks collectively decided to ignore a job posting for a higher-paid team leader position.

• Activists in Iowa used a petition campaign to end the program.

• In Milwaukee, members wore T-shirts that said, "I am already on a team—the Teamsters."

Nancy Crittenden says that besides getting rid of team concept, the campaign served the purpose of strengthening the union for the bigger battle ahead: "No one in our center had ever experienced a strike. We teamed together to get rid of their team concept, and the strike really brought us together as a team for the union."

But here's a little secret you should know: no matter how much time you spend at the office, there's no way you can take care of all the stuff that comes in.

By making work site visits take precedence, you send a message that your priority is one-on-one organizing, and that other officers and activists are expected to follow suit. Make a schedule for visiting sites. Set a time and don't be late! When you arrive, don't visit the boss first. Always call key union activists to let them know you are coming, and visit with them first. Sometimes hold cookouts in the parking lot and/or have a cooler of cold drinks for the members after work. There is nothing like breaking bread or sharing a cold one with the members to help you keep in touch—it's job #1.

Get your whole leadership team out in the field in contact with the members. Make sure someone covers company picnics, sports, and social and family events.

The Budget

Whatever flowery promises are made in election leaflets, the real priorities are revealed by the local union's budget. If training stewards is a top priority, you will be able to tell it from the funds allocated. A union that says "organizing is job one" but devotes one percent of its funds to recruitment is not serious. If you are not versed in principles of accounting or the details of budgeting, then you must get assistance, because the budget will reflect your most important policy decisions.

Creating a budget:

Forces you to plan;

Lets people in charge of certain areas know what resources they can expect;

Helps prevent over-extension in plans and promises;

Provides a system of monitoring and control; and

Provides an overview of priorities.

Your primary income is dues. Dues income will be increased by new organizing, but not without making a significant investment first. The priority you place on new organizing should not be based on expecting an immediate cash-flow advantage, but on power considerations—how will organizing this shop strengthen our local and

Build mobilization and involvement into the budget.

More leaflets, newsletters, meeting places close to work locations—all these cost something. If you want rank and file assistant stewards, you will have to budget for training. Fight the notion that any time someone does something for the union she should be paid "lost time." But you also have to be prepared to partially compensate people who give up lots of work time to take on key union responsibilities.

Publicize your plans and changes.

Publicizing what's new and moving helps to change members' expectations and helps them hold your feet to the fire.

Check pay and perks.

Nothing contributes more to bureaucratization and breaking the link between leaders and members than significant pay and lifestyle differences. Some locals have a policy of equal pay for all full-time

the labor movement in general. You can raise money for specific projects through the sale of T-shirts, hats, buttons, or advertising in the local's newspaper. Even for a popular reform administration, special assessments will be hard to get through unless the case for the specific need is very clear and strong.

Although certain expenditures are usually treated as "fixed"— per capita dues to the international, mortgage payments on the union hall—take a look at them anyway. It may be the international will rebate part of the per caps for special organizing projects. The hall may be your most expensive asset, and it could be more valuable if sold and the money used to benefit the members. Selling the hall is not a move to take lightly or quickly, but it might make sense if the demographics of the local, or the workplaces represented, have changed since the hall was first established.

The union may have a fair amount of surplus funds stashed way. Having some cushion to help balance out income and expenditures during difficult periods is desirable. But beyond that, there is no point to showing that you can accumulate big savings. Use it for the strengthening the union. Use it for organizing new members.

[Material here owes much to Teamster activist Rob Hickey and training programs provided by the Teamster Rank and File Education and Legal Defense Foundation.]

staff, based on the pay of members in the largest unit in the local. Union-leased cars are very visible; they should be utilitarian, not luxurious. Have a realistic expense policy so that people who spend their time doing union business do not find themselves in debt.

Become familiar with procedures of your international.

Every international provides resources for local leaders. Some of it is essential nuts and bolts that you need to get down pat. This includes dues payments, procedures for grievance handling, and various international union reporting procedures. If you don't get them right, things can grind to a halt, or worse, embroil you in time-consuming technical and legal difficulties. The trick in many internationals is to separate out the kernels that you need from all the junk that stems from a business-union approach. That's where advice from other reformers in local office can be invaluable.

Review administrative procedures.

The philosophy of the union is embedded in how it carries out day-to-day activities. Are the union officers accessible, or do members who call get ignored, brushed off, or sent on wild goose chases? Do the officers and staff act like the union belongs to them or to the members?

Like it or not, you must pay attention to administrative procedures. Always ask, What is the flow? What do members see? Draw flowcharts for:

> Handling a grievance
>
> How a member's question is handled
>
> What happens when a member volunteers for union activity
>
> What happens when a member reports some unusual employer activity (new or leased equipment, large transactions with a previously unknown company, ...)

Then check and revise policies on use of resources: what are the guidelines on reimbursements to members or staff? Who can rent the meeting hall, when? Check particularly policies on the use of credit cards and expense allowances. The tone you must set is that the resources of the local belong to the members and cannot be wasted by anyone, least of all the officers or the staff. At the same time all union services and facilities must be available to the members on as open and fair a basis as possible.

Administrative policies should be written and available to all members so that they understand what the standard is and help hold staff to that standard.

Regular, well-planned staff meetings are a must. This is your opportunity to gather information and give clear direction and evaluation. Write a meeting agenda and distribute it in advance, after encouraging staff members to bring up suggestions for it. In between meetings, communicate with your staff regularly.

Administrative Policies

Some items you'll need to cover to create both the appearance and the reality of fairness and to keep things running smoothly:

Staff Rules

Vacation scheduling, sick days, holidays, funeral leave

Comp time, work schedule, office hours

Reimbursement of expenses, car expenses

Meals and meetings

Per diem and out of town expenses

Frequent flyer miles

Pay period

Christmas bonus

Telephone etiquette

Phone log policy

Proper use of voice mail

Answering pages

Filing and retrieval

Shipping and mailing

Office security

Inventory control

Personal use of cell phones, union vehicles, credit cards

Personal use of copiers, computers, Internet

Smoking in the office

Dress code

Grievance-Handling and Organizing Staff

Grievance processing rules, grievance log

Shop visits

Access to confidential records

Union rep's daily activity log

Union rep conduct

Services to members vs. non-members

Returning calls

Operating in another union rep's area of responsibility

Members

Solidarity fund for fired members

Member travel to grievance hearings and arbitration

Lost-time wages

Use of toll-free numbers

Special occasion gifts

Member sickness or death

Use of hall by members

General

Sexual harassment policy

Responsibility for communications with other groups in the community

Accounting for sales of union merchandise and materials— jackets, T-shirts, books.

Decision-making on kind and amount of strike assistance for other unions

Appointments

Depending on your local's structure, you may have to appoint business agents or stewards, pick benefits specialists, even hire clerical and janitorial staff. You have committee jobs to fill. And you'll have informal appointments, too—people who will serve as your resources, spokespersons, or agents on various issues (technology, education, certain departments or locations). Don't underestimate the importance of any of these jobs.

And don't underestimate the fact that those doing these jobs when you took over were people trained by and probably loyal to the officers you replaced. While some may be quite competent, honest, and grateful to finally have a more aggressive or more aboveboard administration, others may still think of themselves as agents for the old guard and actively try to get back to the good old days. After all, your reform means that the union is going to work a lot harder for the members, and that is going to mean more work for the staff.

Look for two criteria when making appointments:

1. Loyalty to the program of reform

2. Competence in the job

(Note that competence can be learned.)

Don't confuse loyalty with ass-kissing. You want people who will tell you the truth as they see it. You want people who can think and act independently. But they have to be in basic support of the program. The most competent organizer is of little use if he is trying to undermine members' control of the union.

Try to make your appointees "look" like your membership. Pay special attention to ensure that minorities, women, and any others who may have been treated as second-class citizens in your local are well represented.

Appointments are also a way of sealing arrangements of mutual support with various groupings within the union. You want to reach out as far as possible, but not so far that you fall over. That is, you don't do yourself any favor by bringing in people who will later embarrass you or work to undermine you or the reform program.

You may have to fire a staffer, or de-appoint a committee member, and train someone new. This is preferable to having someone in the office that you don't trust to carry out the members' reform program. Of course, you need to respect any contractual obligations that may exist.

Some locals hire outside contractors to take over responsibilities like putting out the local newspaper, public relations, and even bargaining. These arrangements are usually part of the mainstays of business unionism. Plan to bring these jobs back to the members; they are crucial skills for developing new leaders. Even if a member requires a little more technical training, she understands the problems of the job better than a professional consultant and will better understand and communicate with the membership. If you need to bring in outsiders, make it a limited number for a limited duration, with training your people at the top of their priorities.

Look for opportunities to spread appointments out. For example, within a budget, it may be possible to have several rank and file assistant business agents instead of one full-time BA.

One of your biggest problems will be appointments in joint labor-management programs. You may have dozens of these jobs, negotiated by the international or the previous leadership. They may include quality, attendance, training, employee assistance, and health and safety. All too often union appointees to these positions end up sounding and acting like management. You need to have a long-range plan for how the union will operate in these programs, up to and including dismantling the injurious ones. In the meantime, you need to have people in them whom you can trust, to tell you what's going on and carry out a pro-union course. For more information see Labor Notes' *Working Smart.*

Dealing with the Old Opposition

After a tough and grueling election campaign, one of the hardest things to do is to maintain the campaigning spirit while shifting the definition of who is the opposition. During elections candidates will make some pretty vicious attacks, many of them personal. It can be very easy for your supporters to view an election victory as the license for payback: "screw those who didn't support you." On the other hand, sentiment among a large portion of the membership will be to put all past history aside, "end the politics," and get on with the job of running the union. Both may be big mistakes. One of your first tasks in the planning process is to evaluate the forces in your local and determine an appropriate strategy for each.

We can't stress too much that this cannot be seen in terms of a "leadership to leadership" discussion and arrangement between the new officers and the outgoing slate. What counts is the long-term effect your relationship with the opposition will have on members— their participation in the union, or their cynicism about it. What Jed Dodd, a leader in the Brotherhood of Maintenance of Way Employees, says about dealing with management also applies to talking with political opponents within the union: "Don't say anything in a private conversation that you wouldn't say in front of a membership meeting." You want to be as inclusive as possible while maintaining commitment to the program you were elected on.

As much as possible, you want to make it possible for former opponents or fence-sitters to sign up with your side and the reform program without having to grovel. In fact, you may want to make immediate overtures to some of the forces and possibly offer them positions in your leadership structure. You'll want to include people who have a needed skill or knowledge, or who have a base among some group of members, if they're likely to buy in to the new program.

It's a tough balancing act, because you run the risk of loyal supporters getting angry if they are passed over for what seems to be a reward to someone on the other side. It means your leaders and activists have to have common agreement that the issue is not "to the victors go the spoils," but rather creating the strongest possible leadership for the battles to come.

Be careful. Bringing in former opposition leaders may weaken your ability to turn the union around. They may not be in agreement with enough of your program, or be more concerned with building their own following, so that the net result is immobilization.

Some of the people you defeated were not bad people. They may have been burned out, or they just believed in a traditional business unionism. If they don't want to come over to your side and help, allow them the option of fading away gracefully. There is no value in rubbing their faces in defeat and mobilizing them into opposition.

It's likely some opponents will choose not to join you based not so much on policy differences as on historic factors, different departments, different cultural groups, different job classifications, and so on. Normally you should gracefully accept their self-definition as independent from your forces, and attempt to work with them on specific items of agreement.

A special case is the opposition we call the "old guard": the group of former leaders who were so invested in being the leadership that their only concern is discrediting you so they can get back into office.

It would be nice if the old guard would just fold its tents and go away after the election. But it is not likely to happen. First, they have the democratic right to criticize you and prepare for the next election. And although democracy and the membership may be the furthest things from their concerns, they will get the benefit of legitimate member support for the idea of honest opposition.

Second, since your election means an end to sweetheart deals with the company, the old guard is going to find plenty of management support. In the lead-up to 1997 UPS contract bargaining, for example, management was caught (on tape) conspiring with an old guard official to undermine the union negotiating committee. An old guard opposition group in your local may also get encouragement, advice, or financial support from officials of other locals and perhaps the international who want to prevent the spread of a rank and file movement for reform.

Dealing with the old guard after you take office can be tricky. You don't want anything that you do in response to them to intimidate members or discourage member discussion. Constant battles at membership meetings can turn off members who want to be involved. Trading charges of corruption will just convince many people that union activity is a waste. You have to make the tactical decisions when to fight them and when to ignore them.

You also need to be prepared for charges of "undemocratic" if you stop the old guard from dominating discussion at a union meeting, or if you deny them their favorite trips or other perks. They may try to set up situations so that you look bad in front of the membership. You have to take all this into account, but keep focused on the long run. You have to be firm and move on—ruling people out of order if need be—even if some members, who don't know the whole history or situation, feel that you are heavy-handed. In the long run the truth will be evident but you cannot allow them to tie up the union while this happens.

Here are a few more tips on dealing with the old guard:

Be clear on your democratic obligations. Your obligations are to the membership and to carry out their program. The former officers have all the rights of members but no special rights just because they are former officers. They do not have the right to special dealing with management or special treatment by the union. You have limited resources, such as a small budget to send members for training. Be sure you use it for members who are developing into new leaders and not to quiet old guard complainers.

Keep the spirit of the election alive. It was the election issues that motivated the members; try to stick to these issues, not personalities. If you work on the issues it will remind people why they repudiated the old guard. Let the old guard expose themselves for being cranks and having no program. Figure out their base of support and work to take it away.

Do clean surgical strikes. When you do fight them directly, be prepared to do a quick but thorough job. If the issue is finance, from your audit of the books and records do a short report to the membership. Make sure that the report gets wide distribution. Have copies when you visit work sites and especially have it ready for your first general membership meeting. Thoroughly explain the corruption and make clear that you will not tolerate it. For example, if they wrote union checks to local liquor stores, adult night clubs, or similar establishments, take the canceled checks down to the local copy shop, blow them up to poster size, and have them on display for the first meeting.

Be prepared for membership meetings. Do everything you can to get your people there. If the old guard is active, make sure that your people have prepared in advance and understand the issues, and have floor leaders assigned to handle each. Consider serving food or at least coffee, juice, and snacks prior to the meeting. Hold a rally in the parking lot prior to your first meeting after you take office. Have plans to handle disruption. Remember in all this that your goal for membership meetings is to facilitate members carrying on the union's work, not to debate the old guard.

Reformers: Do You Need an Independent Reform Caucus After Winning Office?

Much of this chapter has been aimed at giving an emphatic "yes!" to that question. Keeping a caucus organized in support of reform leaders' program is often necessary to the program's success and to leaders' political survival. The caucus provides votes on policy where needed and trained troops to carry out some of the necessary volunteer work. This support is key even where local opposition is weak; as reformers in the Teamsters, UAW, and UFCW have found, old guard officials of the parent union may work hard to undermine local reform leaders.

We can imagine a union where a reform caucus becomes irrelevant: where there's overall agreement on the union's direction, and a strong culture of members deciding that direction; where members freely organize around short-term issues, such as for and against some contract proposal or political endorsement. But you won't be there when you first win office.

Keeping a reform caucus active after winning an election has been difficult in most places. Partly that's because many people believe that good union leadership does indeed make the caucus unnecessary; its role is certainly a lot less clear. Partly the difficulty is maintaining a truly independent caucus when the main leaders have now become officers. The tendency is for some of the caucus

Balancing the Pressures

Victor Reuther, one of the founders of the United Auto Workers, addressed the TDU convention in 1992 after Ron Carey first won election. On members' minds was whether they still needed TDU now that a reformer had won the presidency.

Holding one hand in the air, Reuther used the other hand to apply pressure till it bent over. That was the pressure of the employers, the government, the business-union traditions, and the day-to-day problems. "Ron Carey depends on the members to keep putting pressure on the other side," said Reuther. "That is why we need TDU to continue and grow." How right Reuther was.

to operate solely as support for those officers, and other caucus members to lose interest.

Yet keeping an independent caucus is important, if difficult. For one thing, no one's perfect. While we don't suggest that the reader would ever be tempted to take a kickback or stray from the members' priorities, union officers face many gray areas. Good people can differ on what's proper. An independent caucus keeps officers on track with what the members approve of or don't. Also, we may as well admit that there are plenty of examples of good people going bad. You and other officers are subject to huge pressures, including overwork, management attempts to compromise you, and corrupt influences. An independent caucus helps maintain an anchor point in the rank and file and in the principles of reform.

You may also need to wage an ongoing fight against the old guard in your local. The employers and the old guard may have too many interests at stake to allow you to act unchallenged. As officers of the local, you have to carefully represent everybody. But an active rank and file group can both defend you and expand the reform movement in areas in the local where reform is weak or where there are poor representatives.

By its independence a caucus can maintain closer ties to the ranks. That may be necessary for the caucus to maintain its credibility. Ours is a cynical society, and we're too used to thinking of politics as about individuals, not ideas. If the caucus has an independent life—its own meetings and newsletter—it helps show that it is about certain ideas, not just keeping its allies in office.

The caucus's independent life also provides additional opportunities for leadership training: rank and filers taking responsibility for everything from the caucus's newsletter content to planning meetings, and learning the basics of organizing as they do.

More important, the caucus will be a place for gloves-off discussion of union politics: why certain people promote certain policies, and what's good and bad about their stance. Caucus meetings can help rank and filers sort out the debates going on in the local, where they stand, and why. The same kind of discussion may be needed about national or international union policies and elections. Again, local officers may feel constrained to be diplomatic in their criticisms of higher officials, while rank and file caucus leaders can be more blunt.

Caucus activities will change in the new situation. Remember that much of your past work was the education and organizing that the union should have been doing—and will start doing now because of its new leadership. But the new leaders will have difficulties and make mistakes; the caucus will still need to fill in on the union's work where, for example, an old guard supporter gets elected steward, or officers make an appointment that doesn't work out.

Within the local, an independent caucus can take the lead, discussing and initiating local action and policies. They may propose bylaw changes that would help the reform process, or formulate contract demands to present to a demands meeting. This would normally be in communication with local leaders, but on the caucus's initiative. Thus the leadership load is shared and democracy is strengthened.

Finally, union reform has to spread beyond the local or it cannot survive. One goal of the caucus should be to help members of other locals push their leaders in a reform direction—or elect new ones. Many contracts, grievances, and decisions about jurisdiction are settled at higher levels of the union. Reform needs to spread beyond your union and throughout the labor movement.

A new, reform-minded leadership may be working hard to build the kind of local union where issues are so constructively debated, and members so actively involved, that an independent rank and file caucus is redundant. But that's a very difficult goal. Experience shows an ongoing reform caucus is needed to get there.

New Officers' Checklist

Immediately after winning election you need to plan and assign a wide range of tasks. Many can be started during the lame-duck period; others can be planned now and implemented after you take office. How much you can accomplish during the lame-duck period depends partly on how cooperative the outgoing officers are.

Following is a list of tasks gathered from several local unions. They are not necessarily in the same chronological or priority order—or even the same tasks—that would fit your situation, but they should be a helpful guide. Many of these tasks can or should be done before you are sworn in. Following the list of tasks is an Assignment Sheet you can use to ensure follow-through.

Report back to members right away. Distribute a post-election leaflet. Set up a web page, e-mail, or newsletter communication to activists.

Arrange leaves of absence. Request a leave from your employer for the length of the transition period and term of office, asking current officers to intervene if necessary and using applicable contract language.

Hold a strategic planning meeting. Arrange for uninterrupted time with your broad leadership team to look at the big picture.

Audit the books. Have an independent, union-friendly CPA check out the books and prepare a report suitable for publication to the members. Do it right away so you can make a presentation at your first membership meeting. Use handouts and big charts to clearly establish the record and baseline of your administration. Send out an abbreviated report to the members to show how you plan to change things. Ask the accountant to locate all funds and all accounts.

Secure office space in the hall. Your presence at the union hall is important during the transition. Learn what you can, and keep your eyes open.

Plan first issue of union newspaper. If the local does not already have one, start one. Have the articles written so you can get it out during the first two weeks of your new administration. Be sure to include articles by or interviews with rank and file members. By what is said and how it looks, your newsletter must signal the priorities of your administration.

Determine the status of all current negotiations, strikes, organizing drives. Develop a plan to maintain continuity—or to make big changes.

Determine and plan your immediate priority campaigns. Is the first priority a contract campaign, an organizing drive, a program to reactivate the union in some area? Whatever it is, a campaign that involves members is critical to bringing the union together.

Fill in your map of the local. (This is the map you probably used during your campaign.) Complete information on the number of members, the stewards, and the names of your key supporters at each work site.

Make plans to strengthen the stewards system. Begin using the Stewards Survey and look toward a stewards newsletter and stewards council.

Know where to get help. Draw up your list of experts and consultants. Become familiar with the support services available from the international. Schedule a visit to other reform locals. Arrange for an experienced reform officer to meet with your leadership and answer nuts and bolts questions.

Take inventory. Have a written inventory of all supplies, equipment, etc. Review the report with your trustees. Your international probably has required procedures for inventory.

Make arrangements to change locks, passwords, and signatures on accounts. Send written notification to the outgoing officers and staff to turn in all records and equipment belonging to the local.

Write a preliminary budget. Review the past administration's spending over the last three years. How they spent members' money was their "mission statement." The same will be true for you. Remember this as you set your policies; make your plans first and then make out your budget.

Guard the hall. You or some of your trusted supporters may need to discourage theft and vandalism before you take office. As a last resort, post a guard in the parking lot. Notify the police of what you are doing.

Prepare new business cards and letterhead. Have it at your union printer ready to go on day one.

Contact the staff. Determine who does what jobs and what problems they have. Find out their ideas on improvements. Familiarize yourself with all contracts and personnel policies. Prepare to make changes as necessary.

Line up additional/temporary help. You may need help in the office, with contract negotiations, or handling grievances. Bring in help to deal with any backlog of work.

Review all standing committees. Review their function and who is on them. If they are appointed, replace leaders as necessary.

Review bylaws, constitution, and meeting rules. Go over key ones with your leadership. You may even want to practice chairing in anticipation of your first membership meeting.

Look over past records of meetings. You will need to know about past decisions and policies for running the local. Ask the outgoing officers for cooperation. Make a list of all policies or actions that need to be continued or modified when you come into office. Make this part of your first executive board meeting.

Review all contracts. Study all contracts administered by the local. Note all expiration dates. Make a chart. Familiarize yourself with the grievance procedure in each.

Know the employers. Start a working file on management personnel with whom you are likely to be dealing. Note both personal and professional information.

Contact all benefit plans and trusts. Let them know you will be taking office. Ask for training if you have any trustee responsibilities.

Contact the heads of state or regional bodies of your international. Write a letter to introduce yourself and ask for the relevant bylaws and a schedule of meetings. Introduce yourself to the AFL-CIO Central Labor Council and to leaders of other unions with whom you expect to start working.

Review all contracts for services. Make changes where necessary in maintenance agreements, supply agreements, cleaning contracts, etc.

Contact the retirees club. Familiarize yourself with the club's officers and activities. The retirees are often a great source of experience and help for organizing and for political and contract support.

Plan for modernization. Computers, voice mail, pagers, cell phones—make the new technologies work for you.

Audit all subscriptions. Cancel inappropriate ones and order the ones that will help your staff and members.

Assignment Sheet

Hint: You can list several types of jobs in the Task column. Include overall-coordinator-type jobs dealing with big assignments ("Plan Strategic Planning Meeting"), as well as specific tasks that fall under the bigger jobs ("Arrange meeting space for strategic planning meeting"), or that stand alone ("Order monthly bundle of *Labor Notes*"). In either case, be as specific as possible. Write down "Interview stewards using Stewards Survey" and "Evaluate grievance tracking system," not "Rebuild stewards system." Don't forget to delegate!

The "Report To" item may be either an individual or a body such as the executive board.

Task	Assigned to	Report to	Date for First Report	Date for Completion	Notes

7. Structures and Bylaws

Structure means how people and committees within the union work together to make decisions and carry out responsibilities—the kinds of things usually specified in constitutions or bylaws. Here we consider: what's the best size for the union? Who gets to vote? Which is better—appointment or election? How much should officers be paid? How much autonomy should locals have from their internationals? What's the role of internal appeals procedures?

Although some unions separate out "constitution" and "bylaws," here we will use the term "bylaws" to cover both kinds of documents on the local level—general principles, structure, membership rights, and specific procedures such as the conduct of meetings.

See Appendix 5 for some suggestions on workable bylaws.

One Structure Doesn't Fit All

The 10,000 members of the Northwest Airlines flight attendants' union, Teamsters Local 2000, live in cities across the U.S. and are constantly on the move. A union structure that allows them to participate in and control their union will be different from one that suits a local of 100 people at a one-shift machine shop.

A union structure should take into account the size of the bargaining unit(s) and how many there are; how geographically dispersed the work sites are; work schedules; access to communications on the job (e-mail, phone); historical divisions in the union, such as by skill or classification; and traditions. How much personal contact can the officers expect to have with each member? How difficult is it for stewards to stop by the union office for needed information? If the union is large and spread out, structures like stewards councils are needed so that secondary leaders can help with communication between top officers and the ranks.

The most important basis for structure is what best organizes members to take on their own employer. Structure should enable members to make decisions together at the appropriate level, usually within a work site or employer-wide, or both, rather than based on geography. If you work for the Elm Street Plant of the Acme Machine Tool Co. in Cleveland, it's more important for you to meet regularly with people from the Acme plant in East Cleveland than with those from the Elm Street Bakery.

How many membership meetings need to be held, and what kind? Most unions hold at least one per month, but sometimes the meetings are set up for particular "crafts" or bargaining units instead of the whole membership. Some locals hold only craft or unit meetings, never allowing members from different workplaces to meet together. The effect is that members neither get the chance to know others' problems and extend solidarity, nor meet other activists who may want to join a reform caucus. Local-wide communications among the members—everyone from the Elm Street bakers to the East Cleveland machinists—is necessary for democracy, even if it requires extra meetings to deal with workplace-specific problems.

In these times of rapid mergers, the employers' identity may change frequently, and the union should keep up. Because of traditions it may be difficult to change the current structures in the short run—for example, multiple unions representing different sections of the workforce within a single employer. The best you may be able to do in the short run is to find work-arounds such as joint bargaining committees.

Union Mergers: Is Bigger Better?

The AFL-CIO is promoting mergers among affiliates. We've seen a rash of internationals merging and more and more giant locals covering large territories. Or local union authority is shifted to regional bodies such as statewide councils. Some mergers make sense, like the creation of UNITE! by the Amalgamated Clothing and Textile Workers and the International Ladies Garment Workers Union. Others seem a bit bizarre from a jurisdictional standpoint, such as the merger of a rail union (Brotherhood of Firemen and Oilers) with the Service Employees, or the Practical Nurses Federation of Ontario affiliating with the Laborers. This merger trend is worldwide;[1] its root cause is an inability to organize new members.

Many mergers are based on the simple premise that bigger is better. It's certainly true that the labor movement as a whole has lost power as we've lost members. Bigger is indeed much better when it comes to the total size of organized labor. But it doesn't follow that bigger unions are necessarily more powerful in taking on employers than would be the same number of members organized into smaller unions.

Just as important, today's merger wave means unions are giving up their potential for jurisdictional specialization. Since most international unions will accept—or actively seek—affiliations from anywhere, we are rapidly heading toward a labor movement made up of several large, general unions. Coordinated bargaining in the health care industry, for instance, needed more than ever since employers have grown and consolidated so in the 1990s, is a distant dream now that nearly every major union organizes health care workers.

When officials propose an amalgamation, the question to ask is how will such a move affect democracy and power? Although democracy and power aren't separable in practice, we'll look at the notion that bigger-is-more-powerful first.

Does Size Matter?

Advocates of mergers make their arguments based on power or efficiency:

A bigger union is a stronger union in dealing with employers. It depends. Is the UAW stronger in dealing with General Motors because it also represents a significant number of Indiana state employees? Are Indiana state employees stronger because their union has hundreds of thousands of auto workers as members?

Some Indiana state employees may have thought so when they

voted to join the UAW. Traditional ideas about service unionism—
that the union is an outside agency hired by the workers—make it
seem that the staff and leaders of a big, powerful union can come in
and face down the employer, while the members sit back. If the

Flint Glass Workers Reject Merger

In the summer of 1998, leaders in a small industrial union took
a close look at their own union's identity, effectiveness, and size,
and whether they'd be better off merged into a much larger union. In
spirited convention debate, delegates of the American Flint Glass
Workers Union decided to reject a merger with the United Food and
Commercial Workers. In doing so, "the Flints" helped clarify some
of the drawbacks to the merger trend now sweeping U.S. labor.

The AFGWU's national leaders called a special convention to
consider the proposal. They set an agenda including slide shows,
speeches by UFCW officials, and even a talk by John Sweeney. But
delegates said "no" to all that, and voted to substitute their own
agenda—more time for discussion and fewer speeches, including
none from John Sweeney.

"Some people felt bad about turning John Sweeney away, but
they were mad they weren't being given a chance to speak" on the
merits of the merger, said Local 1007 Financial Secretary John
Nicholson.

The merger was voted down by more than three to one.

Why Not?

Some local leaders heard about the merger months before the
convention through informal conversations. Officially, the national
officers were saying nothing. Local activists spread the word and
organized a network to oppose the merger. They started from the
view that the merger wasn't needed.

Says Tim Tuttle, a national rep, "Some of us didn't believe the
UFCW was a match for the Flints, as far as like industries or common employers." The union represents workers in factories making
glass containers, light bulbs, and other products. Besides, says
Tuttle, "we service our members as well as any larger union."

The Flint Glass Workers did have problems. Union membership
had dropped from a high of 30,000 to 18,000, through industrial
restructuring that wasn't matched by new organizing. That loss put
pressure on the union's treasury. Merger opponents decided the

Teamsters are strong against the trucking companies, they can take care of the Tender Care Nursing Home, right?

Well, no. A union's strength depends largely on a mobilized

---

answer was to do more organizing, and perhaps cut some expenses at the national headquarters, before giving up their union's ghost.

They also began to talk about what could be lost through the merger. The AFGWU is a 120-year-old organization, one of the first members of the pre-AFL Knights of Labor. "It's hard to tell you over the phone," says Tuttle. "There's a real passion...There are families in this movement where parents, grandparents, great-grandparents were in this union."

Yet its small size means that "there are UFCW locals larger than our entire National," as Andrew Slipp, the anti-merger secretary of Local 1007, put it. As a small piece of a much larger union, local leaders feared their union's heritage would be lost.

So would, it seemed, a good bit of their union's democracy. The ten AFGWU national reps are elected by the convention every three years. In the UFCW, as in most major unions, those reps would be appointed. The reps are seen as an important link in a union with locals as small as a dozen members.

"How much attention would a twelve-man mold shop get in an organization with 1.4 million members?" asked Tuttle. In the AFGWU, he says, "We know our members by name...Members in the small locals get as much help as those in large locals like in Corning."

Most members first learned of the merger talks from a column written by Slipp in the national newspaper. When delegates arrived at the special convention, they got their first look at the agreement. Nicholson says, "People said 'we should have gotten that two or three months ago and had a chance to decide before we got here.'"

The lack of consultation with the ranks also fed a distrust of national leaders' motives. According to Slipp, the first information given to national reps was a comparison of their own prospective pension and health benefits. "We felt people were trying to line their pockets," says Nicholson.

"I don't want to say we shouldn't merge ever. But we ought to try to run the union on our own first. The officers in there now aren't doing the job."

membership. An international with members in many different industries contributes to that strength if international leaders understand each industry and make a priority of the issues of each. If the union is democratic and promotes strong leadership in each of its diverse sectors, its diversity need not be a liability. But if the concerns of Indiana state workers were ignored by the UAW leadership, the UAW's activity against General Motors would be of little help to Hoosiers.

In dealing with an employer, it's not size that counts as much as density. Say an employer, Acme Widget Co., has 2,000 workers. A union of 2,000 Acme workers is strong against this company. But a union of 10,000 members is weak against Acme if it has only 100 members in the whole widget industry.

Further, the advantages of size have to be balanced against other considerations. Example: The Steelworkers international is considering forcing a merger of some or all of the five locals at a single steel complex in Cleveland owned by LTV. On the surface, this seems like common sense. The separate locals are holdovers from the process of company conglomeration: two represent workers at what were old J&L Steel operations and three represent workers at former Republic Steel sites. It would be good for all the workers in the same location dealing with the same management to hold common membership meetings and deny the company the opportunity to whipsaw them.

But representation on the Steelworkers' national bargaining council for LTV is based on one vote per local, regardless of size. Unless other changes are made, a merger will cost members of the five Cleveland locals four-fifths of their voting power on bargaining priorities. These five locals have recently been more militant and willing to stand up against the company and the international officers than most. Reducing their voice reduces the democratic culture in the union by shifting power toward the international and away from an alternative vision. The locals will end up weaker against the employer.

A bigger international has a bigger research department and a larger force of international staff. A larger research department does not help you if its responsibilities are spread over many more industries and workplaces. The number of researchers and computers devoted to your industry may even be less than in a smaller, more homogeneous union. That's because in large unions, the biggest sectors get the most attention from international staff; the UAW research department spends most of its time studying the auto industry, and much less on health care or breweries. And political pressures—where the votes are—mean the relative amount of attention to different industries may not even be proportional to the membership; the smaller groups are easy to ignore.

The same thing is true with staff reps. Say two unions each have

An Approach to International Union Unity

In 1997-1998 leaders of the United Paperworkers International Union and the Oil, Chemical and Atomic Workers held merger discussions. The merger was fairly controversial because most observers, including OCAW activists, credit OCAW with a much more democratic culture than UPIU.

One OCAW local president outlined an excellent way to approach the issue:

Rather than raise objections or criticize any such future proposal out of hand, I've been telling folks that if it ultimately passes the following character test, they can expect to hear me speak out in favor of adopting it at the appropriate time, and if it doesn't, they can expect to hear me speak out against it, plain and simple:

Does the proposed merger document call for committing a higher total percentage of the merged International Union's operating budget to organizing, and does it clearly define organizing as our number one priority? Does the proposed merger document provide a mechanism for meaningful rank-and-file review and input into decisions made between Conventions by the International Officers? Does the proposed merger document call for a sustained level of funding for the Labor Party, and for the continued support of its objectives? Does the proposed merger document call for a commitment to rank-and-file membership ratification of all individual Collective Bargaining Agreements, and contain provisions which continue to guarantee a reasonable degree of Local Union autonomy?

Will the merger of the two Unions result in an organization where the rank-and-file is better positioned to fight for further improvements in their own conditions of work, and [is] more completely supported when they are forced to defend their past gains? In my view, these are the basic issues which would have to be properly addressed before I would ever consider becoming a vocal proponent of a merger with the UPIU, or with any other Union for that matter.[2]

100,000 members and a staff of 100; each union has one staff member per 1,000 members. If the two unions merge, you have a much bigger union (200,000) with a much bigger staff (200). But you still have only one staff member per 1,000 members. And a merged international union usually decides to save money by downsizing the merged staffs.

A bigger strike fund gives you more power against the boss. This argument could make sense, depending on the bigger union's strategy. If the union runs like a business, evaluating the cost-benefit ratio of every move, then there's no particular advantage here. The strike fund and staff may be bigger, but they have to cover more workers, and committing a disproportionate amount of the strike fund to a smaller struggle wouldn't be rational. This is the way most unions make decisions.

However, if the union strategy is to be unpredictable and militant, occasionally going to the wall for its members, the larger strike fund can be a valuable weapon. The union makes it clear that it will mobilize all resources, money and people, *on principle* against any employer who tries to break the union; the union will lose money and risk everything to make it so costly that the employer will certainly lose. Faced with this "irrational" union behavior, few employers will accept certain destruction (or, in the public sector, political backlash), even if the union would exhaust itself in the process. In this scenario, a bigger strike fund does make the union more powerful, because the threat of severe damage to the employer is more credible.

But the dollars in the strike fund by themselves don't make the union strong. This strategy works only if the members can be mobilized for such fights. If the members are not willing to make the necessary sacrifices, then the larger strike fund is of no particular value. In other words, this strategy requires a high degree of internal democracy—which, as we argue below, is often compromised in big general unions.

The better unions today operate somewhere between these two styles. Even if they choose the more militant strategy, union leaders must make decisions on when and where to go to the wall. If there are many local contracts, as in most internationals, then many struggles will be going on at once. The union can't put all resources into each of them; the strike fund and resources get parceled out. If a small group of social workers has affiliated with the giant Widget

Makers Union, it's unlikely the Widget Makers will put a high priority on a struggle with the social workers' employer.

A bigger union will have more political clout. Political clout for whom? Clearly the top union leader who heads the merged union will have more clout with a congressperson than she had before, based on the larger membership and a larger political action budget. But is this any more clout than the two leaders of the un-merged unions acting together? Or one person representing a coalition of unions?

Merged unions can make economies of scale in administration, accounting, and computer systems, and can better shift resources to organizing. Possibly so, but without changing a union's culture, hiring more staff is an ineffective way to boost organizing. The best organizers are activist members who can convince others that their union is strong. Will the merger produce more such members, or more bitter and disenfranchised ones?

The efficiency argument does make sense for unions in the same industry, the two major teachers' unions, for instance. The National Education Association and the American Federation of Teachers have a long history of competing for new members, and not enough history of sharing information and ideas. A merger based on a plan that strengthens membership control could stop the competition and duplication of work.

Democracy and Accountability

Larger unions present clear drawbacks in terms of democracy. In locals that are widespread geographically, with members in many different industries, it's much harder for members to pressure leaders or to elect new ones. Compare the difficulty and expense of an election campaign in a one-work-site local to one with members in hundreds of workplaces across a large state. Since in the larger local only the officers and staff can become experts—rank and file members only know their own workplace and contract—alternative leadership is easily squelched. In an international union covering many industries, the same difficulties arise. It's hard for local leaders and rank and filers to communicate well enough to pressure top leaders, much less launch an election challenge.

One argument sometimes heard for mergers is that "you only need to have one set of officers instead of two." If officers are a burden on the membership, then this argument makes sense. But if union officers are leading, and well connected to the rank and file, then having more is better (up to some common sense limit). Consider, for example, a situation where five small locals in the same international represent workers in different companies in the same city. Five sets of local officers and executive boards provide five times as many opportunities for members to move into leadership positions. More hands on the plow, more members involved. As far as payroll is concerned, chances are that all the officers of the separate locals will be volunteers. But a new amalgamated local may well decide to have full-time paid officers.

Solidarity Without Merger

The goals that advocates of mergers say they want—power and efficiency—are good ones. But often there are more effective ways to reach them. A more convincing way to develop political power, for example, with or without merging, would be to ensure that the union's official position actually influences how the members vote, talk, volunteer, and contribute. Politicians today know that many members do not follow union leaders in politics, and that union endorsements often don't mean that much. The goal then is to increase members' identification with the union, so that when the union does take a position on a candidate or legislation, politicians can expect members to act. Again, this means democratic process, so that political endorsements are what "we" do in the union, not "they" the leadership by themselves. Any move that cuts down on members' feeling that the union belongs to them—and mergers can be such a move—weakens the union in politics.

One way to reach the goal of efficiency without merging is to organize multi-local bodies that share staff and administrative work. When different unions exist at a single workplace (usually a poor situation), they can set up joint bargaining councils and stewards councils and effectively act as one on the local level.

Solidarity can be organized whether members are in the same union or not. Activists in one general union, the Canadian Auto Workers, which has members in rail, fishing, retail sales, and casinos, as well as auto plants, say direct contact between these sectors at union conventions and elsewhere makes it easier to organize solidarity for each other's struggles. But cross-union contacts and organization need not be under the umbrella of a national union. Jobs with Justice, Labor Notes, the Labor Party, and local strike support efforts bring workers together. The AFL-CIO's Union Cities program and emphasis on central labor councils could also help fill the gap.

The main hurdle to cross-union solidarity is often officials' desire to protect turf. In the railroad industry, leaders of the conductors' and engineers' unions (the UTU and the BLE) have a long history of disputes over jurisdiction. When the UTU struck the regional Soo Line railroad in 1994, BLE officials urged their engineer members to cross the picket lines. But none did. In spite of the tensions among rail union officials, rank and file cross-union solidarity committees had been built in several areas, including Minneapolis and St. Louis. And while in 1999 the teachers' unions merger is up in the air, local and regional affiliates of the two unions are working together on common issues like charter schools. Such activity should become the rule, not the exception.

Better Is Better

Some unions, like the Canadian Auto Workers and parts of the Teamsters, gain a reputation for openness and willingness to fight for their members that helps them grow. People want to join not because these unions are big, but because they seem strong: it's not "bigger is better" but "better is better." What counts is solidarity, first within the bargaining unit and then with other workers; this depends very much on democracy and membership involvement.

So is smaller better? Not always, by any means. Some opposition to mergers is motivated by mistrust of change, or by officers hanging on to positions they fear will be eliminated. Skilled and professional workers sometimes prefer separate unions thinking they'll get a better deal if not linked with their unskilled co-workers.

Sometimes small militant locals or unions fear to merge into bigger ones that are more conservative; they want to preserve the level of democracy they've built. But if it's possible to use the merger to create a stronger union for workers in their particular industry, it's a mistake for militants to huddle together in a separate union. This is obviously a tough judgment to make: how much will a small, militant group be able to affect the larger union? What might they lose in the process? In sorting these questions out, members of the smaller, more democratic union should keep in mind that others in the industry must be involved in their militancy if their own efforts are to succeed.

Indeed, the merger process itself may provide the basis for new discussions on democracy within the involved unions. Merging requires unions to look at their structure and operation and consider changes. While this usually goes on at the top, activists can use the process to get an expanded hearing on proposals for democratization. In the proposed merger of the Auto Workers, Steelworkers, and Machinists, reformers from all three unions are seeking to put forward the best features of all. For instance, the fight for a direct membership vote for top officers in the new union, long a goal of UAW reformers, will be aided by the fact that this is the current procedure of the USWA and IAM. When the 1998 NEA convention turned down a proposal to merge with the AFT, part of the reason was delegates' belief that NEA structures were democratic and that these would be changed under the proposal. (Delegates approved the idea of merging, but asked for a different proposal on structure of the new union.)

What Size Locals?

The best size for a local union is the biggest size that corresponds to the relevant employer structure and at the same time allows workers to meet and make decisions on common interests. Locals that cover nearly a whole state or a large number of jurisdictions, such as exist in the Teamsters, UFCW, and SEIU, make involvement too difficult.

A local representing a single workplace, even it it's small, makes sense where employment is relatively stable. Workers share common concerns, can easily communicate and make decisions, and can directly observe the functioning of their leaders. They of course need intermediate structures to link them with other locals within the same employer and the same industry. Where an industry is based on small work sites, such as a school system, the restaurant industry, or the smallest of all, home care, geographically defined locals may make more sense. Geographic locals are certainly needed where workers shift around a lot, as in construction trades. But geographic locals need to pay extra attention to workplace organization, the far stronger form of structure.

Large statewide or regional local unions make little sense without a strong internal structure that is truly local. For instance, within the California State Employees Association, which is one giant SEIU local, members are organized into "district labor councils." These might be a single building in the state capital, or a whole town elsewhere. These councils recruit new members and handle first-step grievances, thus avoiding some of the drawbacks of giant locals.

Rational Reorganization

Good reasons for merging are based not on size but on whether the new structure fits the tasks.

• Does a proposed merger unify forces in dealing with an employer? Does it align the organizational structure of the union along the lines of its main employer enemies?

• Does the structure make it easier for leaders to lead and for members to hold leaders accountable?

• Does it promote the development of new leaders at the work site?

• Does it make it easier or harder for workers to understand and make decisions for the union?

These are not the questions many leaders are asking today. Bigger-is-better is a useful rule only from the point of view of dues collectors. In gaining members this way, unions spread themselves too thin to understand and deal with the industry and job issues their members face. More important, workers in any one industry are divided by different structures, different contracts, and different union procedures—undermining their power to organize against the boss. Merger mania gives unionism a bad name and reinforces the anti-union propaganda that unions are interested in members only for their dues dollars.

The labor movement does need reorganization badly, but not hit-and-miss mergers to create large general unions that can represent no one really well. (The same holds true for organizing drives. Since the Teamsters is largely a trucking, delivery, warehousing, and manu-facturing union, what sense does it make for them to organize hos-pital workers?) Let the trade union movement reorganize along the lines of one industry per union, and one union per industry. This way each national employer, or each division of a conglomerate, is faced with one strong union, rather than an array of weak ones that can be pitted against each other.

Unfortunately, this won't happen soon; power against employers is too far from the minds of too many union officials. That's just one more reason why union democracy is not the job of any one union but a necessity for the entire labor movement.

Local Autonomy vs. National Coordination

While bigger unions don't necessarily mean more power for members, local union autonomy—independence from international or national union authority—doesn't necessarily build democracy either.

Making decisions at the lowest possible level does have much to recommend it. The closer people are to decision-making, the easier it is to organize to affect the decisions. Still, experience shows that local autonomy, as the term is used in the union movement, can be very undemocratic. For one thing, it can mean the "right" of locals to undermine conditions for the rest of the union by signing sub-standard contracts. Also, "local autonomy" is often used to mean the rights of local union officers—not the ranks.

For instance, local autonomy was the rallying cry of the old guard in the Teamsters after reformers took over the international in 1992. Wasn't the international violating local autonomy when it put locals in trusteeship for leadership corruption? If the international wanted to force locals to help fund national organizing campaigns, weren't they stepping on local sovereignty? Weren't the locals that refused to support the 1994 strike against UPS in mid-contract simply exercising their right to local autonomy?

Gus Bevona, long-time president of SEIU Local 32B-32J in New York City, held up the flag of local autonomy to oppose certain programs proposed by the international in 1996. Bevona agreed that since many employers are now national and international, the international should be more involved in contract bargaining. But in a widely distributed letter, Bevona demanded that "the final say with respect to all collective bargaining agreement provisions remains with the locals." More rights for his members? In Bevona's local, members don't have the right to vote on contracts; his demand was that the "final say" remain with Gus.

Bevona was also quite concerned that international staff would be holding education programs in his local, but without his control. International staff would then be in "personal contact" with members, and might select members for training that were "working to undermine the policies of the local union administration" (i.e., dissidents).

These concerns about local control of education are valid if we believe that Gus Bevona, who goes to work in a chauffeur-driven limousine paid for by the members' dues, is more responsive to the members than is an outside educator. In truth, neither is accountable to the members of Local 32B-32J, but the educator may have more interest in helping members gain skills.

Bevona's geographic closeness to his members does not mean that he has more understanding of the problems of the rank and file worker than does a national leader. More important is the social distance—Bevona's high pay and pampered lifestyle, his personal power in the local, and his tight hold on office. If members have no alternatives to choose from at the local level, it is quite possible that local officers represent members' interests no better than national officers do.

But there's a more important reason for rejecting local autonomy as a principle: unions should make decisions at the level appropriate to the issue involved. Bargaining against national and global corporations should be done at the national level, for example. A local union in a multi-local company has no right to cut its own deals if those deals undermine the other locals. To make such a deal denies the right of the majority (everyone else) to exercise power against the employer. An article of the UAW constitution, for example, (unfortunately not enforced) quite properly requires the international union to prevent locals from undermining prevailing conditions:

> The International Executive Board shall protect all Local Unions who
> have succeeded in establishing higher wages and favorable conditions
> and have superior agreements, so that no infringement by Local
> Unions with inferior agreements in workplaces doing similar work may
> be committed against the Local Union with advanced agreements.[3]

Power vested in an international union to control national pattern bargaining is clearly appropriate to the task. On the other hand, shifting power to the international union on local questions is often undemocratic. In the UAW, again, many representatives who handle clearly local issues are appointed by and responsible to the international union. The issue is not local autonomy versus central control, but the level appropriate for exercising power.

Intermediate Bodies

Most unions maintain some sort of council or regional body at a level between the local unions and the international. Such bodies can provide useful networking and information exchange between local officers. They can provide a channel for feedback from locals to the international, and a place for local officers to debate national or international strategies. They may provide regional coordination of national programs like a get-out-the-vote campaign.

Or they may simply be a source of extra salaries and perks for certain officials. The Teamsters closed their four U.S. Area Conferences in 1994 because they were both useless and expensive (costing about $15 million a year) The conferences had been founded about 50 years ago to deal with regional trucking companies, but the major trucking employers are now national and the conferences had become dinosaurs.

Regional bodies may be relevant for bargaining in industries where employers roughly correspond to regional union structures—although the main examples of such industries—telephone, rail, and electric power—are changing fast to more national structures. For similar reasons AFSCME locals representing workers at single departments or agencies are grouped into district councils for bargaining with city and state governments.

Problems of democracy in these intermediate bodies are just as difficult as in a large international union, and in some ways more immediate. Such bodies often essentially take on the representation function, but the leaders are seldom directly elected. They are one step removed from the members; local officers usually choose the intermediate-level officials. Leaders of the Association for Union Democracy have said that intermediate bodies that do representation should be subject to the same legal requirements as local unions, namely, direct election of officers at least every three years.

Meanwhile, reformers in unions with powerful intermediate-level officers must face this extra challenge. Because a local presidency is a less powerful position in such unions, that position may be less jealously held by old guard officers and more attainable to reformers. The extra step is then to identify and work with other local leaders to change the council/region/federation. Local leaders and members have waged campaigns to reform some AFSCME district councils. In the Brotherhood of Maintenance of Way

Employees, members of the Pennsylvania Federation (who build and maintain track for major railroads in the northeastern United States) campaigned for and won the right to directly elect their federation officers. Since then, the Pennsylvania Federation has been one of the most militant and effective parts of the union. Certain Teamster locals got together in the mid-1990s and formed two new joint councils (groupings of local officers in a city, state, or sometimes larger area). Typically, officers of joint councils, who are elected by other local officers, are paid full-time salaries on top of their local union salaries. The new joint councils pay officers either nothing or a minimal amount ($3,000 to $6,000 a year), providing resources for organizing while keeping dues low.

People and Positions

The duties, powers, and compensation of elected and appointed leaders are questions that cause unions some of their most heated debates. For instance, a Los Angeles SEIU local, 399, was put in trusteeship after reformers won the executive board seats. The big controversy that brought intervention by the international was a difference between the new board and the old president on who the staff members would be. In UFCW Local 304A, when a new president found that local union policy prevented his unilaterally firing the business agents without cause, he assigned the BAs to sit in the company cafeteria and count how many workers wore union caps.

Officers' Pay

High pay and perks can contribute to an unhealthy separation between the viewpoints of officers and those of members. In most U.S. unions the pay for top international officers is many times higher than members', generally over $100,000 per year and sometimes two or three times that. Many local officers and some staff are paid at a similar level.

Expense reimbursements can also help provide a high standard of living—meetings at resorts and union business conducted over expensive dinners. But that can't be determined from the expense figures alone; a leader who travels to see members and carry on legitimate business will incur high expenses too.

Sometimes high pay is accomplished through multiple salaries: one person may receive full-time compensation for positions at local, intermediate, and international levels at the same time.

One Teamster who received multiple salaries was Frank Wsol, a Chicago local official who made $250,000-$450,000 a year in the 1990s. How did this high pay affect his outlook? After he was accused of plotting with UPS to get a dissident member of his local

TDU's $100,000 Club

Officers' salaries have been a reform issue in the Teamsters for decades. The issue is not just the money spent; high salaries represent a great divide between the members and the officialdom. The great majority of those making over $100,000 per year are viewed as self-serving fat cats.

To publicize just who is making how much money off the members' dues, TDU prints an annual list it calls the $100,000 Club. The club lists Teamster officers with earnings above that mark, the total amount for each, and where they got the salaries.

In the Teamsters, and in some other unions, it's common for officers to receive multiple full-time salaries from two or more different affiliates: local union, intermediate bodies, and the international. The $100,000 Club is the only place these salaries are added up for a full picture of officers' income. Doing the research to put it all together requires checking hundreds of union financial statements (LM-2 forms).

In 1991 the $100,000 Club included 189 people, who made $27.3 million total in salaries. In 1992, a reform administration took office, led by Ron Carey. Carey couldn't affect salaries paid by locals, joint councils, and regional conferences. But he did press international appointees—international reps, organizers, division heads—to accept only one salary; nearly all did. And he requested that international executive board members forego their constitutionally mandated salary if they received another from a local union.

The new administration also closed the area conferences, an outdated extra layer of bureaucracy (and source of salaries), and trusteed many of the locals where the fattest cats were adding illegal abuses to their multiple salaries.

These moves, in combination with rank and file reformers winning control of more locals, took a bite out of the $100,000 Club. In 1998, the club was down to 132 members taking home $16.8 million total; the number of people in international positions in the club was cut from 89 to 26.

fired, Wsol told a reporter that the UPS worker had gotten his job back after eleven months, so no harm was done anyway. Wsol seemed to have little idea of the difficulty someone might have going so long without pay if he hadn't been making $300,000 a year.

Frank Wsol may be an extreme case, but too-high salaries do change officers' viewpoints. If we limit officers' pay to the same level as the top grades of the people they represent:

• Members will not choose to run for office for the pay. They will try for leadership positions because they care about the union and believe they can help members accomplish something.

• Leaders' standard of living will be the same as that of the people they represent. They will continue to live in the same communities and deal with many of the same daily problems as their members.

• The financial cost of losing office will not be as great, so the pressure to hang on to a position by suppressing democracy will be lessened. (Some unions use term limits to address the problem of officers getting addicted to their higher-paid jobs. The worst case is when, as in many Teamster local agreements, the contract has no language giving officers the right to return to their former jobs. Incumbents have more incentive to cheat on elections and it's riskier for challengers to attempt a run.)

The United Electrical Workers (UE) is the only national or international union we know of that explicitly limits officers' pay to members' level, a fact that the union proudly uses to recruit new members:

> The salary of the three top leaders is limited by the UE Constitution to the top wage paid in the industry. (That is currently set at less than $43,000.) It's hard to think or act like a big shot on a worker's wage."⁴

In most unions you'll get an earful of arguments, including from some members, for high officer salaries. Some ideas about officers' pay are closely tied to the business-union approach, where the officers and staff are the union and their job is to "service" the members. For instance, some say about officers' pay, "You only get what you pay for." In other words, if we don't pay our leaders and staff what they are worth in the marketplace, then the most talented people will take jobs working for corporations and we will be stuck with less competent people working for us.

One need only read the business press to see that executive pay does not correlate with what executives produce. Their pay has more to do with internal politics, luck, and family connections. Just look at the pay structure in your company or agency and chances are that "you get what you pay for" won't stand up. Besides, for the union to pay leaders high salaries is not a protection against talent drain, since management can always pay substantially more.

What about the argument "management thinks in terms of money; they'll think we don't respect our leaders if we don't pay them more. And if our leaders don't have the respect of the company they can't do a good job for us." Management will respect our leaders when they feel the impact of a mobilized rank and file. When management understands that union leaders are not in it for personal gain, then they have to deal with the real issues and give up on the sweet talk and personal perks.

"If we don't pay our leaders well enough they will be more vulnerable to the temptations of corruption. Pay them enough so they have something to lose if they're caught with their fingers in the till." This argument is also made for pay raises for government officials.[5] But the evidence is ample that if you are on the money track, you always need more than you have now; officials who have been caught embezzling from their unions were not the lower-paid ones at all.

This problem of seeing union office as a steppingstone to a higher standard of living is at the heart of both corruption and the failed conception of business unionism. It divides the leaders from the members and by placing leaders in an elite group, serves to excuse all manner of repression.

A workable course is to keep officers' salaries close to, if perhaps somewhat more than, what members earn. We might pay officers a bit more if there are hidden expenses of being an officer. Time on the road can mean extra expenses for childcare and clothing, for instance. Also, a union salary does not include extra pay for the tremendous amount of overtime required. In industries where overtime is standard, becoming a union officer should not require a pay cut.

"Shouldn't we pay officers more to compensate for the difficulty of the job, the stress, the weekends sacrificed, and the near 24-hour on-call status that we expect?" Working for the members does have its difficulties, but it also has many more intangible rewards than most jobs. A retired UE official compares his job to members' jobs:

> First let me tell you something where we have it all over you. We officers, organizers, business agents, district presidents have it all over you as far as the job is concerned. When you walk through the gate every morning you hate to do it. If you did not have to earn a week's pay you would never go near that gate...Instead of going to work every morning for the boss and hating it, I've been getting up every morning and going to work on a job I like to do—not because all is pleasant, not because we don't get our brains beat out, not because it's all victories and no defeats; but through victories and defeats, through joy and tears, we've been doing what we like to do. And that's where we have it all over you guys."[8]

Even for those, like caregivers or professionals, who may love their jobs and believe in their work; even for those, like clericals, whose work environment is already as safe and comfortable as the

Obtaining Your Union's Financial Report: the LM-2

Private sector unions and those that represent federal workers are required to submit annual financial statements to the U.S. Department of Labor on a form called the LM-2. LM-2s tell officers' and staffers' salaries and expenses. They also list for each officer any other union affiliates from which they've earned $10,000 or more.

Unions are required to make LM-2's available to members on request. The forms are also available from the Department of Labor for 15 cents per page. (Requests for 30 or fewer pages are provided free. LM-2 forms for local unions are typically 10-20 pages.)

When requesting an LM-2, give the full name of the union, including its international and its local number, and the city and state where it's located. Write to U.S. Department of Labor, Office of Labor-Management Standards (OLMS), Room N-5616, 200 Constitution Ave. NW, Washington, DC 20210. Phone 202/219-7393. Fax 202/501-6780.

The OLMS also has field offices in 25 cities that can provide some LM-2s; check your local phone directory under U.S. Government, Department of Labor, Office of Labor-Management Standards.

union office, there are still intangible gains from being elected. For many people, the increase in personal recognition, appreciation, and development makes becoming a union officer a step up no matter the pay.

And aren't these the only rewards we'd encourage potential officers to seek? If we view unionism as a movement, then the first criterion for capable leaders is that they think in terms of the group's progress, not just their own. If someone sees union office as a method of getting a raise, we can expect that after the election they'll still put their own interests first.

The Executive Board

In many locals members view their executive board as a rubber stamp for the top officials, perhaps a political payoff. In a democratic union the board is a key part of the leadership team (discussed in Chapter 6). Board members fill various roles according to their expertise and constituencies, and each feels responsible for staying in touch with members, providing information and seeking input. Seldom do bylaws include any structure to assure this happens.

Here are a few points to watch out for. One is salaries. Reformers need to look at both the amount of salary and whether the board member is actually doing any work for it. Especially for international unions and intermediate bodies, board seats may be no more than a way for top officials to reward friends with an extra salary.

Another point is the size and make-up of the board. Executive boards can be too large. A board of 20 or more members seldom functions as a group; instead, a smaller group acts as the real leadership. The decision-making process is clouded: one member thinks he needs to present a proposal to the whole board, while another with inside connections realizes she needs only to convince the real leaders. If the board is large, its actual leadership should be a clearly-defined steering committee.

Writing a bylaw on the makeup of the board can be vexing. Most locals elect board members at large. In a local with dozens of work sites, this makes campaigning difficult and can tend to exclude racial and gender minorities and members from smaller locations. On the other hand, deciding a formula that will ensure fair representation on the board is nearly impossible in large, diverse locals. Often this question is decided informally through election slates: candidates for local president have a much better chance running with a slate that is reasonably representative of the membership. If a districting of the local can be agreed on—say each board member represents about equal numbers of workers—it will make the board more effective.

Most bylaws do address the role and responsibilities of the board. Sometimes no one reads this section because the board is so closely allied with the local president that it's not an issue. Then opponents win a majority of board seats. If the bylaws are not clear on what decisions the president can make himself and which must be approved by the board, there's trouble. Clarity on rights and responsibilities can make it possible for political opponents to function together in leadership positions.

Role of Staff

Besides leaders and ranks, another group has great influence in unions: the staff. In this section we use "staff" to refer to people appointed or hired to work for the union in both representational and non-representational capacities, not those elected to a paid position.

Union staff work is like few other jobs. It's not like working for a company: good union staff feel they're part of a cause. In fact, even if hired from outside the union, staff should be members of it, with all rights and privileges of membership, to reinforce that connection. From clerical staff to reps, staffers should work as a team with elected leaders, putting in practice a certain vision of how the

Staff Are Not Outside Politics

A founding member of an SEIU local remembers working hard to compose the most democratic bylaws possible. Members decided that full-time officials could become too politically powerful, so the bylaws provided for a full-time executive director who answered to an elected rank and file board.

The executive director used her position, however, to build a political base in the local that allowed her to challenge the board's authority. Far from being politically neutral, the executive director joined a slate and won international office.

Any staff member who has either ambition to move up in the union structure, or commitment to a certain vision of unionism (or both), will play a political role in the union. We have not seen a structure that could keep staff outside politics.

union should be run. This means it's not usually possible to treat union staff like civil service employees, as if they're above and beyond the politics of the union. The staff that carried out the last leadership's agenda won't be committed to a new way of doing things and won't succeed at it.

Because of their expertise, good staff members provide one kind of leadership. One of their leadership responsibilities should be to help recognize, encourage, and train new rank and file leaders—people who are leaders in the workplace. This can be a tough situation for a staff member who perhaps thinks she is the logical choice for moving up when there is, say, an opening on the executive board. But workplace leadership is of crucial importance to the union and probably a more important addition to the current board than the staff member's broader knowledge. Staff need to recognize the limitations of their own type of leadership.

An occasional problem for reformers who win election is to find themselves faced with staff hired by and beholden to their predecessors. Perhaps the staff organizes a union just before the reformers take office, saying they're looking for fairness under the new leadership. In reality, the staff may be looking for security in a well-paying, up-to-now-cushy job; staying in a rep's position is also a good way to help get their old guard friends back in office.

The best situation is when the staff and the membership relate to each other as more than employees and employer—they act as different parts of the same movement.

Appointed vs. Elected Positions

Which local positions should be elected and which appointed? In most unions descended from the CIO, stewards—the people who handle the first level of grievance handling, whether part-time or full-time—are elected by the people they represent. Unions in the AFL tradition, including the Teamsters and construction trades, generally have the principal officer appoint stewards and business agents.

These first-level representation positions, whether volunteer stewards or full-time reps, would be better filled through elections. Though there are strong arguments for appointing, they are outweighed by the need for clear, open accountability to the members they should be organizing and representing.

There are three arguments for appointed stewards and business agents. First is a natural concern about politics entering into grievance handling. Everyone should be represented fairly, and if the business agent has to run for office he'll tend to favor his supporters over his opponents.

In truth, that's many people's experience of grievance handling: the in-crowd gets more attention to their problems. But favoritism is not reduced in locals with appointed reps; it's often exaggerated. The rep answers to the appointing (elected) officer, not directly to the members. Therefore the rep is still in a very political position of needing to keep her boss in office to keep her job. And at the same time the rep is protected from members' displeasure since it may require a whole new local leadership to force her out.

It's far easier to replace a rep who is elected by only that part of the membership she represents, and such reps, although they have a "political" job, tend to be more sensitive to members' needs. And since representation work is necessarily political—union politics is about how representation gets done—it's helpful to bring the politics out into the open through elections.

The second argument for appointing reps is that the top leaders and shop floor reps need to work as a team. The elected leaders make the decisions, as mandated by the members, and the reps implement the policy. This is not simply a matter of being on the same page for what to tell the employer about a certain issue. It's also a matter of carrying out a shared vision of how the union should function. If the elected leaders are committed to involving the members in contract campaigns, and one rep is telling members to relax, he'll let them know when negotiations are done, democracy is thwarted. The leadership is undermined in the job they were elected to do.

This is a strong argument, but it's also an argument for a winner-take-all kind of union governance: to ensure teamwork, just let the members elect the top officer and let him appoint the board, reps, staff, stewards...

That's going too far, of course. Democracy requires the possibility of minority voices being included in the leadership. And even within the majority, while leaders have to work together, we don't really want them all to think alike. There is value in diversity: different viewpoints and different interests. Appointments tend to emphasize loyalty and similar thinking.

As far as stewards and reps are concerned, the need for rank and file members to know very clearly that they have a direct say in who represents them on the job is crucial to their feeling ownership of the union—so crucial that it's more important than the teamwork goal. For other staff positions the need for leadership teamwork makes appointments appropriate: administrative, clerical, technical, or organizing positions, for instance.

The third reason sometimes given for appointing reps is that the members are not able to make good choices. Perhaps the job is technical, like a rep who specializes in health and safety grievances, and members aren't expected to know enough to judge the expertise of candidates. Or perhaps it seems the number of elected positions is simply too much: members can't be expected to keep track of the platform and record of too many candidates. Or it may be argued that a mostly white or mostly male membership will only elect their own, and people of color and women will be closed out of the leadership.

Where Appointing Stewards Is Democratic

Where local unions want a high number of stewards, appointing them can essentially mean recruiting them, and elections aren't too meaningful. The CWA, for example, recommends one steward for every ten members. If that means several stewards in the same department, members can select the one they want for a particular grievance; several stewards can work together on group grievances.

In CWA Local 4309 in Cleveland, for example, local officers suggested stewards elections but the idea didn't get much interest from members. The local's practice is to appoint anyone who volunteers and meets certain basic requirements; then they're each provided with training. The requirements for being a steward are fairly minimal, but are set out in advance to avoid problems: stewards must attend five of eleven monthly membership meetings, and must not be actively seeking promotion into management.

Said one Local 4309 officer, "We wish we had the problem of more than ten percent of our members wanting to become stewards."

The problem of technical expertise can be partially handled by requiring some minimum achievement to be able to run, say completion of a certain training program, and then making that program accessible to any interested member. In addition technical assistance can be made available to the person once elected. Remember that for experts, how much they know is only part of the question. The more important point is what they do with the knowledge, and the members are fully qualified to judge that.

Keeping track of individual candidates for dozens of positions could be a problem and does limit the practicality of holding elections for all positions. But you can be sure that members will be interested in learning about anyone who wants to be their steward. Adding this position to the ballot will in no way overwhelm the electorate.

Another way to keep track of numbers of candidates is through slates. Slates tend to ensure a leadership representative of races, ethnicities, and genders within the local, since the slatemakers have their eye on drawing a wide range of votes. A slate that includes people of color and women is attractive not only to these groups but to others who understand the need for inclusion.

In conclusion, local union positions that bear direct responsibility for grievance handling—building members' power on the job—should be elected by the members they represent. Positions where the work is technical and not easily observed by the members are better appointed by elected leaders. Positions that are both technical and representational, like health and safety rep, should be elected. Training should be available and members should be encouraged to take it whether or not they've decided to run.

Who Should Vote?

One member/one vote is a valuable principle of democracy. It embodies the notion of equality and the central importance of the individual's views rather than how much he or she pays in dues. But there are times when exceptions to the rule help the union. For instance, many unions stretch the definition of member to include those on organizing committees working to gain union recognition in their workplace.

Retirees

While retirees' experience is invaluable, they are also cut off from the realities of the current workforce. What level of influence over union policy is democratic?

Retirees have paid their dues, not only literally but in terms of sacrificing to win the benefits and wages we have today. We want them to be active union members because their experience and tradition—as well as their numbers and activity—make the union stronger.

Retirees also have an interest in bargaining. Many depend on the union to negotiate improvements in pensions. At the same time, retirees are not involved in the day-to-day life in the workplace. Their direct interest in bargaining does not include working conditions or compensation for active workers. It may be difficult for retirees to fathom the level of speed-up and erosion of union work rules that current workers are undergoing today. Often the only contact the retirees have with the local is through one or two officers.

Retirees and Reform

The California State Employees Association, SEIU Local 1000, includes about 30,000 retiree members. The high number is partly because of its history as an association before affiliating with SEIU, and partly because the dues for retirees are fairly low.

The main active employees section, the Civil Service Division, represents about 80,000 workers but has many fewer actual members. Thus, the retirees, with full voting rights, have almost equal influence in the CSEA as the active workers.

In the early 1990s, a reform movement grew in the Civil Service Division among members who wanted the union to organize among the ranks for militant contract campaigns. The Caucus for a Democratic Union won the offices of the Civil Service Division in 1996.

Two years later at the 1998 CSEA convention, the Civil Service Division leaders had the support of about two-thirds of their division's delegates. But they still lost important votes on the floor to a combination of retirees, the minority within their division, and other smaller divisions—all led by the top CSEA leaders. This happened at a time when the big issues facing the CSEA were about how the

This means that retirees tend to play a conservative role in union politics, defending the status quo and, understandably, seeing workplace issues through the prism of their experience in previous years. For example, as people of color or women became majorities in their workplaces, the retiree vote in some instances has helped maintain the white or male character of union offices.

In the long run, it is the active members in the workplace that give the union most of its power, including the power to win benefits for the retirees. Active workers have to take most of the risks; their daily work life depends on current contracts. It is to these workers that the union must respond first and most immediately.

Can the union do that and still keep the benefits of retirees' experience? The answer lies in recognizing and representing retirees' special needs. They should have their own meetings and elect their own leaders. They should elect their own representatives to executive boards and special committees. They should not vote for union offices and convention delegates.

Civil Service Division itself should operate to get a long-sought contract with the state; yet the overwhelming majority view on this question among Civil Service Division delegates could not prevail.

The division's elected leaders sought control over their own budget, including staff appointments and activities. The retiree delegates voted as a block against these proposals. The retiree officers were very concerned about maintaining the status quo because Civil Service Division dues subsidize retiree activities, mostly lobbying on state pension fund issues.

The top leaders of the CSEA, meanwhile, saw their control (and perks) threatened by a movement from below in the Civil Service Division. They successfully united the retirees with a minority of delegates from the Civil Service Division and others to maintain their positions and block the reformers' program.

The CSEA structure recognizes the common interests among active state workers and retirees by joining them in the same organization under the same leadership. But it fails to recognize the ways the two groups' interests may diverge. In doing so, the CSEA denies active workers control over their own bargaining and grievance handling—and thereby makes it harder to pressure an anti-union state government and harder to inspire nonmembers to join.

At the same time, we need to make sure that retirees have opportunities to understand what's happening at the workplace and to participate in union committees and other union activities, to make full use of their experience, activity—and free time!

Special Sections of the Membership

When different job classifications within the workforce have, or feel they have, very different experiences and needs, the challenge to democracy is to represent everyone in a way that most strengthens all. Here we'll look at an example in which a union used a hybrid of organizational arrangements to unite the numerically small, but powerful, skilled workers with the large mass of production workers. The UAW's ability to do this helped make industrial unionism work.

Part of the UAW's arrangement reflects equality: each member has one vote for regular officers and delegates, everyone pays dues at the same rate, and all dues money goes into the same pot.

Part reflects a federation relationship; skilled workers get say-so beyond their numbers. The trades in each plant, even if small, elect their own bargaining representative, and they have their own national bargaining council and formulate their own special demands. And part of the arrangement is a coalition relationship; until the late 1990s at least the understanding was that a contract could not be ratified unless it was approved by both skilled and production (the rules are complicated and their interpretation disputed).

In this case the coalition/federation approach was used to include a powerful minority. It could also be used for a segment of the workforce that the union seeks to organize into the unit or to involve more actively, such as office or technical workers in an industrial plant, or field workers in a local dominated by central office workers.

No 'White Knight': Appeals Procedures and Government Agencies

The reader may have noticed a certain omission thus far: nowhere do we list government agencies or union appeals procedures that can take care of eliminating undemocratic practices. You've certainly caught on to our strong view that democracy is for the members to build and maintain. No "white knight" can democratize your union; it depends on an organized membership.

That said, there are legal-type processes that may sometimes offer a tool for organizing. If an election has been stolen, and members are mad about it, a new one ordered by the Department of Labor may make members more determined to make changes. If petitions and testimony by the rank and file pressure an internal review board to find in their favor, these members' stance is vindicated, plus their faith in their own organizing is strengthened.

One trap reformers sometimes fall into is putting energy into winning a case that is of limited value by itself. Yes, you were right that the chairperson shouldn't have ruled you out of order, but who cares two years later? But the main mistake unionists make when looking at these options is to hope that they can operate independent of the powerful forces in society or in the union. Government is influenced by the money of corporations, and union review boards at the international level tend to be closely tied to the union's administration.

"Bill of Rights"

The main federal law covering democratic rights within unions is the Labor-Management Reporting and Disclosure Act of 1959 (sometimes called "Landrum-Griffin" after its co-sponsors). The LMRDA covers unions that have members in private industry; strictly public sector unions may be covered by state laws on civil service. Many legislators who backed the LMRDA did so for anti-union reasons, hoping to rein in unions they perceived as too powerful by placing some restrictions on officials. They included members' rights as a cover, to give the appearance of fairness to the working people who make up unions. Still, the LMRDA does give members rights that are valuable for democratizing—thus strengthening—unions.

LMRDA Title I lays out these rights. They include the right to fair elections, to free speech on union issues, to meet together as a caucus on union matters (like electing a certain candidate), and to freedom from discrimination in representation. The union must follow its own constitution and bylaws.

Occasionally, reformers have enforced some of these rights for important gains: getting a stolen election overturned or gaining full information on a tentative contract before the vote. But this can be a multi-year process; it's not unusual for an officer's term to be half over before an election rerun takes place. And the staff of the Labor Department, responsible for enforcing the LMRDA, are often too busy to investigate "small" cases or are hesitant to anger high-ranking labor officials. Nevertheless, it's best for reform activists to know their rights in case officials abridge them and the evidence is clear-cut enough even for government functionaries.

One place it's especially difficult to enforce legal rights is where a rank and file reformer is unfairly disciplined or fired by management. Then hostile officials, hoping to be rid of the reformer themselves, may handle the grievance with a certain lack of enthusiasm. Under the law, the reformer is entitled to representation. But the courts have chosen over the years not to try to decide what is good versus poor representation; the union rep need only go through the motions of handling a grievance. Thus these cases, known as "duty of fair representation" cases, are not impossible but notoriously difficult to win.

For more information about enforcing legal rights within the union, or help finding an attorney who might be willing to represent you, contact the Association for Union Democracy (see Appendix 6).

You can get a copy of the Landrum-Griffin Act by writing to the U.S. Department of Labor, Washington, DC 20216; or visit their web site: www.dol.gov.

Case Study: The UAW Public Review Board

Most unions have some form of appeals procedure written into their constitutions, intended to cover cases like election protests or union-imposed discipline. Decisions made on the local level can be appealed to bodies higher up. Often, the highest decision-making body is the union's convention; sometimes another body has this authority. The UAW Public Review Board is the best of the latter approach. Under the UAW constitution, a member's appeal goes first to the local union, then to the International Executive Board, and then to the PRB. The PRB is made up of respected outsiders such as lawyers, professors, and clergy. It has a high degree of organizational independence from the union apparatus and considerable authority. Consequently, over the years some union reformers have given the PRB much praise and called the UAW a model on this score.

Although there is much to be learned from this arrangement, the

UAW PRB shows the limitations of an appeals procedure as a route to union democracy. The board seems to be effective in helping the union leadership limit individual financial corruption and unethical behavior. But it offers no significant correction to policies that severely limit internal democracy, and in practice serves to defend the leadership against serious challenges. Partly this is due to the PRB's outlook, partly to its legalistic role. As we note elsewhere, there is no set of bylaws or restrictions that can force union democracy; member control comes more from the union's culture and day-to-day practice than from any formula that can be set down in bylaws. The PRB cannot change a local's culture; it can only decide matters that can be outlined in bylaws. And even when a legal ruling outlining members' rights would clearly help, the PRB draws back.

For instance, open debate is closely associated with democratic rights. As the PRB itself eloquently argues: "Legitimate debate among union members...is the lifeblood of any democratic institution. Stifle it and the institution will inevitably be crippled or even die. In the name of policy conformance, legitimate political comment ought not be censored."[7] The board has defended UAW members' right to freely criticize union leaders and to print and distribute their own leaflets. But where locals include different companies or plants widely separated, members have no ready access to the members in other locations or to retirees, who also vote. Thus "legitimate debate" could be greatly aided by access to the union newspaper; a healthy democracy requires this. A certain amount of space could be set aside for internal discussion and including a variety of views appears. Certainly all widely held views in the union should be heard.

On the other hand, every member cannot expect the right to publish her views in the newsletter whenever she wishes. In its rulings, the PRB notes the problem of the one extreme as the excuse for adopting the other. In a case where an elected official wanted to criticize international union policy in the local's newspaper, the board confirmed the right of union officers to determine "wisely or no, that articles representing only a certain viewpoint shall appear in the paper."[8]

One of the most important functions of the PRB is to give members a way to appeal the handling of grievances. What makes this meaningful is that in the UAW's major contracts, the companies

agree to recognize a PRB decision that a grievance should be rein-
stated.[9] The PRB rightfully restricts its role in grievances to questions of procedure, not bargaining policy. But it has a particular view
of grievances that reinforces the UAW's servicing-model unionism.
In one ruling, for example, the board makes a point based on what it
believes is a common assumption:

> A decision whether to arbitrate a grievance is not after all a political
> question. It is not a matter of rallying the troops to a cause. To
> decide this issue requires an evaluation of the facts of the case to
> determine whether there is a realistic possibility that the Union can
> prevail.[10]

This reflects the narrow view of unions that they are a legal service in an industrial court. Deciding to push a grievance based only
on guessing the arbitrator's decision is a recipe for conservatism.
This kind of narrow legalism keeps the union from relying on members to help push the envelope and keeps the ranks out of the
process. Instead of deciding which grievances to pursue based on
what helps a campaign for union priorities, we turn the issue over to
lawyers to analyze arbitrator decisions.

Almost all cases that come before the PRB are appeals from
decisions of the International Executive Board, and almost all decisions uphold the IEB. Of the approximately 120 appeals between
September 1993 and March 1996, about 92 percent upheld the IEB.

These numbers by themselves are not an indictment. But an
examination of cases involving organizational and policy challenges
to the union's leadership shows a pattern of subservience to the
IEB.[11]

A Model Appeals Procedure

Although an appeals procedure can't create democracy, all
unions need a fair one, no matter how democratic they are. The procedures of a number of unions, including the UAW, make a good
starting point in designing an international appeals procedure. The
following features are important; many of these points also make
sense for inclusion in local union bylaws.

• A membership bill of rights should be specific about the functioning that members have a right to expect from their union, including the right to a level playing field in union elections.

• Procedures should be streamlined and written without jargon,
and should not require lawyers at any stage, although outside assis-

tance is permitted. The union should issue educational material detailing how to use the procedures. A good model is the booklet *Internal Union Hearings: a Handbook for Trade Unionists,* published by the Canadian Labour Congress.

• An ombudsperson should be available to advise and assist members in the process.

• The appeals procedure must be backed by the contract. It does no good to appeal the withdrawal of a grievance if the company will not readmit the grievance into the procedure.

• The appeal body must have sufficient power to see that its decisions are enforced, to avoid suspicion that decisions against the union administration will be sabotaged by the administration. It should have separate staff and some enforcement and implementation powers. Special care must be taken to see that reintroduced grievances are in fact pursued.

• Similarly, the individual member must have certain rights to make sure that his/her interests are respected in the execution of decisions. The UAW PRB has proposed some possibilities, including the right of the member to be independently represented at grievance negotiations and arbitration, by an attorney or other representative of the member's choosing.

• No union member or staff member serving on an appeal body should be eligible for promotion within the union, for appointment to a new union position, or to stand for election for a higher-level union office for two years after service on the appeals body has ended.

• Where a full-time appeals body exists (such as the PRB), some mechanism should be created to keep it in touch with the realities of the workplace and union life. Some members of the body could come from the workforce. The body can schedule occasional visits to workplaces.

• Members should have appeals options. In the UAW a member can choose between the PRB and a "Conventions Appeals Committee" made up of randomly selected convention delegates. The existence of options helps pressure any one appeals mechanism from becoming too cozy with the leadership.

Bylaws Reform

Although the bylaws by themselves can't give members power, bylaws outline practices that may help or hurt that goal. Pro-democracy reformers may see bylaws changes that would help build members' power, but they should be careful not to go overboard working on bylaws changes. For one thing, it will be impossible to fix all the language or omissions that could someday lead to problems; there is no perfect set of bylaws, and an attempt to fix all problems would create a document so complicated it would be useless.

Just as important is the fact that most members don't care about legalities and technicalities. If they don't see how bylaws changes could help them on the job, they're unlikely to make an extra effort to get to a meeting on amendments. If the members where you work don't respect their appointed stewards, proposing a bylaw amendment for elected stewards may help activate them. But if they like the stewards well enough, such an amendment will seem irrelevant.

Bylaws campaigns may help build the union and the reform caucus if it's clear how the change would improve members' power on the job. For instance, members of Teamsters Local 556 at the Iowa Beef Processing plant in Pasco, Washington started organizing for a bylaws change after the chief steward told a worker there was nothing the union could do about his case. The worker had been over-supervised and disciplined while he was injured. He asked the local president to appoint a new chief steward who would stand up for him, and co-workers collected 500 signatures supporting the request, but the president refused. Hundreds of members then drove over an hour to attend a local meeting so they could vote for a bylaws amendment for elected stewards. One of the chief organizers of the bylaws campaign, Maria Martinez, was elected chief steward. With new stewards, the 1,200 workers started organizing an information network on the processing floor and a lawsuit over the company's refusal to pay for time spent on preparation and clean-up. The bylaws campaign was simply a step toward being able to do this organizing.

See Appendix 5 for some suggested bylaws. Just remember that the goal is to remove barriers to democratic culture in the workplace.

Notes

1. See Gary N. Chaison, *Union Mergers in Hard Times: The View from Five Countries,* Ithaca: ILR Press, 1996.

2. Kelly Quinn, "Did Somebody Say McMerger?" *The Organizer* Electronic Edition, August 1998, Vol. 3, No. 2, OCAW Local 1-675, www.geocities.com/soho/atrium/5258/.

3. UAW Constitution, Article 19, Section 6.

4. UE website: www.ranknfile-ue.org/uewho.html. December 23, 1998.

5. Gary Becker, "Want to Try to Squelch Corruption? Try Passing Out Raises," *Business Week,* November 3, 1997, p. 26.

6. Remarks of Secretary-Treasurer James J. Matles at 31st UE Convention, June 9, 1966 (in UE pamphlet "What Should Union Officials Be Paid?" p. 8).

7. UAW v. Local Union 599 UAW, Region 1C (PRB Case 942, decision issued March 26, 1992) pp. 6-7.

8. Plyer v. Local 599 UAW, PRB Case No. 238 (1961), reaffirmed in PRB Case 942, p. 238.

9. This can be good for the members if the appeals procedure itself works well. Otherwise, the main effect is to shield the companies from legal action by union members. The contract provision was developed after the courts ruled that requirements that union members exhaust internal remedies were only relevant if the internal remedy could change the result. *(Clayton v. UAW,* 451 US 679 1981).

10. Lesa Soncrant v. Local Union 1889, UAW Region 2B (PRB Case No. 1177, decision issued October 1, 1997) p. 5.

11. For a longer discussion on this see Mike Parker, "Appealing for Democracy," *New Labor Forum,* Fall/Winter 1998.

8. International Conventions and Elections

The larger the organization, the harder it is to make it democratic; this certainly applies to unions. For most members, international or national union leaders seem beyond their influence. Yet the international is the face of the union to most of the world, and the international's effectiveness makes a difference in all members' day-to-day work life.

This is most obvious for those who work for a national or multinational corporation, or whose industry is covered by a pattern labor agreement. Among truck-driving Teamsters, the connection was clear when TDU started in the 1970s because members were upset with national contract bargaining. Members of the New Directions Movement in the UAW likewise could organize against the international's pro-team-concept policies, which affect auto workers daily. In the UFCW, the reform caucus REAP (Research, Education, Advocacy, People) started among meatpackers who saw their pattern contracts—bargained by the international—on a fast downslide; later some of the retail clerks, who are roughly half of the union, began to agree that the same policies at the top were hurting their regional and local bargaining.

In unions where most bargaining is handled locally, it's more difficult for reformers to convince members that they should get involved in a movement to make changes at the top. But democratic reforms at the international level would indeed affect working conditions.

For one thing, even where employers are local, as with city governments, the policies set at the top can determine how the local union reacts. When management wants to privatize, does the international advocate trying to underbid the contractor, or building a community coalition? On which strategy, pursued locally, can local officers get help through literature, staff time, or training?

Second, autocratic international officers depend for support on a network of local officers who are directly responsible for contracts. In exchange for local officers' support, international leaders provide subsidies, staff, and backing on jurisdictional questions or in case internal charges are filed. They may also agree to "local autonomy" in the form of not sending international auditors to check the local's books. If a reform administration withheld these favors—or, better yet, started aggressively promoting member involvement—it could loosen a local leader's grip on office and/or open the door for local members to make changes on their own. For example, as described in Chapter 1, the reform administration in the Teamsters international didn't count on old guard local officers to mobilize members for the UPS contract campaign. The international hired rank and file UPS workers as campaign organizers and sent them on the road. Headquarters sent bargaining updates to every UPSer's home and videos to all the stewards to share with co-workers. Campaign paraphernalia was sent first to the locals and then if necessary to rank and file activists.

Nearly every major U.S. union operates like a one-party state. The leadership may or may not form an official organization, like the Administration Caucus in the UAW. Either way, international officials with their supporters in the locals cooperate to maintain a tight grip. How do these ruling parties maintain their control?

One reason they can do so is the sheer size of the job of overhauling an international. Headquarters controls the publications, the staff, the convention agendas. Reformers have far fewer resources. The fact that so few unions have a lasting national opposition caucus—much less one that's won big victories—is testament to the difficulty of the challenge. And, as we will argue below, many international union constitutions are not designed for democracy. A third factor is international officers' selective use of staffers, grievance handling, and bargaining services to reward friends and punish those who step out of line.

For example, the UAW International leadership appoints thousands of union representatives and holders of full-time positions in labor-management programs. In the Teamsters, before reformers were elected in 1991, the regional and national grievance panels—half-union, half-employer committees—were used to remove many reformers who were fired under false pretenses; some panels remain a mixed-bag and the potential for such retribution still exists. The UFCW leadership has been known to help local officers who are in jeopardy from rank and file reformers by imposing trusteeships and excluding locals from pattern bargaining.

This book won't go into the nuts and bolts of building a national or international reform caucus. Circumstances in different unions vary too much. Here we'll look only at two tools reformers have used—conventions and elections for officers—and the arguments for and against different systems.

Conventions

Most international conventions function as a rubber-stamp on top leaders' policies. How can that happen?

The first step to a rubber-stamp convention is delegate elections that aren't based on real convention issues. Though it need not be the case, usually the international leadership determines the key decisions to be voted on at the convention. But are these announced to the ranks before they elect their delegates? Are candidates for delegate expected to say how they would vote on the important questions? Not at all. Usually voters know next to nothing about what questions delegates will decide, nor do delegate candidates announce their stance on issues or candidates in advance. There is no opportunity for accountability to the members.

The United Electrical Workers (UE) encourages delegates' accountability by giving them a reason to report to local members after the convention: locals have the right to vote to overturn convention decisions. It's very unlikely this would happen, but the principle is there that convention decisions should be brought home and discussed.

In a few unions, lack of accountability is exaggerated by the fact that many delegates are not elected to that position at all; they are local officers who are automatically delegates by virtue of their position. Where locals may choose through their bylaws to elect dele-

Quickie Election 'a Sham' at IBEW Convention

[The following description of the IBEW's 1996 convention is excerpted from *Union Democracy Review,* the newsletter of the Association for Union Democracy, issue 109, November 1996.]

When the IBEW convention opened around 9:00 a.m. on Monday, September 16, in Philadelphia, the delegates were lulled into a mood of comfortable normality by the usual boilerplate routine: the Higgins invocation, the host VP speech, the Mayor, the building trades rep, the state AFL-CIO honcho, plus a Marine marching band. Then, softened into relaxed inattention by an inspirational entertainment show, the delegates were poorly prepared for the sudden acceleration of unexpected events that soon followed. It must have been around 10:30 when J.J. Barry, international president, took over the podium to trigger his secretly crafted plan to paralyze his critics and opponents.

Barry moved so quickly that even his own supporters who knew what was coming were taken by surprise. The rules committee came forward: ten procedural points plus 14 sub-points, offering what seemed to be a normal lengthy agenda, except for one little joker providing for the election of top officers as a "special order of business" that same first day. The delegates did not realize that the election would begin within minutes after the adoption of those rules. There was a fast "discussion": four speakers, all for the rules, let's get the election over with and get down to the serious convention business, no one recognized to speak against, question called, rules adopted, bang bang. Barry announces that the election will now take place, and turns the chair over to VP Ed Hill to conduct the operation.

But it went so fast, no one is ready. The chair calls upon Delegate Comer, who is supposed to nominate Barry, but he isn't there. Somewhat flustered, the chair calls upon Tommy Van Arsdale to do the honors, but someone yells out that he is not a delegate. The chair switches: will Ed Cleary come to the podium? But he is not there either. Finally they find some other living body actually present. By this time most of the five minutes allotted for Barry's nominator have expired. In half a minute, Barry is formally nominated.

gates, they should do so. If the international constitution requires local officers to serve as delegates, as in the UFCW, these officers should organize discussions of convention issues in advance, get

Then delegate Duane Moore of Local 477 is recognized, the first oppositionist to get the floor. He was originally supposed to nominate the insurgent candidate, Mike Lucas, to run against Barry. But Moore announces that because the opposition has had no chance to present its views on anything to the convention, he makes no nomination and Lucas will not run. "This is a sham and not a democracy at all," he concludes.

Chairman Hill calls for other nominations. None. International Secretary Jack Moore tries to make a motion to cast one unanimous ballot for Barry, the unopposed candidate, but he is stopped. Puzzled, he asks, "Will there be a ballot with nobody on it but President Barry?" Confusion. The convention comes to a brief halt while the ruling powers hold their discussion off the record. The convention comes back to order and the chair announces that, willy nilly, Lucas will be forced onto the ballot. It's now about 11:00. Effectively the big election is over, although it takes a little more time to go through the motions of voting by open, recorded, non-secret, electronic balloting. Barry is elected with a weighted vote of 587,263. Lucas, the un-nominated candidate-despite-himself, gets 117,381, about 16.5 percent of the total.

What's The Hurry?

Why the unseemly rush to install Barry as the first major order of business of the very first session of the very first day before the delegates could catch a breath? For one thing, it seems obvious that the administration was determined to avoid a secret ballot election.

Lucas's challenge had rallied a surprising extent of openly expressed support from IBEW locals. Moreover, many locals supported his position on issues that would presumably come to the floor. Several locals had endorsed resolutions for a secret ballot. If, before the election, there had been a serious discussion on issues and then a secret ballot, Lucas would have had a chance to upset the administration and win the election. Barry's supporters would not risk it.

Apparently, the election railroad at the convention was the last straw. Resisting administration pressures, the delegates voted finally to amend the constitution to provide for a secret ballot in future elections.

input from members, and then report back how they voted.

Whether or not they have to run for delegate, local leaders usually are delegates; thus most conventions can be considered a gathering of local officers. If most local officers are honest and well-meaning, why do they tolerate the top-down, often self-serving control of many international leaders?

Perhaps we should ask "why not?" If a local leader sticks his neck out opposing this or that proposal from the international leadership, he takes a big risk for little reward. The risk is retribution, through withdrawn support or worse, which may have a harsher impact on his members than on the officer. If there's no organized national reform movement in the union, the gain, a better international union, seems unlikely anyway. To most local officers, even if they disagree with the international's direction, it's just not worth it to put up a challenge. And, of course, many local officers either agree with the international leadership's direction or benefit personally from their international's current distribution of resources (appointments, salaries, power to quell dissident members).

Secret Ballots at Conventions

It's easy to make a case against secret ballots at conventions: delegates should take responsibility for the decisions they make, and be held accountable to the folks back home. But the question of secret ballots arises from time to time among reformers, as a way to lessen the possibility of intimidation (or vote buying) by those in power. And the question arose for delegates to the National Education Association's 1998 Representative Assembly (convention). NEA delegates have secret ballot voting on leadership and bylaws; concern about proposed open balloting at conventions was part of the reason they rejected the plan that year for merging with the American Federation of Teachers.

In the International Brotherhood of Electrical Workers, reformers argued that international officers had maintained their power by being able to retaliate against individuals and locals that voted against them. They made a secret ballot one of their key planks— and won (see the box).

That the IBEW incumbents have no use for democracy is clear. For now the secret ballot provides an opening for building the movement. This is a good example of reformers' assessing democratic procedures in a non-abstract way: looking at the immediate impact, while also recognizing the potentially damaging long-term effects—because a secret ballot at conventions is a poor idea in general.

Why? First, a secret ballot removes the members' ability to control their delegates by rewarding or punishing them for how they voted at the convention.

Second, it's not likely delegates can really keep their views hidden. At a convention where leadership is contested, delegates are asked to "declare" their support in many ways. Stickers or buttons are distributed; local leaders are asked and expected to endorse a candidate.

Also, each side proposes resolutions or constitutional changes that demonstrate the direction their candidates would take the union. At the Teamsters convention in 1996, for instance, Hoffa backers proposed changes aimed at weakening the international, while Carey's reform delegates backed a code of ethics for pension plan trustees. For the SEIU convention the same year, where a contested election for president was expected until the last weeks before the convention, Andy Stern's campaign for president was closely tied to the international's proposals on funding for organizing and political action. If we don't want all these votes on policy and direction to be held by secret ballot, it's difficult for delegates to avoid taking some public stand.

If they've been pressured to publicly take the incumbents' side, what force might push delegates to turn against the incumbents in a secret ballot? Their deeper convictions? Hopefully, yes. A more sure force would be the opinions of the members back home. But since the incumbents run the convention, they are more likely to know how secret ballots were cast than are members. Delegates can make wonderful statements for the consumption of their constituency, while proving to the higher-ups that they voted the "right" way. Under circumstances like this, a secret ballot could actually aid intimidation and vote buying.

National Elections: At the Convention or by the Members?

Should members vote directly for international officers, or should they vote for convention delegates, who in turn vote for the top officers? The issue is hotly debated. In unions that use the convention system, "members' right to vote" is often a central plank of reform groups. Top officers of most large unions, if confronted with the question, say the convention system is working better than would direct elections.

Some unions do, and many could, operate democratically with a convention system. But for most major U.S. unions, changing to a direct election for international officers would provide an opportunity to rebuild the union on the basis of member control.

The best known case of changing from a convention vote to direct election is the Teamsters. When the Justice Department sued the union under the Racketeer Influenced and Corrupt Organizations Act, part of the settlement struck between the old guard and the government was direct elections for the top leadership. The first such election, in 1991, allowed TDU and the Carey reform slate to win the membership vote and sweep the international offices, even though, that same year, they were able to win only about 15 percent of the convention delegate seats.

Some other unions that use direct elections are the Laborers, Machinists, Steelworkers, Mine Workers, and Postal Workers. Those that use convention elections include the UAW, SEIU, OCAW, UE, Communications Workers, Canadian Union of Postal Workers, and Canadian Auto Workers. These few examples illustrate that direct election of international officers in no way guarantees rank and file control.

In the Teamsters, democratic forces were able to use the government-ordered elections as an opportunity to take control of their union. But the elections by themselves—without a rank and file movement like TDU—would have, at best, removed some of the more blatant corruption but left standing an old guard bureaucracy. In Chapter 2 we describe how, by contrast, federally supervised elections in the Laborers, with no organized reform movement, produced little benefit for the members.

Similarly, direct elections in the Steelworkers or Machinists do not seem to stimulate, let alone guarantee, a democratic culture in these unions, any more than exists in the UAW, CWA, or SEIU (although direct election of district directors in the Steelworkers has contributed to more independence for district directors). Conversely, some unions that use the convention system—UE, OCAW, CUPW—are among the more democratic unions, not because of their election method but because of other reasons that have promoted a more democratic culture.

Arguments for the Convention System, and Responses

1. It's too hard for rank and file members to know or observe the functioning of top officers or candidates. National media with its bias against labor cannot be counted on for accurate information. How can members make informed choices? At least convention delegates have the opportunity to discuss issues with each other and evaluate the candidates firsthand.

2. Direct national elections put a premium on publicity and money. This could lead to the influence of corrupt forces outside the union. A recent example is the financing scandal in the Carey campaign for Teamsters president. Despite the reform nature of the Carey administration, the need to counter the old guard's easy access to money opened a segment of the Carey campaign to corrupt practices.

3. Direct election undermines the authority of convention delegates. If you want a convention to have power and set policy, then you want the delegates to choose and control the people who will implement the policies.

4. Dissidents can campaign for convention delegate instead of for top offices, and then elect their candidates at the convention. If the members want a change, they can vote for convention delegates who will make change.

5. The members will not vote for women or minorities, so there will be no way to have diversity in the leadership.

A convention system made more sense years ago when many unions originally established their structures. Back then, travel and long distance communications were costly and slow. Unions had developed primarily around local or plant concerns. Bargaining was local. With national unions serving more as federations, their officers seemed distant and of secondary importance to most members. Even though national corporations had become more important by the time the CIO unions were founded, many still took on the old structures.

Today the issues facing unions—contracting out, downsizing, whipsawing—are common to almost all workplaces in an industry, and unions often confront national or international companies that have global strategies. The link between national politics and the fate of unions is also stronger. Since the actions of national unions directly affect members' work lives, choosing their own top leaders becomes a matter of immediate interest to members, and a good way to draw them into the life of the union.

Responding to the arguments above:

1. The convention system was set up before national radio, television, video tapes, web sites, and easy national travel, when it truly was harder for members to have knowledge of candidates and issues within unions. (By contrast the International Typographers Union, which started direct elections in the 1890's, had the benefits of a literate workforce, easy access to printed communications, and a highly mobile membership.[1])

Voters today can decide on the big issues without eyeballing the candidates personally.

Nor does the convention system guarantee that delegates get a thorough look at candidates and platforms. At the 1992 UAW convention, for instance, the reform caucus New Directions' candidate for president, Jerry Tucker, was not allowed on the convention floor nor permitted to address the delegates whose votes he was courting.

2. It's true that direct elections cost money. The cost of printing and mailing ballots is not so large; the bigger expense is the campaigns. A national or international campaign for office is a major organizational and fundraising project. There is a danger of external forces—employers or potential vendors—getting involved in direct election campaigns, just as there is a danger of employer influence in most facets of union life (including a tightly contested convention vote: employers illegally intervened in many Teamsters delegate races in 1991 and 1996). Education and watchful eyes among the members, though, are healthier antidotes than shutting down a potentially democratic process altogether.

The possibility of corruption by money is not really the question here. It's actually easier to buy an election under the convention system, because those with goodies to distribute can buy off a few delegates more easily than the whole membership.

Also, a serious campaign for top offices under the convention system could cost just as much money as a direct election. The reform movement could take its campaign to the members by running for delegates in every local; the incumbents would of course mount a counter-campaign. The UAW New Directions Movement attempted such a national campaign for president in 1992, and to counter it the incumbents' Administration Caucus asked each staffer to donate $500 to their campaign. The money argument against direct elections is really an argument against any campaign at all that goes to the members.

3. The argument about preserving delegates' authority is made to convention delegates themselves—the ones who have to vote on changing election methods. It carries weight with that audience, who like to hear that they've made the trip to Las Vegas for some reason other than partying, but not with rank and filers. Few union conventions act as real legislative meetings. Most are highly orchestrated affairs with plenty of fluff, entertainers, and politicians designed to fill up the sessions. No-holds-barred debate over the issues facing the union is more likely on the shop floor than on the convention floor, if members have the chance to choose between two truly different alternatives.

4. While such a union-wide campaign for delegate seats is possible, it puts an unnecessary layer between a member's opinion and her vote. In addition, trying to run a national candidate through delegate races means the campaign must have people willing to run in every local, or most of them. With direct election, members can vote for the opposition candidate even if the campaign organization is not yet strong in their local.

5. Leaving aside the fact that a large percentage of union members *are* women or minorities, the argument that direct elections will not see to these groups' needs is really only one form of the more fundamental argument that the membership is ignorant, easily swayed by gossip and personality, and easily set against other members. The grain of truth is that racism and sexism do exist among union ranks. But this argument misses completely one of the virtues of democracy: election struggles tend to force people to look for support where they normally might not, and form political coalitions. The result is that where minorities or sections of the membership that have been traditionally left out organize themselves, they are generally sought after for leadership slates. It's just good campaign strategy to have a slate of candidates that reflects the membership, and not to write off the votes of racial or gender minorities.

One of the arguments for a direct election is that it seems like a natural, paralleling elections for national office in the U.S. In 1992, the *Detroit Free Press* did a poll of 150 Detroit-area UAW members and found 92 percent in favor of direct elections, or "referendum vote" as it's called in the UAW. (That same year, UAW delegates passed a resolution reaffirming the convention system; resolutions from 21 locals for referendum voting didn't get past the resolutions committee.) Barb Eastman, a New Directions member from Flint, Michigan, told *Labor Notes,* "My members want referendum vote for two reasons: so they can vote [then-president Owen] Bieber out, and because they feel like, 'Why *shouldn't* we have it?'"

Finally, one of the reasons a direct election can contribute toward democracy, as it did in the Teamsters, is simply that it shakes up the system. Many unions have become bureaucratized around their current methods, combined with liberal patronage for those who are loyal and punishment for those in opposition. In this context a thoroughgoing overhaul of the procedure provides a more equal playing field for all forces and opens members' minds about new possibilities for involvement. The demand for direct elections can be an important tool in a movement for reform, although not a substitute for a movement.

At the same time democratic culture is a product of many things, not just election procedures. Where a union has established leadership accountability with a convention system, there may be other factors more worthy of attention—say developing forums for ongoing debate of issues, or including rank and filers on national bargaining committees—rather than restructuring elections in the name of abstract principles.

Outnumbered: Reformers at an "Old Guard" Convention

Attending an international convention as a reform-minded delegate can be pretty frustrating. Your arguments are so clear and common-sensical. Why aren't more delegates swayed to your side?

Though there's plenty of wheeling and dealing that goes on at international conventions, real union politics goes on back home. Delegates who arrive loyal to the top union officialdom are not likely to change—no matter the eloquence of floor speeches for reform. Those committed to pro-democracy reforms will stay that way unless the pressure from staff and officials is more intense than the pressure of their members' expectations.

So how can reformers make use of conventions? The idea that the most important consideration in convention activity is the members back home leads to a couple of guidelines.

For one, reform delegates should keep their program for the convention simple. Choose one or two issues to push. That makes it easy for the members to understand what you're trying to do and to see what the result was. It's also a lot easier for you to talk to members about how your proposals will help them get power on the job (the whole point!). Instead of a leaflet that discusses 27 different amendments, concentrate on a message like "International Officials Block Right to Vote on Contracts!" As always, be careful that your literature is about building workplace power. "International Officials Misuse Robert's Rules" will draw yawns.

Second, the convention may allow you to meet delegates from other locals who share your viewpoint. They may be making proposals similar to what your group supports, or you may notice a certain delegation cheering for your speakers. Those are important people to make contact with for the future, but don't count on being able to form coalitions for this convention that weren't begun before the first gavel. That happens, but not often.

If the main audience for your convention is the members back home, why take the (often considerable) effort to speak from the floor? Two reasons: a good speech from the floor helps remind reform delegates why they're doing the right thing, which helps them resist the pressure they may be facing from the international. Floor debate also helps your group plan how they'll talk to the members back home about the outcome.

At the Teamsters' 1996 convention, for instance, a proposal was made to drop the word "Brotherhood" from the international's official name. Backers talked about inclusion, about recognizing and welcoming women as full-fledged Teamsters. Opponents warned about the expense of ordering new stationery. In the end, the proposal was defeated. But reform leaders, especially among flight attendants, food processors, and office workers, had a good synopsis of the two sides' view of women members.

International conventions can be demoralizing for reformers. Though many people may tell you in the hallway they're glad you're speaking out, top leaders may win votes by a shockingly large majority. But if you can showcase a few key issues, the convention process can help a reform caucus show they're in better touch with the members than are the leadership and their supporters. That will build members' power in the long run.

Notes

1. Seymour Martin Lipset, Martin Trow, and James Coleman, *Union Democracy: the Internal Politics of the International Typographers Union,* Garden City, NY: Doubleday, 1962, p. 42.

Appendix 1.
Being Effective at
Union Meetings
(When the Officers Think
They Own the Union)

In a democratic union meeting the chairperson encourages participation and fairness and, most of all, makes it possible for the members to make the important decisions. The chairperson uses the rules to make it easier for people to have their say. This appendix is for members of unions where, in contrast, the leaders think the union belongs to them. They don't like union meetings. They try to keep those who disagree with them from participating, and they or their favorites do most of the speaking. They use the rules to try to intimidate and confuse members, and misuse the rules when convenient to prevent the members from making decisions the officers don't like.

When your local is run this way, you cannot expect simply to show up and have your issues fairly heard and voted on. You need to make special preparations in advance: choose your issue and define your goals for the meeting; organize support; become familiar with the rules governing the meeting; and prepare for speaking—who will speak about which points. Of course, the union meeting should be just one part of your overall strategy for building your group—the more important organizing will go on back at work.

Let's take a look at each of these items.

Define Your Goals: Pick One or Two Issues

A smart local officer can label someone who always has a long list of complaints as a crank, a nut, or (worst of all) a politician. If you bring up all the changes your union needs, you are likely to be talking about matters that many people in the local know nothing about. This makes it easy for officers to pick your weakest or least understood issue to focus on and turn the majority against you.

Therefore, to prepare for a union meeting, pick one or two issues that have wide support or directly affect a lot of people. If you only complain about technical violations of the bylaws you may get a reputation as a nitpicker.

Be sure that you raise positive issues (propose a holiday party for the kids, an organizing drive at a competitor, a contract demand for more relief workers) as well as negative ones (questionable union expenditures). You don't want a reputation of just being a naysayer, of opposing the officials on everything just because you are against them, or an "out-of-office politician." In fact, sometimes the most effective approach is to build your proposals around something good that your officers have written or an international union policy ("organizing is job one").

Focusing on one or two topics can sometimes cause problems in a group if people think you are concerned only with one leader's favorite issue. In your group you should discuss which issues to bring up, and decide democratically.

You and your supporters should be clear on your goals for the meeting. Especially when you are just getting started, your goal may be simply to raise an issue so that members can find out about it. Or you may just want to put the union leadership on the spot so they can't claim later that they didn't know about a problem. It takes time to build support, and often many meetings. You may accomplish a lot even without winning a motion.

Organizing Support

The key to winning anything at a union meeting is simple: numbers. Numbers of people voting on your side, numbers of people speaking on your side, and numbers of people who understand your issue and will create a climate of interest and support at the meeting.

To get people to the meeting, put out a leaflet, post notices, phone-tree, and, most important, talk one-and-one. Tell members what you propose to bring up at the meeting, how it affects them, and why you need their support. You may want to emphasize that you are only asking for a small commitment; you may want to warn them that the wrangling at the meeting may be unpleasant, but it will be worth it if we can get our issue passed.

While there may be an occasional advantage to springing your issue on the meeting as a "surprise," this is seldom effective. Surprises make it impossible to organize in advance and thus to really get people to understand what's at stake. Of course, one way undemocratic officials hold onto power is through "surprises." So one of the jobs of your group is to anticipate the issues that will be brought up by the officials and give them advance publicity. This way the members are better prepared for the meeting, and you get the respect for informing them.

When you organize the activists in your group or the members with a particular concern about the issue, the secret is to make sure that everyone has a job. Here is a list of jobs to distribute:

> Prepare the flyer explaining the issue
>
> Distribute the flyer
>
> Contact other members and encourage them to attend the meeting; for example, set up a phone tree
>
> Prepare fact sheets, copies of contract language, or other materials for the meeting
>
> Distribute these at the meeting
>
> Make the motion
>
> Second the motion
>
> Speak on different aspects of the motion
>
> Watch the rules for violations

If you spread these jobs out you will start with a solid core who cannot easily be ignored.

Rules and Parliamentary Procedure

Although it may not be apparent, the basic idea behind parliamentary procedure is to allow the body to take action. It is a democratic idea, because it provides a way for large groups to make a decision that counts. Without this approach, many meetings would consist of nothing but aimless discussions that would go on and on and resolve nothing. Then, later, a small group would make the real decisions.

It is for this reason that all the rules in parliamentary procedure are built around the "motion." It is by using motions that you get things done at a meeting.

Sometimes people will say, "We complained about that problem at the last two meetings, but nothing was done." Of course nothing was done, because no motion was put on the floor. No vote was taken that would have directed the executive board to take action by a specific date and report back to the membership by another specific date, for example.

You should not always seek to put forward a motion, however. If your support is low, you might just make a suggestion to the executive board. You may plan to ask good questions about some matter. These are questions of tactics. You need to get a feel for when to press ahead with a motion and when to have more modest goals.

Check to make sure you know of any special procedures for getting issues heard at membership meetings. Some locals may require advance notification to the executive board, or all motions in writing, or a first reading of a motion at one meeting followed by discussion and voting at the next.

Check your local bylaws for anything that might be relevant. You may have more rights than you think.

Here are some tips on Robert's Rules for those who are operating from the floor. See also Appendix 3.

• The maker of the motion gets to speak first on the motion.

This rule is in Robert's Rules of Order Revised (#3). If the chairman has the habit of immediately speaking to any motion put on the floor, or calling on a favorite, or just cutting off debate, it is useful to know this rule. The same section of Robert's also makes clear that a person cannot speak a second time while someone who has not spoken wishes to speak.

• An appeal of the decision of the chair can reverse a ruling that you are "out of order."

If you are ruled out of order unjustly, this is your basic remedy. Remember, it is worthless to try to overrule the chair if you do not have the votes. But if you do have support, this rule can help make the point that you won't accept arbitrary rulings lightly. (See Appendix 3, but many local bylaws have specific procedures on this.)

• Be careful on reports.

If the meeting "approves the minutes" or "report" of the executive board or any other committee, you are approving whatever is included in those reports. If the Building Committee, for instance, recommends building a new union hall and their report is approved, then the body has authorized the local tó spend the money for a new building. In most cases where the membership meeting has the right to overrule an action of a board or committee, this is the place to do it.

What's more, you can move to amend the report of a committee or a recommendation of the executive board, as a way of bringing up your issue. Suppose that the report says, "The executive board appointed Kelly to be sent to the skilled trades conference." You may move to amend the report to say that two trades people should be sent, and that they should be elected by the membership meeting. You can also build on what the board has included in its report. For example, the board's report might mention that it received and filed a letter from a local on strike, requesting support. You might amend the report to contribute a certain amount of money to the strikers.

Sometimes you can use the reports that are given at the beginning of the meeting to your advantage. For example, if your local has a regular agenda point called "Communication" or "Correspondence," you can get your issue brought up on the floor simply by writing a letter to the executive board on that topic.

• Don't get wrapped up in the rules.

It could create the impression that you or your group is concerned with trivial matters. Others may think you are just a show-off or some kind of politician. Use your knowledge of the rules sparingly.

The best policy is for your group to have one or two parliamentary experts—people who make it their hobby to know the rules, bring a copy of them to the meeting, and are able to back up challenges to the arbitrary actions of the chair if the occasion arises. This is one of the jobs to assign when you are preparing for meetings.

Appendix 2.
Leading a
Membership Meeting

This appendix is for local officers who want their union meetings to involve the members and to be working meetings that set the stage for action. A successful meeting requires far more than a strong chair who knows Robert's Rules of Order. Most of all, an effective meeting requires planning. For more pointers, see also the section on membership meetings in Chapter 4.

A good union meeting requires several elements:

1. A core leadership group that plans how to make the meeting work

This could be the executive board, or, if the union is polarized into non-cooperating factions, then the majority faction and its supporters must do the planning and take responsibility for providing leadership during the meeting itself.

2. A set of clear goals for each meeting, prepared by the leadership core

Hold the discussion of goals well before each meeting.

Content Goals

1. What are the critical issues that must be addressed, for example, updates on contract campaigns, a move by management, rumors? These may or may not require motions. If the meeting is focusing

on a particular segment of the membership this month, what are the issues relevant to them?

2. What can we expect that other members will raise? How should these be handled?

3. What important decisions must be made at the meeting?

4. What activities/actions will follow from the meeting? The meeting should adopt or continue a plan that includes useful activities for all interested members, including, for example, fact-finding, petition gathering, phonebanking/communication, leaflet distribution, selling raffle tickets, group grievance, shop floor action.

Process Goals

While "process"—how well the meeting runs and feels—cannot be a substitute for content that addresses members' needs, how that content is handled often makes a big difference in how much members are willing to be involved and in how much control they have. Different goals require different processes: A meeting taking a strike vote should emphasize unity and determination. A meeting hearing the first reading of proposed contract demands should emphasize breadth of ideas and imagination.

Here are some possible process goals for union meetings:

Members have both the sense and the reality that they are making critical decisions.

Members get important information.

New members participate.

Sectors not previously involved participate.

There's a sense of unity; members are fired up.

There's a sense of democratic organization; minority points of view are heard and debated.

Members are recognized for work they've done.

3. Advance planning

a. Use the network of natural leaders, the stewards, e-mail, and the union website to get out information on the meeting in advance—the reasons that members should be there.

b. Most reports do not have to be read at the meeting. Print them up, distribute them in the workplace in advance so members can discuss them. Use meeting time for questions or amendments.

c. Put the important items first on the agenda.

d. Be sure there is a "New Concerns" time on the agenda where members may get up and state a concern without having to formulate a motion. The officers write down the problem and get back to the member both personally and at the next meeting in announcements or a report.

e. Plan for a meeting short enough so that it ends with social

Prioritizing Agenda Items

In a healthy union any number of issues could come up at the monthly meeting. Preparing a good agenda that deals with the most important issues assures members will participate on those issues. Suppose we have 20 possible items to deal with in one hour. Consider all the ways we could deal with this problem on the spot:

1. Robert's Rules: take them in the order that the makers of the motions are recognized. Or spend time on making and passing motions to suspend the rules.
2. Random: Assign each a number and draw lots.
3. Equal time: Assign each three minutes for total discussion and voting.
4. Ignore the time limit: Extend the time of the session and take time away from something else.

All of these are unsatisfactory and at least in some sense unfair. The worst thing to do is to use most of the precious hour trying to decide which issues should be taken up. The best procedure is to do some preplanning and prescreening of motions. Then other alternatives become possible:

5. Combine motions that are similar.
6. Consider together motions that are addressed to the same subject.
7. Prioritize the motions, to tackle the most important first or for longer times.
8. Sample different issues, say one important to each section of the membership.
9. Refer some motions to committees, and some to individuals for action.
10. Allow more time for some motions and less time for others.

Prescreening of this sort is leadership. To be effective, it must be done by bodies respected by the members, preferably elected leaders such as the executive board, but possibly special bodies such as agenda committees or resolutions committees.

In sorting out meeting priorities, planners must consider both how important something is and how controversial it is. Very important items must be dealt with, but it's possible they won't take much meeting time if most members are in agreement. Things that are both important and controversial require much more discussion time.

time afterward. This gives members the opportunity to firm up what they have to do and to meet one another. A meeting that dribbles out means most people will not be certain what their ongoing role is, and it is simply demoralizing for those remaining to the end.

f. Invite guests from sister unions in the company or industry and introduce them. Just the presence of such guests helps to remind members of the bigger picture.

g. Assign people to make reports, motions, and supporting statements for each critical content point on the agenda. If necessary, assign floor leaders to handle debate and amendments on particular issues.

In addition, check with known spokespeople for opposing points of view on the questions coming up, and with others whose position is not known but who should be consulted or who should be encouraged to speak. Get agreement on procedure and times. Make sure time is allowed for newcomers and others who may wish to speak on the key points.

h. Figure out what written materials in advance or at the meeting would help members understand the issues (e.g., proposed agenda, contract proposals, motions).

i. Make sure the facilities are checked out: sound system, chart pads, seating, overhead or other audiovisual equipment, beverages and food.

j. If you are inexperienced or expect a tough meeting, walk through some scenarios (see sample exercises at the end).

4. Good chairing

Preparation is essential to a good meeting, but once the meeting starts, the chairperson is critical. The chair is never just an impartial, neutral rule-enforcer. Rather the chair has to continue all the filtering and prioritizing functions that were started before the meeting. The chair must be the leader of the meeting, looking for ways to help the meeting and the union reach its goals and for ways to involve members in the speaking and decisions. When the meeting is getting off the subject or dragging, the chair's job is to get the meeting back on course and move on. When things get complicated, propose a procedure to simplify. When the debate is sharp and focused, it's up to the chair to remind members of their common aims and the unity that must result from the meeting. No matter how heated or interesting the discussion may seem, it is up to the chair to remember that there are members perhaps attending their first union meeting who may not understand the issues, the in-group jargon, or the procedures.

5. Good leading from others than the chair

If you are a leader of the core group, even if you are not chairing there is a lot you can do to make the meeting effective. See that those who had assignments from the pre-meeting planning take care of them. Pay attention to the content of the meeting and be prepared with amendments or motions. Remember that the person who is chairing may be preoccupied with procedure and needs to avoid too much intervention on content. Help set the tone of the meeting by paying attention, helping keep the discussion on track, and applauding appropriately.

Help out when there is trouble by going quietly to the members who seem to be having difficulties with a procedure. Show them the best way to accomplish what they want.

Unless you are in fundamental disagreement with the way the chair is doing something, support the chair. As you know, it is a hard enough job. Often there is more than one good way of doing something. Sometimes it is better to do things the second-best way than to create additional confusion by proposing the best way.

Rules and the Chair

Your bylaws probably spell some out meeting rules, including quorums and the procedure for removing unruly members. Most bylaws additionally specify Robert's Rules of Order except where there is a conflict with other portions of the bylaws. In Chapter 4 we discussed some of the problems with Robert's. If you are stuck with Robert's, check out Appendix 3, so you can use the rules defensively, if necessary.

A good chair should:

1. Ignore the technicalities as much as possible.

The best course is to use and modify in a democratic fashion whatever seems to be the tradition in your union. If seconds are required, ask for seconds. If debate is loose, let it be. Look at the "Simplified Rules of Order" in Appendix 4. They are close enough to Robert's to be familiar, and most people will find them fair.

The ideal would be to keep discussion fairly informal and look for consensus. When there is disagreement over an issue, that is when more formal procedures—motions, amendments, and more structured discussion—are necessary.

Fairness is the key to good chairing. If the members believe you are being fair, they will back you. Suppose a sticky parliamentary situation comes up. The best way to handle it is not to entertain motions to suspend the rules, or to cite some obscure (to most) rule from Robert's, but to simply say:

> I think the fair way to handle this would be let Jane and John each present their point of view for three minutes each. Then we will vote to see which motion we will use as the basis of discussion and amendment. Does that make sense?

Read the membership. Depending on heads nodding, murmuring, expressions, you might ask someone specifically, "John, do you have a problem with that?" If people appear comfortable, you can say, "If there is no objection, that is what we will do." If there is some objection, but it does not seem to be big enough or serious enough to cause you to reconsider, simply say, "OK, as chair I will rule that this is our procedure. Does anyone wish to make a motion to appeal the ruling of the chair?"

This informal method does not contradict Robert's. But more than that, it is effective. Members appreciate it, because they can understand it. It wastes little time on procedure. And the results are almost always seen as fairer than bulldozing something through on a technicality.

2. Use the rules to help people.

Never use parliamentary procedure to show how smart you are or, worse, to make someone else feel foolish.

When you have to use a rule, always explain it. For example, if you have to rule someone out of order, explain how to do things properly. "Brother Jones, I am sorry but I have to rule your motion out of order. Right now we are discussing another motion, but I would suggest you raise that motion right after we have voted on this one."

3. Use "overruling the chair" as a procedure for smooth running.

Never let this seem to be a personal attack on you as the chair or even an unusual occurrence. Rather, you can use it to give the chair more flexibility in making key rulings, because you invite "overruling the chair" as the means to confirm membership support for your ruling. See Appendix 4 for details.

4. Keep the agenda moving.

Periodically, remind the body where they are on the agenda and what is scheduled to come up.

Have another person serve as timekeeper who will publicly signal speakers when they have one minute left. If there is a time limit for an agenda item, write the ending time on a chart pad below a clock, so everyone can see how the time is going.

If the meeting is large and you are using microphones, have speakers line up at microphones, but maintain the right to call on those who have not spoken much or who reflect a point of view not well represented in the discussion.

5. Encourage spirit in the meeting.

It is important that the meeting be able to express its sense of unity and solidarity. Applause, laughing together, or voting on issues is part of this expression and should not be cut short.

Ask for applause for recognition of particular contributions, particularly newly participating members.

All issues about the running of the meeting are about the rights of the members, never about your personal authority.

If a member is unruly, make it clear that this behavior is disrespectful to all the other members there and worse, prevents them from getting their important business done. Never get into a personal power struggle between you and the person who is out of order. If you have to ask someone to leave, put it to the body: "Shall we ask Henry to leave if he cannot take his seat and allow others to talk?"

6. Set a tone of fairness and openness.

The chair sets the tone. Be attentive to the speakers, be respectful, applaud. Try to keep the whispered conversations at the podium to a minimum, although they may occasionally be necessary.

Under Robert's the chairperson of a meeting technically has regular voting rights in either a secret ballot or an open vote. In the case of an open vote, the chairperson may vote whenever the vote would make a difference, not only to break a tie but also to create a tie (which means the motion is defeated). Similarly, the chair has the right to speak on substantive issues just like any other member.

In general, we recommend that the chairperson avoid both of these. It is hard to maintain the stature of a fair and unifying chairperson for the meeting as a whole while speaking as a strong partisan in a debate. Besides, it is hard to pay attention to the content while you are trying to think ahead about procedure and problems. It is best to take yourself out of the partisan role and leave that to others; it's a good way to develop leadership in others. If for particular issues you must be the partisan leader, then by all means let someone else take the chair.

Leading a Good Meeting: Exercises

The following exercises are designed to help a leadership core group prepare for situations that may arise at a large meeting.

Before doing these exercises, do two things: change the situations and issues so they are closer to your own. Then list and prioritize the core group's goals for the meeting (as described in the text).

These problems assume a sizeable local membership meeting or convention session, and that a member of the core group is the chair.

1. Speaking too long

John, a newly active member, is speaking much too long, describing something that happened at his work site. In his enthusiasm, he is not paying attention to the notices by the timekeeper that he has gone over. He keeps saying, "I am almost done" and keeps going. The meeting is beginning to get restless and a little bored. The member is an excellent activist and recruiter. You hate to cut him off.

As the chair how might you handle the situation?

As a non-chairing leader of the core group how might you help?

2. The disruptive member

George is mad about the defeat of a proposal that he supported earlier. He makes the same motion again. The chair rules him out of order. The member persists, saying that he has a democratic right to make the motion, and why are we acting like dictators, and he doesn't need to come to union meetings just to have people rule him out of order.

As the chair how might you handle the situation?

As a non-chairing leader of the core group how might you help?

3. Plans break down

The meeting is going well, with a good discussion on whether to adopt a letter of understanding with management to combine certain classifications and establish training. A member rises and accuses the chief negotiator (who is not the chairperson of the meeting) of taking a payoff to jam this down the members' throats. He claims to have proof, which he will present right now. There is now considerable doubt and confusion.

As the chair how might you handle the situation?

As a non-chairing leader of the core group how might you help?

4. Rules confusion

Jill makes a motion to support a rally in Washington, D.C. concerning some upcoming legislation. Another member makes a motion to table to the executive committee. Somebody immediately jumps up with a "point of order" and says that it is a violation of democracy not to let people vote on the original motion.

As the chair how might you handle the situation?

As a non-chairing leader of the core group how might you help?

5. Complicated motions

The Education Committee has presented a motion to publish an introductory booklet about the union for new members. A draft has been available. Several members rise to make various points about the booklet, mostly of a minor or detailed sort. One deals with an interpretation of the union's history. Another deals with the method for calling a steward, a third deals with functioning of union committees. Some are saying they want to amend the booklet. More members are lining up to comment on the draft.

The session is running long without an end in sight. While some are intensely interested in a particular point, many in the hall seem bored with the wandering discussion and would like to move on.

As the chair how might you handle the situation?

As a non-chairing leader of the core group how might you help?

Appendix 3.
Hints on Using Robert's Rules of Order

At the end of this appendix is a table summary of Robert's Rules of Order Revised,[1] handy in dealing with sticklers for particular rules.

Even where the bylaws specify Robert's Rules, in most situations we recommend that they be ignored in favor of common sense and fair play. We are not fans of Robert's Rules and argue that they are not very democratic. We also suggest better ways to approach chairing a meeting (see Chapter 4 and Appendix 2). Similarly, if you are dealing with a bureaucratic chairperson, we urge you not to rely on technicalities to protect your rights (see Appendix 1).

However, although we are not fans of Robert's Rules, it may be useful to know that he was a lot better than those who stand up at meetings and disrupt them by citing technicalities in his name.

Robert well understood the principle that the rules were made to assist the meeting, rather than the meeting being held to use the rules. In other words, if by tradition a union meeting allows back and forth discussion to clarify points, and this practice is evenly enforced, then this is more important than the fact that this violates Robert's procedure for discussion.

In fact, many of the additions and changes made in Robert's revised versions were answers to the self-styled parliamentary experts who liked to confuse meetings by showing off their expertise by introducing technicalities.

Here are some citations from Robert's Rules Revised that you could cite when the chair is running the meeting in a bureaucratic fashion or others are obstructing business, or, conversely, when you are chairing and trying to do it in a common sense way. These are from a section describing the duties of the chairperson.[2]

> No rules will take the place of tact and common sense on the part of the chairman.
>
> The chairman should not permit the object of a meeting to be defeated by a few factious persons using parliamentary forms with the evident object of obstructing business. In such a case he should refuse to entertain the dilatory or frivolous motion, and, if an appeal is taken he should entertain it, and, if [he is] sustained by a large majority he may afterwards refuse to entertain even an appeal made by the faction.
>
> Know all about parliamentary law, but do not try to show off your knowledge. Never be technical, or more strict than absolutely necessary for the good of the meeting.
>
> [It is the chair's duty] To assist in the expediting of business in every way compatible with the rights of the membership, as by allowing brief remarks when nondebatable motions are pending, if he thinks it advisable.

The Basics of Robert's

Knowing a few basic rules, if applied fairly and supplemented with common sense, will get you through running a meeting under Robert's most of the time. There is no provision in Robert's for a parliamentarian. If a member plays such a role, he or she is strictly advisory to the chairperson. It is the job of the chair to interpret the rules.

• Before discussion begins, a motion should be made.

> The maker of the motion gets to speak first.
>
> Only one motion (or amendment) is considered at a time.
>
> There may be an amendment to an amendment, but no further levels.

• A motion to limit debate or move to a vote ("call the question"), or a motion to suspend the rules:

> is not debatable.
>
> requires two-thirds to pass.

• A motion to table:

is not debatable.

requires a majority vote.

• A motion to refer a motion to a committee or to postpone it to a certain time:

is not a motion to table and is treated like an amendment.

Appealing the Ruling of the Chair

An important procedure from Robert's for the chairperson to understand is the motion to appeal the ruling of the chair (Robert's Rules Revised #21). Such appeals should be seen as normal procedures and not a big deal or a personal attack on the chairperson. This procedure is what allows the chairperson to be a strong leader while at the same time keeping control of the meeting in the hands of the members.

• Any ruling by the chair may be appealed.

• The appeal must be done immediately following the ruling of the chair, before other business (another motion or report) is considered.

• The chair is not required to step aside for an appeal and should not do so. (If the step-aside tradition exists in your local, discard it, so as to reduce the barriers to using this important procedure.)

• The rules for debating an appeal under Robert's are quite complicated and should be ignored. See "Other Motions" in Appendix 4 for a suggested procedure.

Notes

1. Henry M. Robert, *Robert's Rules of Order Revised,* New York: Morrow Quill Paperbacks, 1979 (note this is a direct reprint of the 1915 edition). Robert's Rules Revised is by far the most commonly used version, but there are also books in circulation based on the 1893 version or the 1990 "Newly Revised" edition. One useful attempt to simplify the rules is available on the web from the University of British Columbia Psychiatry Department www.psychiatry.ubc.ca/dept/rulesord/contents.htm. See also Mary A. Devries, *The New Robert's Rules of Order,* New York: Signet, 1989, which is an attempt at a modern-language version of the 1893 edition. The Robert's Rules Association (which backs the "Newly Revised" version) maintains a web site at www.robertsrules.com.

2. *Robert's Rules of Order Revised,* Section 58.

Basic Parliamentary Procedures[1]

Types of Motions (in order of precedence)

To Do This:	You Say This:
Adjourn meeting	"I move that we adjourn."
Call an intermission	"I move that we recess for ..."
Complain about heat,noise, etc.	"I rise to a question of privilege."
Temporarily suspend consideration	"I move to table the motion."
End debate and amendments	"I move the previous question."
Postpone discussion	"I move to postpone the discussion until..."
Give closer study to something	"I move to refer the matter to committee."
Amend or substitute a motion	"I move to amend the motion by..."
Introduce business	"I move that..."

More Motions (no order for those below)

To Do This:	You Say This:
Protest breach of rules or conduct	"I rise to a point of order."
Vote on a ruling of the chair	"I appeal the chair's decision."
Suspend rules temporarily	"I move to suspend the rules so that..."
Avoid considering a motion	"I object to consideration of this matter."
Call for a standing vote count	"I call for a division." or "Division!"
Request information	"Point of information."
Take up a matter previously tabled	"I move to take from the table."
Reconsider a hasty action[11]	"I move to reconsider the vote on..."

Notes to Table:

1. This summary sheet is adapted from one used at the 1998 Labor Party First Constitutional Convention.
2. If lost, may be reintroduced; if won, a motion to "Take from the table" can be introduced after passage of some business.
3. Unless vote on question has begun.
4. Unless the committee has already taken up the subject.
5. Unless the motion to be amended is not debatable.
6. Unless the chair submits to the assembly for decision.

(From Robert's Rules of Order Revised)

May you interrupt the speaker?	Do you need a second?	Is it debatable?	Can it be amended?	What vote is needed?	Can it be reconsidered?
No	Yes	No	No	Majority	No
No	Yes	No	Yes	Majority	No
Yes	No	No	No	No Vote	No
No	Yes	No	No	Majority	No[2]
No	Yes	No	No	Two-thirds	Yes[3]
No	Yes	Yes	Yes	Majority	Yes
No	Yes	Yes	Yes	Majority	Yes[4]
No	Yes	Yes[5]	Yes	Majority	Yes
No	Yes	Yes	Yes	Majority	Yes
Yes	No	No	No	No Vote[6]	No
Yes	Yes	Yes[7]	No	Majority	Yes
No	Yes	No	No	Two-thirds	No
Yes	No	No	No	Two-thirds[8]	Yes[9]
Yes	No	No	No	No Vote	No
Yes[10]	No	No	No	No Vote	No
No	Yes	No	No	Majority	No
Yes	Yes	Yes[12]	No	Majority	No

7. Except when relates to transgression of speaking rules, priority of business, or during a division, or if pending question is undebatable.
8. A two-thirds vote against consideration.
9. Only successful votes against consideration.
10. Only when clearly necessary.
11. May only be made by one who has voted on prevailing side and on same or next day.
12. Unless the motion to be reconsidered is not debatable or after previous question has been ordered.

Appendix 4.
Simplified
Rules of Order

Virtually all unions use Robert's Rules of Order. Yet few people who chair meetings understand and follow the rules, and only a tiny part of the membership understands more than the barest outline. This defeats the number-one democratic value of having rules—that everyone knows how to accomplish their goals and what to expect.

Here is a set of rules that will serve most local union meetings. They require only a few pages and can easily be distributed to all members. Although Robert's Rules is a whole book, the Simplified Rules include most of the rules and concepts that unions, in practice, actually use from Robert's. In addition, these rules emphasize democratic practices and remove some of the undemocratic features in Robert's. The emphasis is on helping members be involved.

It is usually not worth the affront to tradition to try to formally amend the local union bylaws to adopt these rules. Instead, the rules proposed here could be adopted as the informal "short form." In most locals, the interpretation of Robert's is quite loose anyway.

One way these rules are simpler than Robert's is through the consistent use of majority rule, rather than two-thirds or more, on all motions. (The exception is those issues on which the local bylaws require a larger majority, such as amending the bylaws.) Rules requiring more than a majority vote (two-thirds, three-fifths, three-quarters, unanimous) are intended to protect minority rights, but in practice, they multiply the power of already powerful minorities so much that they can thwart majority rule. In the long run, minority rights can be protected only by the care and respect of the majority. So in these Rules, instead of requiring a two-thirds vote to end debate, for example, a majority is allowed to do so, but only after the chair asks who and how many still wish to speak.

These same rules, slightly modified, can be used in very large meetings and conventions. The main changes would be (1) to require seconders for motions and when calling for a vote count, (2) to require submission of motions in advance, and (3) the use of a "convention committee" to sit throughout the convention and make recommendations for adjusting the agenda or other procedural problems. Teamsters for a Democratic Union (TDU) has used such a set of rules at its national conventions for twenty years.

Simplified Rules of Order

I. Purpose

The purpose of these rules is to allow the maximum democratic participation in meetings.

In meetings, as in all phases of union democracy, leadership is an essential part. The chair is the leader of the meeting. Therefore the main job of the chair is to help the meeting and its members conduct business and accomplish goals. The rules are a way to achieve these goals and are not an end unto themselves. Therefore the chair and meeting attenders should be allowed considerable flexibility in proposing implementation.

II. Agenda Preparation

A. The proposed meeting agenda will be made up by the executive board or through a procedure established by the board.

The proposed meeting agenda will include all motions submitted to the board by members in advance, unless the member withdraws the motion before the meeting. The board may recommend time limits and limits to debate on such motions as part of the agenda proposal. The executive board will set an order for the agenda as appropriate, except that items held over from previous meetings take precedence over any non-emergency new business.

The proposed agenda should include the full text of short motions and brief descriptions of longer motions and reports. The agenda may include proposals for procedures, such as time limits for specific discussions and how to handle voting.

B. Availability

The main points of the meeting will be provided with the announcement of the meeting, and the full meeting agenda will be available before the meeting.

Committee reports and background material should be available before the meeting.

C. Approval

Adoption of the agenda is the first order of business at the meeting. A member may propose to amend the agenda to change the order of business or the procedures. There may be one speaker for and one against each such amendment. The chair may allow a second person for and against.

Amendments and adoption of the agenda will be by majority vote.

III. Voting

A. Methods

1. Voice vote
2. Standing or hand vote (on request of any member)
3. Count. Because a vote count takes so much time, this will only be done when the chair finds a standing vote too close to call, or when at least ten percent of the members attending second the call for a count.

B. Definitions

Unless otherwise provided, all motions, both substantive and procedural, require a simple majority for passage.

A simple majority is achieved when more than 50 percent of those voting vote yes. (Examples: if there is a tie, the motion is defeated. If 31 vote yes, 30 vote no, and 50 abstain or do not vote, the motion is passed.)

IV. Main Motions

Unless another arrangement has been made, one motion is considered at a time. If someone makes an amendment, it will be discussed and voted on before going back to the main motion or other amendment. (There may be an amendment to an amendment, but there may be no third-level amendments.) However, when two or more motions or amendments are directed to the same point, procedures may be proposed by the executive board or chair, subject to approval by the meeting, to consider two or more motions or amendments together.

V. Discussion

A. Individual

Unless otherwise provided, each speaker will be limited to three minutes. No speaker will speak twice on the same motion when others are waiting to speak for the first time. The chair may ask someone who has already spoken to answer a question if it would clarify matters, and the person who made the motion may be allowed to sum up.

B. Total

Where no time limit for the total discussion has been proposed as part of the agenda, the chair must propose one.

C. Content

The discussion should be relevant to the motion on the floor.

VI. Other Motions

Like all other motions, those below require only a simple majority to pass. Where a motion is normally non-debatable, the chair may suggest some limited discussion if there appears to be substantial confusion in the body.

To Table

Not debatable.

Postpones further discussion and decision indefinitely (can be reintroduced in a very short time, or never). (Tabling is not used for sending a motion to a committee or for changing the time for consideration. See To Refer.)

To Refer (for example, to a committee) or To Postpone (to a specific time)

Limited debate (e.g., two speakers for and two against a proposal).

To Reconsider

Must be made by someone on the winning side.

Limited debate unless the procedure is suspended.

Procedural

For suggesting a procedure to handle a certain point (for example, to extend the time for discussion, or to consider two motions together).

Not debatable except on recommendation by chair.

To End Debate and Come to a Vote ("to call the question" or "to move the question")

Must be made by someone who has not yet spoken on this motion.

Not debatable.

Before taking the vote on ending debate, the chair must first ask for a show of hands of those who wish to speak, so members may make an informed decision.

To Adjourn or Recess

Not debatable.

The chair may ask or answer questions regarding pending business, to help members understand what they are cutting off if they adjourn the meeting.

The chair may entertain non-debatable motions for referring pending business before holding the vote on whether to adjourn.

The chair may entertain motions for setting the next meeting, if not already scheduled.

The chair must first ask for a hand showing of those not wishing to adjourn before taking the vote.

To Overrule the Chair (also called "to overturn" or "appeal the ruling of" the chair)

Must be called out immediately after the chair's ruling, before other business is conducted.

The chair does not have to step aside.

The chair should explain her ruling, the person appealing speaks, the chair responds. If the matter looks very controversial, the chair may take speakers for and against before her final reply.

The vote is then immediately taken in the following way: "All those in favor of upholding the ruling of the chair, please say 'aye.' Opposed, say 'no.'"

The chair plays an important role in keeping the meeting moving along by suggesting procedures and making rulings in ambiguous situations. Normally the chair should be allowed this authority and flexibility. The check on this authority is the motion to overrule.

VII. Quorum

The required quorum will be established in the bylaws. (If one is not specified, there is no quorum requirement.) A call for a quorum may not be shouted out or interrupt a speaker, but must come after being recognized by the chair. The chair will check for a quorum by show of hands or count, in the same manner as voting. A call for a quorum is out of order for ten minutes after a previous quorum call. If a quorum is lacking, the following business is still in order:

Motions directed toward getting enough members for a quorum

Motions about when to meet again

Motions to refer business to the executive board

Good and welfare

Motions to adjourn or recess

VIII. Miscellaneous Points

Normally, people will speak in the order that they are recognized, by raising hands. Certain circumstances make it necessary to get recognized more quickly. This is accomplished with one of the following points. All may be made by shouting out. However, you may not interrupt someone while they are talking except for Personal Privilege and a Point of Order to appeal a ruling of the chair. If the chair feels an individual is abusing these points, she does not have to recognize the abuser.

A. Point of Personal Privilege

To be used only when there is difficulty in participating in the meeting, such as inability to hear, too much commotion, smoke, etc. May not be used as a way of getting the floor to answer a criticism, even if you believe you were misunderstood or misquoted.

B. Point of Procedure

To be used to move to change the procedure (e.g., to propose that we have two speakers for and two against this motion).

C. Point of Order

To be used to call attention when it is felt that the chair or the body is deviating from the previously adopted procedure (for example, "Our procedure calls for our coming to a vote at this time.") May also be used to challenge a ruling of the chair.

D. Point of Information

To *ask* a question of the chair. May not be used to ask a question directly of another member (There is no such thing as a "point of clarification" or any other special way to give information, except to be recognized by the chair in the usual manner.)

Appendix 5.
Suggested Bylaws

While good bylaws by themselves will not make a union democratic, bad ones can be a stumbling block. They can prevent members from controlling their representatives and union policies, keep members from becoming more involved, or protect corrupt practices. When reformers take over a local, they may find it necessary to modify or work around the bylaws. Campaigns to change bylaws can also be an organizing method; drives to win the right to elect stewards, for example, were vital to the early days of building TDU.

When reforming bylaws, it is tempting to propose revisions that will prevent all evil experienced up till now and that can possibly be predicted in the future. This is not a good idea. First, the simpler the structure the better. Democracy works best when based on a common understanding of how things work. Complicated procedures make the workings of the union hospitable only to lawyers and those who enjoy procedural wrangles. Second, many different traditions can help make the union strong and democratic. It is important to be respectful of these traditions. For example, a local may long have used a permanent election committee whose members hold no other office, take the job very seriously, and carry out fair elections. Other methods may be preferable in the abstract, but more is to be lost by destroying a workable tradition than can be gained with a slightly better procedure.

Lean toward keeping the bylaws as simple as possible. They

should include the principles of the union, the basic structure, the specifics of membership rights, and the procedures to be used when divisions become very sharp. When more detailed procedures are necessary, specify that they are to be worked out at the time by the executive board or the relevant committee, and then approved by the membership. This approach provides more flexibility.

However, it is not always possible to have simple bylaws. Most internationals have requirements for what bylaws must contain, and will consider only proposals based on some model or traditional set. In this case you can give members a bylaws summary.

Most bylaws pay a great deal of attention to financial issues. While money questions are important and often a source of corruption, democracy can be undermined in other ways as well. It's just as important for the members to have the right to vote on a letter of understanding with management as it is to check on who authorized $1,000 for travel expenses to a conference.

Following is not a complete list of possible bylaws, but some concepts and model language, some of it taken from existing locals.

Union Mission or Objectives

A sense of vision or mission is what makes unionism a movement. The union's preamble to the constitution can help to define the union's place in the world. More immediately, it can help deal with internal divisions by stating up front a commitment to deal with these problems. The preamble might be a good place to establish a defense of all workers including gay and lesbian members or undocumented workers, for example. This may be where external organizing or being involved in the community is clearly authorized.

Examples:

The Teamsters Model Bylaws:[1]

> It is recognized that the problems with which this labor organization is accustomed to deal cannot be resolved in isolation but require achievement of a broad spectrum of economic and social objectives as set forth above and as the union may determine from time to time.

The United Health Care Workers of Greater St. Louis:[2]

> To unite under one organization, regardless of age, color, creed, disability, gender, health status, nationality, political affiliation, race, religion, sexual orientation, all health care workers under jurisdiction of the UHCW to promote maximum justice in the workplace and in the community.

A United Federations of Teachers chapter for worker educators:[3]

Improving the Quality of Education for our Students. Improving our
working conditions means improving the conditions in which students
learn. Demands like more full-time positions and paid prep time for all
teachers are demands for the conditions necessary for the expansion
of student educational opportunities. We want to increase the
involvement of students and workers in decision-making. We want
our work, our students, and the field of Worker Education to be better respected, better funded, better supported. Organizing to improve
working conditions is a crucial step in that direction.

Definition of Membership

Normally the question of membership is taken for granted: eli-
gibility is defined as members of the bargaining unit. But several
other categories of membership would strengthen the union. Other
than management and plant guards, who are prohibited from joining
the same unions as regular workers, there are really no legal barriers
to expanding the concept of membership.

• Retired members: see discussion in Chapter 7.

• Laid-off members: Members laid-off but awaiting recall
should have full rights but special dues consideration. In some circumstances they should have special meetings and even special representatives on the executive board and/or bargaining committee.

• Employer-separated members: Most unions simply forget
about former members who quit or are fired or laid off longer than a
specified period. But if we want to build the attitude that the union
is a cause that is more than part of the red tape of a specific employer, then it makes sense to keep contact with separated members at
least until they have joined another union. Indeed, people who have
left a good union job can be the best organizers in their new workplace. The concept of associate member makes sense.

• Organizing members: A different form of associate membership can be used where a union is trying to organize a shop but has
not yet achieved recognition. Sometimes the union loses a representation election, but the active workers continue acting like a union,
doing their best to represent fellow workers even without a contract.
This has been called a "minority union." In such a case a lower level
of dues may be appropriate, but members should have full voting
rights. A number of organizations are using this concept, including
the Health Care Workers of Greater St. Louis, the United Electrical
Workers, and community-based workers' centers like Black
Workers for Justice.

• Union staff: Should a person who is hired onto the union staff become a member of the employing union? We recommend yes, especially where the job involves interpreting and implementing union policy. As much as possible, members should view the staff (and the staff should view themselves) as part of a movement rather than employees of an organization.

• Spouses: We recommend including spouses within the definition of members, with reduced dues, the right to serve on committees, and the right to elect a special representative to the executive board. Spouses depend on the union's success as much as the person whose name is on the paycheck. Involving the spouse makes it easier for the employee to be active, and often adds energy and contacts with the community.

Members' Rights and Responsibilities

In addition to the usual rights, this section should include:

Right to information about what is being voted on (see section below, "Contract Rights")

Right to a copy of the contract and all letters of understanding covering the member, and right to inspect and copy any contract or letter of understanding agreed to by the union

Right to a copy of the contract in member's primary language (if significant number of members speak a language other than English)

Right to a taped copy of the contract (if significant number of non-reading or blind members)

Right to inspect minutes and financial records of all union bodies and obtain copies of minutes, subject to reasonable costs

Right to use union facilities for meetings and events on an equitable basis at a reasonable cost

Right to be fully informed about the progress of any grievance or other union action that directly affects the individual member

Right to inspect the status of all grievances

Right to initiate bylaws amendments and recall of officers

Right to be free of harassment, especially that based on race, gender, disability, health status, nationality, sexual orientation, or political affiliation

Right to have notification of all currently proposed motions included in the announcement of a meeting

Right to attend and speak (but not vote) at meetings of other subdivisions of the local

Right to vote by secret ballot in all elections and on all contracts and binding agreements with management

One clause that appears occasionally in union bylaws places too great a restriction on rights: "No members shall make known the internal affairs of the Union to non-members."[4] In other periods such a provision may have made sense. But now it serves mainly to intimidate members and restrict discussion in semi-public forms such as newsletters or web sites. It discourages contact between members of different unions and restricts members' ability to participate in and get help from labor studies institutions or other organizations. If some form of information security is required by special circumstances, the bylaws provision should be very specific in its application.

Membership Meetings

In small unions with a single employer, it is usually possible to have a simple structure with the membership meeting as the supreme body, although even here, geography, shift, or seven-day-operation considerations may require several separate meetings. In very large, more complicated locals, a delegated council structure often takes the place of general membership meetings.

Wherever possible, the membership meetings should play a strong role; this is where the ranks should have a chance to direct officers' actions well before election time. If work schedules make it impractical for everyone to be present at once, then changes to make attendance possible should be a high priority of bargaining.

Here are a few possible bylaws on meetings:

> Membership meetings are the highest body of the union. They
> —must review and approve all expenditures greater than $1,000.
> —may review and approve or reject all actions of the executive board, officers, or committees.
> —may pass motions to direct actions of officers (except that the officer may invoke the privilege of postponing implementation until after the next membership meeting, if the item had not been specifically included in the notification for the current meeting)

The membership should have the ability to direct an officer only if the officer is elected by that same membership. In other words, it makes no sense for a unit to be able, by itself, to direct the action of the president of an amalgamated local. Thus the person who chairs and implements the decisions of a unit meeting should be a person who is elected by the unit.

> Minutes of meetings shall include all motions made at meetings and their disposition, as well as all financial transactions or appointments made. The minutes shall be the official record of the local union and shall be maintained at all local union offices.[5] All minutes or committee reports to be approved by a meeting must be available in writing

at least one-half hour prior to the meeting.

Notification of membership meetings will include the known business to come before the meeting and will be distributed as broadly as practical, including via the local newspaper, web site, posting, and any other methods that will efficiently reach a large number of members. At a minimum, notification for regular and special membership meetings will be provided one week in advance through posting in the workplace. Emergency meetings require a minimum of 24 hours' notice.

Special membership meetings may be called by the executive board or by petition of five percent of the membership. Emergency membership meetings may be called by the president or the executive board.

The local shall provide quality childcare at all membership meetings.

A quorum for a membership meeting properly posted is those in attendance.

Officers and Executive Board

The most effective and most democratic union has a team leadership consisting of a strong president, responsible to a strong executive board, responsible to a strong membership. This means that the president can act, but must answer to and can be reversed by a well-organized executive board, which in turn can be directed and overturned by a well-organized membership.

The executive board is empowered to act for the membership between meetings on all questions except those specifically required to be approved by the membership. This includes reviewing and directing actions of the president.

The executive board will discuss and approve all appointments to committees and all expenditures greater than $500.

Or

The affairs of the Local Union shall be conducted through the authority vested in the Executive Board, subject to the approval of the general membership. The Executive Board shall ensure that the policies and directives of the general membership are being followed.[6]

Sometimes, to overcome a tradition of a rubber-stamp executive board, it is necessary to spell out the tasks for which the board is responsible. In consciously trying to create such a strong executive board, activists in SEIU Local 616 included as specific duties: to oversee the executive director; to hear and act on member concerns; to provide for membership recruitment, communications, and budgeting and auditing; to establish chapters; and to assign and lead committee work.

Traditions will probably guide the selection of officer titles and nominal responsibilities. A local should have many people who are responsible for orienting new members, but formally electing a

"Guide" rarely takes care of this. The best arrangement is for the bylaws not to specify which officer takes which responsibilities, beyond certain basic ones, but for the executive board to assign responsibilities among board members, taking into account individual talents.

The exception to the above is the trustees. We would propose an expansion of their normally assigned duties to include watching how union policy is carried out as well as the handling of money.

> Trustees shall examine the books and report their accuracy and the state of balances. A trustee's disagreement with an expenditure properly authorized by the executive board or membership shall not be a valid basis for refusing to sign the report.[7]

> Trustees shall review directions by the membership and the executive board and include in their report the trustees' estimation of the action taken on these items.

To reduce the possibility of corruption and give members more confidence in the union, anti-pork barrel provisions are useful (see Officers' Pay in Chapter 7).

> The salary and benefits of officers shall be based on the income of the 90th percentile (highest of the lowest-paid ninety percent) of the membership in the bargaining unit during the previous year.

> Increases in officers' and staff salaries or expense allowances may be approved only during the last six months of any regular term of office. Such increases will be effective only after the installation of new officers following a regular election.[8]

Stewards Council

> A Stewards Council consisting of all the stewards in the local union shall meet at least monthly. The meeting schedule and agenda will be coordinated by a Chief Steward elected by the council in consultation with the president. The president (or on occasion a designee) will attend all meetings. The council shall be self-governing within these bylaws and may adopt educational programs, set up subcommittees, make recommendations to the executive board, and discuss grievances or contract problems. The council shall not have the authority to enter into contracts which bind the local union.[9]

Committees

Committees need not be specified in the bylaws. Committees that have nothing to do become hiding places for union rip-offs and patronage. Further, when an issue becomes hot, that is the time to involve new people by setting up a committee on the spot. The bylaws should mention only the elections committee and the contract campaign/strike committee, which are then constituted as needed rather than being permanent bodies. All other committees should also be established as they are needed, and repopulated as situations or interest change.

> The executive board will create and dissolve local union committees as necessary. Committee openings will be posted and volunteers will be encouraged. The executive board will discuss and approve appointments to or removals from the chair and membership of all committees.

Representation of Special Sections

To compensate for past or current problems, it may be desirable to provide special forms of representation for groups within the union who have been left out, say because of geography, or because their unit is small. In the UAW-Big Three, skilled workers have their own representatives and the right to a separate vote on the portions of contracts that affect only them. One large AFT local provides for at-large elections for a representative assembly. To increase the likelihood that representatives include some from smaller districts, the rules provide that the twelve highest vote-getters are elected, but no more than four from any single district.[10]

Union Staff and Employees

In a democratic union, the staff or employees are responsible to the members; the direction of the union will change with elections, and the staff may need to change too. (See "Role of Staff" in Chapter 7.)

> A staff contract or period of appointment cannot exceed the term of office of the appointing officer.[11] Appointed staff and employees may be removed at will by the appointing authority, subject to any grievance procedure or collective bargaining agreement approved by the membership.

Contract Rights

Among the most important (but frequently absent) democratic rights are the power to shape bargaining demands and to have an informed vote on contracts.

> No less than six months prior to contract expiration, the executive board will propose the method and time schedule for gathering bargaining issues and determining the key bargaining demands. The bargaining unit, through membership meetings or delegate assemblies, will adopt a statement of key bargaining demands.

> At least six months prior to contract expiration, the executive board will request volunteers from the membership for a contract campaign/strike committee. The president will appoint the chairperson of the committee.

> All tentative contract agreements, amendments to the contract, and letters of understanding must be ratified by the membership following a meeting(s) with proper posting as a ratification/information meeting.

Many union leaders have used the practice of stating that a rejection of a contract is a vote to go on immediate strike as a method for forcing acceptance. In fact the two are quite separate issues.

> The vote on ratification will not be combined with any other vote such as the decision to go on strike.[12]

The right to vote is only meaningful if the vote is informed. Would anyone stand for an officers' election where the period for nominations and campaigning begins when the incumbents put out their campaign literature, and lasts one day? Yet that is the way we vote on most contracts.

> Within 24 hours of reaching a tentative agreement, copies of it, with additions and strikeouts clearly marked to indicate changes from the previous agreement, will be made available for inspection at all local offices and will be provided either in hard copy or electronic form to any member who requests, and who has pre-paid a reasonable fee to cover duplication and shipment costs.

> The union will prepare and distribute an accurate summary of the tentative agreement a reasonable time before the ratification vote. Minority reports of bargaining committee members, if any, will be included.

> An adequate period will be provided before the ratification vote for consideration of the tentative agreement and for formulation and distribution of alternative views, if any.

Elections

To ensure that the details of election procedures are suited to the union's needs at the time, an election committee can be elected six months prior to the election. It can submit detailed procedures to the membership and gain approval for them.

Only the basics of procedures should be included in the bylaws, including:

• Length of officer terms. We recommend two years.

• Whether elections are to be by mail ballot or walk-in.

• Whether the winner must receive a plurality or a majority. We recommend a majority, in which case a run-off may be required.

• Who is eligible to run. Avoid restrictions such as length of membership, prior experience, or meeting attendance. These may be valid considerations and can be used in campaigning, but it should be up to the members to decide how important they are.

• The right of nominees to be heard, including access to mailing lists and the union newspaper. Most unions agree to mail to the membership, with the costs borne by the candidate(s). A few unions will provide the actual mailing list to any member,[13] but this may raise privacy issues. In either case the union should actively facilitate candidate contact with the members.

> The election committee will schedule a pre-election mailing to all members and will include all materials submitted by candidates. The union will pay for the postage and handling of the first ounce of mail for all candidates. Candidates must provide their own materials and cost for postage and handling above one ounce.

• The method for filling vacancies and calling special elections.

• The method of handling recalls. Out of fear that it will be abused, most unions mandate a recall procedure that is virtually impossible to use. But recall is a basic democratic right. It is the members who have to live with the results. Trust them to shun or punish any abuse of the procedure.

> Members may initiate a recall of any officer by a petition that includes the name and office of the individual to be recalled, the names of the individuals or caucus circulating the recall petition, and the reasons for the recall. The signatures and signing dates of 25 percent of the current membership of the constituency of the officer must be gathered within a 30-day period. A recall vote will be held within 30 days of presenting this petition to the next executive board meeting. If the recall vote is successful, the office will be declared vacant and the normal policy for filling the vacancy will apply. A petition to recall an officer who has already been subject to one unsuccessful recall vote shall require a majority of members signing.

Amendments to Bylaws

Some unions do not allow the members the initiative in changing the bylaws, but only the executive board. Most require a two-thirds vote for changes. We recommend this language instead:

> These bylaws may be amended by initiative of the executive board or by petition of three percent of the membership, with the approval of the majority of the members voting at the second membership meeting after the membership meeting where the amendment was initiated.

Emergency Action

Sometimes union action must be fast to be effective. If the bylaws prevent being able to make an urgent decision quickly, either the bylaws quickly become a dead letter as people find a way to deal with reality, or the union becomes discredited because it cannot respond to members' needs.

> In a situation where the executive board believes that the integrity of the union and the well-being of the membership are at significant risk,

it may by two-thirds vote recommend a temporary suspension or change in the bylaws for vote at the next regular or emergency membership meeting. The temporary action goes into effect if approved by two-thirds of those voting at a duly posted membership meeting and may be in effect for a time no longer than the period required for a normal bylaws amendment.

The executive board may establish procedures and conditions for making emergency decisions including delegation, polling by telephone, and use of the internet.

Notes

1. *Teamsters Proposed Model Local Union Bylaws*, Section 4, October 1992.

2. United Health Care Workers of Greater St. Louis, *Constitution and Bylaws*, Article III, December 6, 1997.

3. United Federation of Teachers, *Bylaws of the Consortium for Workers Education Chapter*, Article II, October 1993.

4. Transport Workers Union Local 100, *By-Laws of the Transport Workers Union of Greater New York*, Article XIX d, November 23, 1987.

5. From *Teamsters Model Bylaws*, Section 11.

6. SEIU Local 616, *Bylaws*, Article V, Section 4.

7. From *Teamsters Model Bylaws*, Section 12.

8. Based on United Steelworkers Local 1343, *Local Union By-Laws*, Article VI.4.f.

9. Based on *Teamsters Model Bylaws*, Section 13.

10. Connecticut State Federation of Teachers Local 4200, *Constitution of the Administration and Residual Employees Union*, Article VI, Section 3.

11. Based on *Teamsters Model Bylaws*, Section13.

12. This was a key bylaws proposal of the New Directions caucus in Transport Workers Union Local 100.

13. Independent Association of Publishers Employees Inc., *By-Laws*, Article VII.2.c, October 1, 1985.

Appendix 6:
Resources

Organizations

We have included here a few of the reform groups or websites in international unions as of 2005. A much more complete list of groups in internationals and locals is on the website of the Association for Union Democracy; see below. You can also do a web search for your union, local, company, or industry to turn up discussion lists or websites.

Association for Union Democracy

AUD provides education, legal assistance, and practical advice to members on their democratic rights to free speech, fair elections, due process, and, where appropriate, fair hiring. It reports on battles for democracy in its bimonthly *Union Democracy Review* and on its website. It helps members to be active in the internal life of their unions. You can sign up for monthly email updates.

AUD's website has links to sites run by rank-and-file reformers in many, many unions. Click AUDLinks. AUD also has a guide to building a good rank-and-file website, with a sample homepage.

104 Montgomery St., Brooklyn, NY 11225
718-564-1114
aud@igc.org
www.uniondemocracy.org

Carpenters for a Democratic Union International
www.ranknfile.net

Labor Notes/Labor Education and Research Project
Publisher of this book—"putting the movement back in the labor movement" since 1979. Publishes monthly *Labor Notes* magazine, $24/year. Holds local meetings, schools, and large biannual conferences that bring together activists from all unions and several countries, for practical knowledge-sharing and a dose of inspiration. Helps workers in the same union or industry get in touch with each other. Call to find out about upcoming Labor Notes events in your area.

7435 Michigan Ave., Detroit, MI 48210
313-842-6262
labornotes@labornotes.org
www.labornotes.org

Longshore Workers Coalition
For members of the International Longshoremen's Association.

PO Box 2130, Charleston, SC 29413-1230
917-647-7751, 843-830-4471, 843-830-6508
http://ilarf.org/

Research-Education-Advocacy-People (REAP)
For members of the United Food and Commercial Workers.

705 Douglas St., Room 250, Sioux City, Iowa 51101
info@reapinc.org
www.reapinc.org

Teamsters for a Democratic Union
Publishes monthly *Convoy-Dispatch* newspaper, $30/year.

PO Box 10128, Detroit, MI 48210
313-842-2600
tdudetroit@tdu.org
www.tdu.org

Books

How to Get an Honest Union Election, by Herman Benson. Order from the Association for Union Democracy, see above. $6.

Running for Local Union Office. Order from Teamsters for a Democratic Union, www.tdu.org/Store/store.cgi. $10.

A Troublemaker's Handbook 2. Chapter 18, "Reform Caucuses and Running for Office." Examples of successful union reform efforts: how they did it. Chapter 19, "Running Your Local." Setting up a member-to-member network, using lost time, educating stewards, leading staff, and building long-term goals into your daily functioning. To order, see last page or www.troublemakershandbook.org.

The Transformation of U.S. Unions: Voices, Visions and Strategies from the Grassroots, Ray Tillman and Michael Cummings, eds. Lynne Rienner Publishers, 1999. An anthology of experiences with and arguments for union democracy. Order from 313-842-6262 or www.labornotes.org. $22.50.

Other Resources

Jerry Tucker, a founder of the New Directions Movement in the UAW and Director of the Healthcare Justice Education Fund, consults with unions and rank-and-file groups. 940 Oak Knoll Manor Dr., St. Louis, MO 63119, 314-968-5534, jtuckernd@sbcglobal.net.

To locate unions in your area or to connect with locals in your international, go to http://biglabor.com/lorsform.html.

To get your local's LM-2, a financial report filed annually with the Department of Labor by all U.S. union locals (except those composed exclusively of public workers), go to http://union-reports.dol.gov/olmsWeb/docs/formspg.html or to www.biglabor.com.

Index